Studies in Ancient Persia
and the Achaemenid Period

Studies in Ancient Persia and the Achaemenid Period

edited by
John Curtis

Ⓒ

James Clarke & Co

James Clarke & Co
P.O. Box 60
Cambridge
CB1 2NT
United Kingdom

www.jamesclarke.co
publishing@jamesclarke.co

Hardback ISBN: 978 0 227 17705 1
Paperback ISBN: 978 0 227 17706 8
PDF ISBN: 978 0 227 90706 1
ePub ISBN: 978 0 227 90707 8
Kindle ISBN: 978 0 227 90708 5

British Library Cataloguing in Publication Data
A record is available from the British Library

First published by James Clarke & Co, 2020

*The Iran Heritage Foundation
is a registered UK charity that
exists to promote and protect
the cultural heritage of Iran.*

Contents

Editor's note

When I became CEO of the Iran Heritage Foundation in 2014, my former British Museum colleague Terence Mitchell asked for my help in publishing an article that was a greatly expanded version of a lecture delivered in 2005. I am pleased to have been able to fulfil that obligation by including the article in this volume, but it should be noted that all views and opinions expressed in the article are those of Terence himself.

Best thanks are due to Lutterworth Press for agreeing to publish this book, to the copy-editor, Dorothy Luckhurst, and to Debora Nicosia who has seen this book through the press. I am most grateful to the Trustees of the Iran Heritage Foundation who have provided a subvention for the publication of this book.

Lastly, it should be noted that that there has been no attempt in this book, apart from the Mitchell article, to standardise the transliteration of names in Persian or in other languages. Instead, the most commonly used forms of the names in English have been used wherever possible.

Terence Croft Mitchell (1929-2019)
Photo by Andrew Cryer, March 2019

Introduction

This collection of essays was intended as a tribute to Terence Mitchell on his 90th birthday but, sadly, he died in London on Easter Sunday, 21 April 2019, one month short of the landmark birthday. This book will therefore be a memorial volume.

Terence Mitchell was born on 17 June 1929, the elder son of the landscape artist Arthur Croft Mitchell (1872-1956) and his wife Evelyn Violet, née Ware. During part of World War II he was evacuated to the United States and attended Holderness School in New Hampshire. On returning to the United Kingdom he continued his education at Bradfield College in Berkshire. His military service was spent as a craftsman in the Royal Electrical and Mechanical Engineers (REME). Following this he went up to St Catharine's College, Cambridge, where he read Archaeology and Anthropology. At Cambridge he was a contemporary of Jeffrey Orchard and Eric Uphill, with whom he remained friends for the rest of his life. His teacher in the history and archaeology of the Ancient Near East was Margaret Munn-Rankin (1913-81). After Cambridge he became a schoolmaster for several years at St Catherine's School in Almondsbury near Bristol (1954-56), and from 1956-57 he studied at Tyndale House in Cambridge. From 1958-59 he was 'the European representative of the Australian Institute of Archaeology'.

In 1959 he joined the Department of Western Asiatic Antiquities at the British Museum at an exciting time when the department was rapidly expanding under the dynamic leadership of Richard D. Barnett. The cuneiformist at this time was Donald Wiseman, soon to be replaced by Edmond Sollberger who succeeded Barnett as Keeper in 1974. Terence was appointed Deputy Keeper at this time. He became Acting Keeper 1983-85, and Keeper 1985-89.

Amongst his principal academic contributions were chapters on Israel and Judah in the revised edition of the *Cambridge Ancient History*, but the work for which he is best known is *The Bible in the British Museum*, a semi-popular book that was first published in 1988 and has been reprinted many times. He has earned the gratitude of the scholarly community by editing for publication no less than three of Sir Leonard Woolley's magisterial final reports on the Ur excavations, volumes 7 (Old Babylonian period), 8 (Kassite and Assyrian periods), and 9 (Neo-Babylonian and Persian periods).

At various times during his life he was a Trustee of the Palestine Exploration Fund, of the British Institute at Amman for Archaeology and History, the London Diocesan fund, and the London Diocesan Board of Finance.

In retirement he divided his time between his house in Mallord Street, Chelsea, and a country house known as Madeira in Wadhurst, Sussex, made occasional visits to the Athenaeum Club, and continued to work on a regular basis in the British Museum as an unpaid special assistant.

He had strongly-held Christian beliefs of an Evangelical nature, but these did not impact on his museological career. He had a particular interest in the Book of Daniel but, regrettably, the commentary that he had been working on for many years was unfinished at the time of his death.

John Curtis

Terence Mitchell's Published Works

in chronological order

'Archaeology and Genesis I-XI', Faith and Thought 91.1 (1959), pp. 28-49

'A Terra-Cotta Ewe's Head from Babylonia', British Museum Quarterly 23 (1961), pp. 100-1

'The Old Testament Usage of *něšāmâ*', *Vetus Testamentum* 11 (1961) pp. 177-87

Edited C.L. Woolley and M.E.L. Mallowan, *Ur Excavations, IX: The Neo Babylonian and Persian Periods* (London: British Museum; Philadelphia: University of Pennsylvania, 1962)

Entries in The New Bible Dictionary, ed. J. D. Douglas (1ˢᵗ ed. 1962, 3ʳᵈ ed. 1996) - Arabia in Old Testament; Ararat; Ark; Arpachshad; Chronology of the Old Testament (with K.A. Kitchen); Eden - Garden of; Eden - House of; Euphrates; Flood; Genealogy (Old Testament); Gihon; Ham; Havilah; Japheth; Methuselah; Nations, Table of; Noah; Shem

Edited C.L. Woolley and M.E.L. Mallowan *Ur Excavations, VIII: The Kassite Period and the Period of the Assyrian Kings* (London: British Museum; Philadelphia: University of Pennsylvania, 1965)

'The Musical Instruments in Nebuchadnezzar's Orchestra', in D.J. Wiseman, T.C. Mitchell, R. Joyce, W.J. Martin, K.A. Kitchen, *Notes on Some Problems in the Book of Daniel* (London: The Tyndale Press, 1965) pp. 19-27 (with pp. 25-27 by R. Joyce)

'Philistia', in D. Winton Thomas (ed.), *Archaeology and Old Testament Study* (Oxford: The Clarendon Press, 1967) pp. 405-27

'A South Arabian Tripod Offering Saucer said to be from Ur,' Iraq 31
    (1969), pp. 112-14

Sumerian Art Illustrated by Objects from Ur and Al-Ubaid (London:
    British Museum, 1969)

'Musical Instruments and Monuments Representing Musical
    Instruments in the Department of Western Asiatic Antiquities', in J.
    Rimmer, Ancient Musical Instruments of Western Asia in the British
    Museum (London: British Museum 1969) pp. 45-48; also 'Music in
    the Old Testament' in ibid., pp 49-51

'The Meaning of the Noun ḥātān in the Old Testament', Vetus
    Testamentum 19 (1969), pp. 93-112

'Review of Acquisitions1963-70 of Western Asiatic Antiquities I', British
    Museum Quarterly 36 (1972), pp. 131-46

Review of B. Doe, Southern Arabia (1971) in JRAS 105 (1973), pp. 61-63

'Ancient Palestine - A New Exhibition', British Museum Society Bulletin
    15 (1974), pp. 13-15

'Old Testament Archaeology: Some Recent Work', Faith and Thought
    101.2 (1974) pp. 142-57

'Sigillography' with J.Ch,. W.W., Encyclopaedia Britannica 15th ed
    (1974), pp. 741-43

Edited C.L. Woolley and M.E.L. Mallowan Ur Excavations, VII: The
    Old Babylonian Period (London: British Museum, 1976) (including
    enlargement and thorough revision of catalogue of objects, pp. 214-
    54)

'A South Arabian Portrait Head', British Museum Yearbook 2 (1977) pp.
    257-58

'Another Phoenician Inscribed Arrowhead,' in P.R.S. Moorey and P.J.
    Parr, eds, Archaeology in the Levant: Essays for Kathleen Kenyon
    (London 1978), pp. 136-53

'Two British East India Company Residents in Baghdad in the 19th
    Century', Zeitschrift für Orient-Archäologie 1 (1978) pp. 376-95

'An Assyrian Stringed Instrument', British Museum Yearbook 4 (1980)
    pp. 33-42

'Israel and Judah until the Revolt of Jehu (932-841 BC)', Cambridge
    Ancient History, III.1 (Cambridge: Cambridge University Press,
    1982) pp. 442-87

'Israel and Judah from Jehu until the Period of Assyrian Domination
    (841-c.750 BC)' Cambridge Ancient History, III.1 (Cambridge:
    Cambridge University Press, 1982) pp. 488-510

'Pottery. a. Phoenician and Punic', in R.D. Barnett and C. Mendelson
    (eds), Tharros: A Catalogue of Material in the British Museum from

Phoenician and Other Tombs at Tharros, Sardinia (London: British Museum, 1987) pp. 50-58

The Bible in the British Museum (London: British Museum, 1988) (several later revisions and additions, most recent, 2016)

'Interpreting the Early Chapters of Genesis', Faith and Thought October Bulletin (1989), pp. 3-9

The Treasure of the Oxus (Zurich: Museum Rietberg, 1989)

'The Bronze Lion Weights from Nimrud', in R. Gyselen (ed.), *Prix, salaires, poids et mesures*, Res Orientales II (Paris: GECMO, 1990) pp. 129-38

'Israel and Judah from the Coming of Assyrian Domination until the Fall of Samaria, and the Struggle for Independence in Judah (c.750-700 BC)', *Cambridge Ancient History*, III.2 (1991) pp. 322-70

'Judah until the Fall of Jerusalem (c.700-586 BC)', *Cambridge Ancient History*, III.2 (Cambridge: Cambridge University Press, 1991) pp. 371-409

'The Babylonian Exile and the Restoration of the Jews in Palestine (586- c.500 BC)', *Cambridge Ancient History*, III.2 (Cambridge: Cambridge University Press, 1991) pp. 410-60

'The Phoenician Inscribed Ivory Box from Ur', *Palestinian Exploration Quarterly* 123 (1991) pp. 119-28

'The Music of the Old Testament Reconsidered', *Palestinian Exploration Quarterly* 124 (1992) pp. 124-43

'Where was Putu-Iaman?', *Proceedings of the Seminar for Arabian Studies* 22 (1992) pp. 69-80

'Shared Vocabulary in the Pentateuch and the Book of Daniel', in R.S. Hess, G.J. Wenham and P.E. Satterthwaite (eds), *He Swore an Oath: Biblical Themes from Genesis 12-50* (Cambridge: Tyndale House, 1993) pp. 132-41

'Furniture in West Semitic Texts', in G. Herrmann (ed.), *The Furniture of Western Asia, Ancient and Traditional* (Mainz: Philipp von Zabern, 1996) pp. 49-60

'The "House of David" Inscription from Dan', *Faith and Thought* 21 (1997) pp. 2-4

'The Persepolis Sculptures in the British Museum', *Iran* 38 (2000) pp. 49-56

'Camels in the Assyrian Bas-Reliefs', *Iraq* 62 (2000) pp. 187-94

'What is the Hebrew Language?', *Faith and Thought* 27 (2003) pp. 6-9

'New Light on the Siloam Tunnel Inscription', *Faith and Thought* 37 (2005) pp. 17-25 (the inscription, p. 25, reproduced upside-down); article repeated (with the inscription the right way up and with further illustrations) in *Buried History: Journal of the Australian Institute of Archaeology* 41: 43-50

'Foreign Words in the Old Testament – Clues to Dating?', *Faith and Thought* 43 (2007) pp. 25-41

Catalogue of the Western Asiatic Seals in the British Museum: Stamp Seals III, *Impressions of Stamp Seals on Cuneiform Tablets, Clay Bullae and Jar Handles* (Leiden: Brill, 2008) with drawings by Ann Searight.

'Nebo-Sarsekim (Jeremiah 39:3) mentioned in a recently noticed Babylonian text', *Faith and Thought* 46 (2009) pp. 25-30 (chronological chart incorrectly contracted); article repeated (with the chronological chart shown correctly and with further illustrations) in *Buried History: Journal of the Australian Institute of Archaeology* 45 (2009) pp. 7-10

'Another Look at Alleged Ancient Bagpipes', in R. Dumbrill and I.L. Finkel (eds), *Proceedings of the International Conference of Near Eastern Archaeomusicology held at the British Museum, December 4, 5 and 6, 2008*, ICONEA 2008 (London: ICONEA Publications, 2010) pp. 33-46

'The Text of the Greek New Testament', *Faith and Thought* 54 (2011) pp. 17-30

'Skin Diseases in the Biblical World', *Faith and Thought* 57 (2014) pp. 20-30

'The Death of Goliath', *Tyndale Bulletin*, forthcoming

'Another Inscribed Arrowhead in the British Museum', Festschrift article, forthcoming

Five Unpublished Persepolis Relief Fragments in the Ashmolean Museum

Paul Collins

Documenting the scattered architectural fragments from Persepolis or Takht-e Jamshid in Iran has been an ongoing project since Richard Barnett (1957) and Louis Vanden Berghe (1959: 152-53) first published details of reliefs from the site in foreign collections. Some thirty years later, the list was expanded by Michael Roaf (1987). Terence Mitchell (2000) made his own important contribution to this diaspora project by detailing sculptures from Persepolis in the British Museum[1]. More recently, Lindsay Allen has been researching the movement around the globe of more sculptures in what she has termed 'fragmentation events' (Allen 2017).

Although the Ashmolean Museum has a small collection of excavated objects from the major Achaemenid site of Pasargadae,[2] it was only in 1982, with the acquisition by purchase of a relief showing the head of a Persian (Fig. 1), that the register books first recorded an object from Persepolis.[3] This sculpture was duly noted by Roaf in his list of fragments

---

1   It is with much pleasure that I offer this note in memory of Terence Mitchell. Terence was enormously welcoming to me, both as a graduate student and during my time as a curator in the Middle East Department of the British Museum from 2006-11; he was a constant source of knowledge and I am especially grateful to him for sharing his lists of stamp seals with me when I was documenting that part of the Museum's collection for online publication.

2   These objects were allocated to the Museum for its support of the excavations directed by David Stronach between 1961 and 1963, for which see Stronach 1978.

3   AN1982.944. The relief fragment was purchased from Major J.C.E. Bowen in 1982. It was probably acquired by Bowen when he was stationed in Iran

Fig. 1. Fragment of a limestone relief
from Persepolis depicting a Persian,
fifth century BC, AN1982.944.
© Ashmolean Museum,
University of Oxford.

Fig. 2. Bas-relief fragment from
Persepolis showing hair or beard
curls, fifth century BC, AN1988.393.a.
© Ashmolean Museum,
University of Oxford.

Fig. 3. Bas-relief fragment from
Persepolis showing part of a rosette,
fifth century BC, AN1988.393.b.
© Ashmolean Museum,
University of Oxford.

Fig. 4. Bas-relief fragment from
Persepolis showing a set of ridges,
fifth century BC, AN1988.393.c.
© Ashmolean Museum,
University of Oxford.

Fig. 5. Bas-relief fragment from Persepolis showing hair or beard curls, fifth century BC, AN1988.393.d. © Ashmolean Museum, University of Oxford.

Fig. 6. Bas-relief fragment from Persepolis showing hair or beard curls, fifth century BC, AN1988.393.e. © Ashmolean Museum, University of Oxford.

(1987: 156). The apparent absence of any other examples of architectural sculpture from Persia in the Museum was made evident in the newly refurbished Ancient Near East gallery which opened to the public in 2009 with this single relief standing for the glories of Persepolis.[4]

It therefore came as something of a surprise when in 2013 a search in the Ashmolean's collections management database using the term 'Persepolis' revealed five small and unassuming pieces of stone sculpture that do not feature in any current survey of fragments removed from the site. The discovery was made by Dr Senta German who was researching objects to support undergraduate classes in Classics as part of the Museum's University Engagement Programme.[5] The accession

---

(1938-47) as Vice Consul; Consul General for Khorasan; Undersecretary to the Resident in Rajputana; and Assistant Consul in Tehran. See Antell, Brown and Vermue 2015. The original context of this sculpture is very uncertain given the generic anonymity of such uniform figures, many of which come from dislocated slabs across the site (Allen 2017).

4   Gilmour 2011.

5   The Ashmolean's long tradition of teaching using objects in subjects such as archaeology and art history has been expanded across the University's faculties with the establishment of the University Engagement Programme funded by

numbers of the fragments indicate that they had been registered in 1988 and handwritten entries by Roger Moorey[6] in the register book for September of that year reveal that he had found the pieces unnumbered in the collections. The group consists of the following pieces:

Hair or beard curls. 9.8cm x 4cm x 3.4cm. AN1988.393.a (Fig. 2)

Part of a rosette. 8.6cm x 6cm x 3.1cm. AN1988.393.b (Fig. 3)

A set of ridges; some of the surface stained by orange soil.[7] 8.2cm x 7cm x 3.1cm. AN1988.393.c (Fig. 4)

Hair or beard curls. 8.4cm x 8.1cm x 1.2cm. AN1988.393.d (Fig. 5)

Hair or beard curls. 10.5cm x 7.5cm x 5cm. AN1988.393.e (Fig. 6)

There is some confusion in the documentation about the provenance of the pieces. Attached to the reverse of one fragment (AN1988.393.d) is a paper label hand-written in blue pencil: 'From the palace of Cyrus Persepolis contemporary with the prophet Daniel'. In contrast, a typed list in the related object record file in the Department of Antiquities describes all five pieces as originating 'from the palace of Darius at Susa'. Although bas-reliefs have been excavated at the fourth-century-BC 'Chaour' palace at Susa, and sculpted stone elements are also known from a number of 'pavilion' sites across Persia (Labrousse and Boucharlat 1972; Curtis 2005: 37), Persepolis is the most likely source of these relief fragments; their grey, marbly fabric visually resembling the stone types used there (Lindsay Allen, personal correspondence). Given the small scale of the pieces, recontextualising the fragments at their source remains a significant challenge.[8]

The modern history of the fragments is only partially recoverable, but there is sufficient information to suggest parallels with known collecting practices that led to the widespread dissemination – largely through dealers – of elements of Achaemenid sculpture though Europe and North America during the 1920s (Allen 2013: n. 5).

the Andrew W. Mellon Foundation. The five fragments from Persepolis have been used to support the following undergraduate classes in Classics: Texts and Contexts 1 (The Persian Wars and Cultural Identity); Aristocracy and Democracy in the Greek World, 550-450 BC; The Early Greek World and Herodotus' Histories: 650 BC to 479 BC (Greek History 1).

6   Moorey was the Ashmolean's Keeper of Antiquities at the time, see Curtis 2015.
7   Based on a preliminary observation by a member of the Ashmolean's Conservation Department, there is no evidence of surviving paint as is known from some Persepolis sculptures, see, for example, Ambers, and Simpson 2005; Nagel 2010.
8   See above, note 3.

According to the typed list, the five Ashmolean pieces were the property of 'Mrs M.S. Johnson-Smyth of 5 Norham Gardens, Oxford' who had gifted them to the Indian Institute[9] of the University of Oxford on 24 February 1927.[10] The final page of a letter written by Mrs Johnson-Smyth to the Curators of the Institute's Museum of Eastern Art is preserved within its correspondence archive[11] and this records that the fragments were – presumably – collected:

> . . . by a missionary from Persia, who also travelled through Mesopotamia.
> They are at present in my house at Canterbury. I can bring them to Oxford next term.
> I shall be much obliged if you will kindly lay this letter before the Committee of the Curators at your next meeting.

Frustratingly, the first page(s) of the letter, which may have provided further information on the collection history of the pieces, is missing.

The ease with which it was possible to collect such fragments from Persepolis during the later 1920s is revealed by the novelist, poet, and journalist Vita Sackville-West in an account of her visit to the site:

9   The Indian Institute was proposed in 1875 by Sir Monier Monier-Williams, Boden Professor of Sanskrit, University of Oxford, to form 'a centre of union, intercourse, inquiry and instruction for all engaged in Indian Studies'. The University took over its management in 1884 and appointed a panel of Curators to oversee it. In 1927 the Institute's library was placed under the control of the Bodleian Library but the Curators continued to manage a Museum of Eastern Art. In April 1961 the contents of the Museum were transferred to the Ashmolean Museum where they formed the basis of the newly formed Department of Eastern Art. By this time, all teaching in Indian Studies was taking place in the Oriental Institute (Bodleian Library 1995).

10   This is confirmed by the Minutes of the Curators of the Indian Institute housed in the Bodleian Library (IN 1/2). Item 6 on the Agenda of a meeting held on Thursday, 24 February 1927 records: 'The gift of certain Semitic antiquities'. The associated minutes (page 162) records the gift of 'certain antiquities from Elam, inscribed, by Mrs Johnson-Smyth'. Mrs Johnson-Smyth and/or her husband may have been alumni of the University but a search for them in the Central Archives was unsuccessful. An investigation of College archives might be more revealing but would be a significant undertaking.

11   This portion of the Institute's archive is held by the Ashmolean's Department of Eastern Art.

Fig. 7. Right portion of a brick with a six-line inscription of the
Elamite King Shilhak-Inshushinak, about 1150-1120BC, AN1988.389.
© Ashmolean Museum, University of Oxford.

A little further and you are in the Hall of the Hundred
Columns, a wilderness of tumbled ruins which in their broken
detail testify to the richness of the order that once was here:
fallen capitals; fragments of carving small enough to go into a
pocket, but whorled with the curls of an Assyrian beard; wars
and dynasties roll their forgotten drums, as the fragment is
balanced for a moment in the palm of the hand. (Sackville-
West 1928: 133)

The pocket size fragments from Persepolis were not the only objects
obtained by Mrs Johnson-Smyth from the travelling missionary. The
following items were also gifted by her to the Indian Institute in 1927:

Right portion of a brick with a six-line inscription of the Elamite
King Shilhak-Inshushinak, about 1150-1120 BC.[12] 7cm x 7.5cm.
AN1988.389 (Fig. 7)

12　For similar examples, see Malbran-Labat 1995: 88; Potts 1999: 206.

Fig. 8. Fragment of a blue-glazed baked clay brick or tile, AN1988.390.
© Ashmolean Museum, University of Oxford.

Fragment of a blue-glazed baked clay brick or tile. 5cm x 3.5cm. AN1988.390 (Fig. 8)

Rectangular terracotta brick, red coloured; 'rosette' in relief on one face. 10cm x 4cm x 3cm. AN1988.391 (Fig. 9)

Hollow-cast terracotta fragment; female head in relief with traces of paint. 9cm x 9cm. AN1988.392 (Fig. 10)

In 1935 the Museum of Eastern Art was reorganised and pre-Islamic antiquities were judged to be outside the remit of the collection. As a result, these nine objects were transferred to the Ashmolean Museum.[13] It would be 53 years before Roger Moorey officially recorded their presence in the collections. The most recent 'rediscovery' of the pieces is fortuitous in that it not only provides an opportunity to publish them for the first time but a planned re-display of the Ashmolean's Ancient Near East gallery in 2019 offers the chance for the Persepolis fragments to be given a public presence they deserve.

13   For which, see Leeds 1935: 8.

Fig. 9. (above) Rectangular terracotta brick, red coloured with a 'rosette' in relief on one face, AN1988.391. © Ashmolean Museum, University of Oxford.

Fig. 10. (below) Hollow-cast terracotta fragment of a female head in relief with traces of paint, probably 1st century BC-2nd centuryAD, AN1988.392. © Ashmolean Museum, University of Oxford.

Bibliography

Allen, L. 2013. 'From Silence: A Persepolis Relief in the Victoria and Albert Museum', *V&A Online Journal* 5. http://www.vam.ac.uk/content/journals/research-journal/issue-no.-5-2013/from-silence-a-persepolis-relief-in-the-victoria-and-albert-museum/ (accessed 10 October 2018)

Allen, L. 2017. 'Everything, in Fact, Was Something Else', *Persepolitan*. https://persepolitan.org/ (accessed 10 October 2018)

Ambers, J., and St J. Simpson. 2005. 'Some Pigment Identifications for Objects from Persepolis', *ARTA* 2: 1-13

Barnett, R.D. 1957. 'Persepolis', *Iraq* 19: 55-77

Bodleian Library. 1995. 'Indian Institute', https://www.bodleian.ox.ac.uk/data/assets/pdf_file/0009/194931/Indian-Institute-IN.pdf (accessed 15 October 2018)

Curtis, J.E. 2005. 'The Archaeology of the Achaemenid Period', in Curtis, J.E., and N. Tallis (eds.), *Forgotten Empire: The World of Ancient Persia*. London: British Museum Press, 30-49

Curtis, J. E. 2015. 'Peter Roger Stuart Moorey 1937-2004', *Biographical Memoirs of Fellows of the British Academy* XIV: 363-80

Gilmour, G. 2011. 'The Ancient Near East Gallery at the Ashmolean Museum, Oxford', *Near Eastern Archaeology* 74(2): 124-28

Haley, A., M. Brown and E. Vermue. 2015. 'John Charles Edward Bowen Author Archive', http://www2.oberlin.edu/library/special/finding_guide_bowen.pdf (accessed 18 September 2018)

Labrousse, A., R. and Boucharlat. 1972. 'La fouille du palais du Chaour à Susa en 1970 et 1971', *Cahiers de la Délégation Archéologique Française en Iran* 2: 61-167

Leeds, E.T. 1935. 'Report of the Keeper of the Department of Antiquities for the year 1935', in *Report of the Visitors of the Ashmolean Museum 1935*. Oxford: University Press, 7-20

Malbran-Labat, F. 1995. *Les inscriptions royales de Suse* (IRS). Paris: Editions de la Réunion des musées nationaux

Mitchell, T.C. 2000. 'The Persepolis Sculptures in the British Museum', *Iran* 38: 49-56

Nagel, A. 2010. *Colors, Gilding and Painted Motifs in Persepolis: Approaching the Polychromy of Achaemenid Persian Architectural Sculpture, c. 520-330 BC* (unpublished PhD Dissertation, University of Michigan)

Potts, D.T. 1999. *The Archaeology of Elam*. Cambridge: Cambridge University Press

Roaf, M.D. 1987. 'Checklist of Persepolis Reliefs not at the Site', *Iran* 25: 155-58

Sackville-West, V. 1928. *Twelve Days: An Account of a Journey across the Bakhtiari Mountains in South-western Persia*. London: Hogarth Press

Stronach, D.B. 1978. *Pasargadae: A Report on the Excavations Conducted by the British Institute of Persian Studies from 1961 to 1963*. Oxford: Clarendon Press

Vanden Berghe, L. 1959. *Archéologie de l'Iran ancient*. Leiden: E.J. Brill

2

Where Did the Persian Kings Live in Babylon?

John Curtis

As is well-known, principally from contemporary sources such as the Cyrus Cylinder, the Nabonidus Chronicle and the Verse Account of Nabonidus, the Achaemenid Persian[1] king Cyrus the Great captured Babylon on or around 12 October 539 BC. Thereafter, the city was effectively under Persian control until the conquest of Alexander in 331 BC, although there were rebellions in the reigns of Darius in 522-521 BC and Xerxes in 484-482 BC. Babylon became one of the most important centres of the Achaemenid empire, together with Persepolis, Pasargadae, Susa and Hamadan, and, as we know from cuneiform sources, Babylon prospered economically under the Persian kings and was an important administrative centre.[2] In the late Achaemenid period there was probably also a mint at Babylon (Meadows 2005: 202, 206, nos 363-64). The city was the seat of a Persian satrap or governor, and according to classical sources the Persian kings spent several months of each year in Babylon.

In view of this 200-year Persian domination of the city, it is very surprising that the archaeological record for this period appears comparatively meagre compared with the preceding Neo-Babylonian and succeeding Seleucid periods. The evidence for building activity at Babylon in the Persian period is also quite limited.

---

1   In this paper the terms Persian and Achaemenid are used interchangeably.
2   The wealth of Babylon in the Achaemenid period is also attested, for example, by Herodotus (I.192; III.92).

To start with the archaeological evidence, it is apparently quite sparse, or at least it has not yet been fully recognised, which is particularly surprising considering that the residential district known as Merkes continued to be occupied during the Achaemenid period (Koldewey 1914: 240, 311-12) and there is plentiful evidence for graves of the Achaemenid period (Strommenger 1964). There are archives of tablets, but they are private archives and temple archives, and the administrative or satrapal archives, if they existed, have not been discovered (Briant 2002: 71).[3] Also, the precise provenance of most of the tablets from Babylon is unclear (Reade 1986a).[4] There are occasional discoveries of interest. For example, there are fragments of a round-topped stele of Darius (Seidl 1976; 1999)[5] showing on one side Darius with his foot on a prostrate Gaumata with two rebel kings roped together in front of him, as on the Bisitun relief. The text on the reverse of the stele apparently reproduces the Babylonian version (or part of it) of the Bisitun inscription. A badly mutilated lump of white stone, apparently in the form of addorsed bull protomes and perhaps a column capital (impost block) of Achaemenid date, was found in an east courtyard of the Southern Palace of Nebuchadnezzar (Haerinck 1997: 30). There is also a hoard of silver currency, found by Hormuzd Rasam, probably at Babylon in 1882, which included coins, a silver jar handle in the form of a winged bull, a silver earring and a silver bowl (Reade 1986b). Haerinck (1997: 32-33) has pointed to clay figurines that may be of Achaemenid date (Koldewey 1914: figs 150, 151),[6] and there are sporadic examples of published pottery vessels that are probably Achaemenid (e.g. Fleming 1989: fig. 3G, with references). Koldewey (1914: 267) notes that metal finger-rings, often with engraved bezels to be used as stamp-seals, became common at this period. Animal designs were particularly popular. Beyond this, there is not a great deal.

The evidence for building projects is not very much more informative. In the Cyrus Cylinder, Cyrus is at pains to stress that after capturing

---

3   See also Pedersén 2011. For references to tablets from the reigns of Cyrus, Cambyses, Darius and Artaxerxes with topographical information about Babylon, see George 1992: passim.

4   Around 25 of the Achaemenid period tablets from Babylon now in the British Museum, ranging in date between the reigns of Cyrus and Artaxerxes III, have interesting stamp-seal impressions. See Mitchell and Searight 2008: passim. See also Altavilla and Walker 2016.

5   See Koldewey 1914: 166. It was found in the Kasr mound, in the area of the Northern Palace.

6   It is possible that some of the many figurines from Babylon published as Late Babylonian or as Hellenistic-Parthian (e.g. Karvonen-Kannas 1995, Koldewey 1914: 277-86) might in fact be Achaemenid period.

Babylon he did not destroy the city, and this impression is confirmed in the Verse Account. Likewise, there is no evidence in the archaeological record of a destruction at this time. On the contrary, Cyrus apparently undertook some rebuilding work. In the Cylinder, he says, 'I strove to strengthen the defences of the wall Imgur-Enlil, the great wall of Babylon, and I completed the quay of baked brick on the bank of the moat which an earlier king had built but not completed its work' (Finkel 2013: 7, lines 38-39).[7] He also apparently restored an important building, but the text is broken at this point (lines 42-3). Thereafter, the textual evidence for Achaemenid building work at Babylon is sparse. Herodotus (III.159) says that, following his recapture of Babylon after the city had revolted, 'Darius destroyed their walls and reft away all their gates, neither of which things Cyrus had done at the first taking of Babylon.' However, Darius may also have constructed a new palace at Babylon according to a tablet dated to the 26th year of his reign (Briant 2002: 170, 908). According to late Greek and Roman authors, particularly Diodorus, Strabo, Arrian and Aelian, Xerxes sacked the temples in Babylon after the Babylonian revolts of 484-482 BC, but the evidence for this is disputed. It is accepted by George (2010) but rejected by Kuhrt (2010).[8] Then, as we shall see, there is a Persian-style building (the 'Perserbau') probably built by Artaxerxes II, but this is much too small to have been a royal residence or an important administrative centre. So, where did the Persian kings live when they were in Babylon and where was their principal administrative centre?

As we have seen, Cyrus did not destroy Babylon, and in the Cyrus Cylinder, he says (line 23), 'I founded my sovereign residence within the palace (at Babylon) amid celebration and rejoicing' (Finkel 2013: 6, line 23). There are also references in Xenophon's *Cyropedia* to a palace or palaces in Babylon at the time of Cyrus. Thus, Cyrus visits the fictional Cyaxares (VIII, v. 17) and tells him that a palace has been selected for

---

7   This seems to be in contrast with the statement by Berossus that Cyrus demolished the outer city-wall after he captured Babylon (quoted by Reade 2000: 202; see also Rollinger 2013: 143-47), unless we presume that Cyrus repaired the inner city-wall while at the same time dismantling the outer city-wall. For archaeological evidence for the (re)building of some of the walls of Babylon in the Achaemenid period, see Koldewey 1914: 177, 182, no. 13.

8   According to Arrian (III.16.4-5), after the Battle of Gaugamela, Alexander hastened to Babylon which surrendered to him: 'On entering Babylon Alexander directed the Babylonians to rebuild the temples Xerxes destroyed, and especially the temple of Baal, whom the Babylonians honor more than any other god. . . . At Babylon too he met the Chaldaeans, and carried out all their recommendations on the Babylonian temples, and in particular sacrificed to Baal, according to their instructions.' On Xerxes and Babylon, see Waerzeggers and Seire 2018.

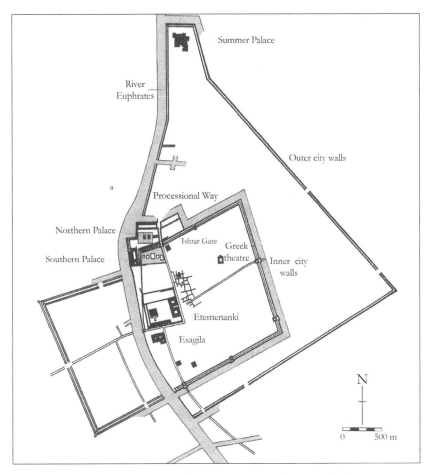

Fig. 1. Plan of Babylon showing location of principal palaces
(from Seymour 2014: map 2).

him in Babylon, so that he might occupy a residence of his own whenever
he goes there, and we are told (VII, v. 57) that, after Cyrus had captured
Babylon, he 'moved into the royal palace and those who had charge of
the treasures brought from Sardis delivered them there'. The implication
is that Cyrus simply took over a palace or palaces formerly used by the
Neo-Babylonian kings (Fig. 1) and that he (and his successors) made use
of them as residential and administrative centres. But is this likely and
plausible? Would the Achaemenid kings have been content to live and
work in buildings which were so closely associated with their displaced
predecessors and where there were constant reminders of their erstwhile

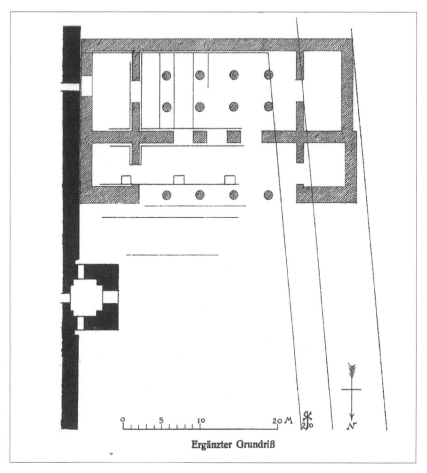

Ergänzter Grundriß

Fig. 2. Plan of the Persian building at Babylon
(from Koldewy 1931: pl. 28).

presence in the form of the inscriptions and so on. It seems unlikely,
so let us examine the evidence for royal residences at Babylon in the
Achaemenid period.

Let us start with the one building at Babylon that is indubitably
Persian. This a small palace or pavilion measuring just 34.80 metres by
20.50 metres on the west side of the Southern Palace of Nebuchadnezzar,
known as 'the Persian building' or the 'Perserbau' (Koldewey 1914:
127-31; 1931: 120-25). It has been studied in detail by Haerinck (1973).
The superstructure of the building was not preserved, but the plan and
associated material were recovered by the German excavators (Fig. 2). It

consists of an inner hall with eight columns which is accessed through a portico on the north side with four columns. The inner hall is flanked by two side rooms, and the portico by two corner towers. The columns are thought to have been of wood, but the column bases were partly preserved. In the inner hall they were bell-shaped but in the portico they consisted of a simple torus. Two fragments of a stone inscription of Artaxerxes II were found in this building (Koldewey 1914: 128-29, fig. 78; Wetzel, Schmidt and Mallwitz 1957: 71, pl. 26, top).[9] The badly damaged impost block referred to above may also have come from this palace. Fragments of stone indicate that originally there were carved reliefs associated with this palace decorated with figural and floral designs. Pieces of glazed brick were also found, with representations of spearmen ('the immortals') and floral designs. These brick fragments were made from sintered quartz in the Achaemenid fashion and not from baked clay as in the Babylonian fashion. The foundations for the floor consisted of a 60-centimetre deep deposit, with the thickest, lowest level made up of pebbles, and pieces of burnt brick, clay and limestone (Haerinck 1973: 112-13; Koldewey 1914: 128). The two levels above this were made in the same fashion but with finer pieces, and the top surface consisted of a very hard, two-millimetre-thick red-coloured layer made of lime and fine gravel.

The different features of this building – the columned hall, the glazed brick decoration, and the red floors – are clear indications that it must be of Achaemenid date. The apadana-style plan finds many parallels in the Achaemenid world (see Stronach 1987) and glazed bricks made from sintered quartz are familiar from Susa and Persepolis. Red cement-like floors are a hallmark of the Achaemenid period and occur at both Susa (Perrot 2013: figs 55, 145) and Persepolis (Schmidt 1953: passim[10]). It is sometimes thought that this palace was built in the reign of Darius (e.g. Haerinck 1975), but the consensus now seems to be that it dates from the time of Artaxerxes II (Haerinck 1997: 28; Briant 2002: 908).

The purpose of this Persian building is quite unclear. In view of its small size, it can hardly have served any useful ceremonial, administrative or residential function, and it is tempting to see it as some sort of pavilion built for the recreation and relaxation of the Persian king or the satrap. However, perhaps it can be better understood in the context of the vast 600-room palace to the east of it, known as the Southern Palace of Nebuchadnezzar and restored at huge expense on

9   Other Achaemenid period inscriptions on fragments of stone from Babylon are also illustrated in Wetzel et al. 1957: pl. 26.

10   For references, see index under 'red-surfaced flooring'.

the orders of Saddam Hussein during the Iraq-Iran war. This restoration was on a gigantic scale, so that now the main entrance to the palace is through a reconstructed arch 30 metres high and many of the walls have been rebuilt to a height of eighteen metres. Herman Gasche (2013) has recently made the very interesting suggestion that the western parts of this building, known as the '*Westhof* and the '*Anbauhof*, were built or rebuilt during the Achaemenid period. He bases this hypothesis on the presence of an architectural feature known as the '*salle à quatre saillants*'. This consists of a room on one side of a courtyard with four pilasters arranged as symmetrical pairs toward the ends of the long sides of the room. There is a wide entrance between the courtyard and the room with four pilasters. It is usually supposed that the purpose of these pilasters is to enable large rooms to be covered over with mud brick vaults. The pilasters would have supported transverse vaults at either end of the room and a barrel vault for most of the length of the room between the two pairs of pilasters. Gasche maintains that the combination of these features, that is the four-pilaster room and the wide entrance, is a distinctively Iranian plan that is first evidenced at Susa in the second millennium BC and found later in the Palace of Darius at Susa (Gasche 2013: fig. 482).

Michael Roaf earlier studied the '*salle à quatre saillants*' and concluded (1973: 91) that:

> after its early appearance in the Middle Elamite period, for six centuries we lose sight of the '*salle à quatre saillants*' with its characteristic four pilasters and entrance on the long side leading on to a courtyard. In the seventh century BC, however, there is a change in Neo-Assyrian palace design, which may be because of the introduction of this architectural form.[11] Thereafter the '*salle à quatre saillants*' has a wide distribution, being found in the Neo-Babylonian southern citadel at Babylon, in Darius's Palace at Susa, at Lachish, and at Persepolis in the fifth century BC.

It is not certain, then, that the appearance of the '*salle à quatre saillants*' at Babylon is a hallmark of Iranian influence but, given that the extreme western part of the Southern Palace is a later addition, it is at least plausible. The later building work is evidenced by the fact that the eastern walls of the *Anbauhof* are not bonded with the western walls of

---

11   Gasche argues (2013: 437) that the Elamite/Achaemenid and Assyrian forms of this plan are different and independent of each other.

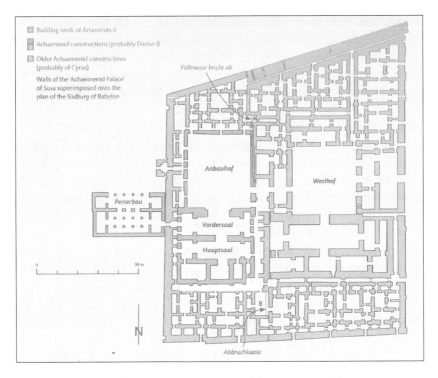

Fig. 3. Plan of the western part of the Southern Palace
(from Gasche 2013: fig. 481).

the *Westhof* (Fig. 3; Gasche 2013: fig. 481). Of course, it might be argued
that any later building work in the Southern Palace could have happened
in the reigns of Neriglissar or Nabonidus, and this possibility cannot be
excluded. Nevertheless, Gasche's argument does seem quite compelling.

There is further evidence for later building work, in this case almost
certainly Persian, in the central part of the Southern Palace. In court 36,
just to the south of the Throne Room, were two brick-built surrounds
for the bases of palm trunk columns (Koldewey 1914: 108-9, fig. 66;
and 101, fig. 63). These sockets were covered with plaster and have
been compared with columns at Persepolis.[12] The columns presumably
supported a roof or awning that that was a later addition to the courtyard.
In the central courtyard (*Haupthof*) of the Southern Palace, Koldewey

12   In the Persepolis report, Schmidt (1953: 28) notes that these column supports
found at Babylon can be compared with columns encased in plaster shells
found in the Treasury at Persepolis.

found post-Babylonian remains consisting of a brick-built tower 11.50 metres square and with walls 3.25 metres thick. Inside were the remains of an altar (?). Koldewey (131: 77) speculates that this building might have been a small temple of the Persian period. Haerinck (1987: 141) compares this building with the temple at Nush-e Jan, the Zendan-e Soleiman at Pasargadae, and the Kabeh-e Zardusht at Naqsh-e Rustam. Erich Schmidt had apparently suggested it could be a fire temple. In any case, it seems likely that that the building was of the Persian period. It seems, then, that the central part of the Southern Palace was certainly in use during the Persian period and probably also the western part. The whole Southern Palace could have been a residential and administrative hub in the Persian period, in which case the small apadana-style building next to it might have been intended as nothing more than a place of escape for the Persian king and dignitaries.

At this point it is interesting to reflect on the fact that Saddam Hussein spent millions of dinars rebuilding the Southern Palace, and the building was opened with great fanfare during the Babylon Festival of 1988. According to Sir Terence Clark,[13] British Ambassador to Iraq 1985-89:

> The diplomatic corps was seated in the Processional Way, by then heavily restored, and we listened to hymns of praise to President Saddam Hussein for Iraq's victory over Iran and to a father recounting to his son the story of the greatness of Nebuchadnezzar, which he likened to the greatness of Saddam. We watched as rows of soldiers and girls dressed in Babylonian costumes marched before us down the Processional Way, accompanied by lit torches and music played on 'Babylonian' instruments, to the far end where two tall palm trees carried the profiled portraits of Nebuchadnezzar on one and the remarkably similar portrait of Saddam on the other.

The great irony here is that Saddam may have been restoring a building that was at least partly Persian.

Gasche also notes the presence of the same architectural feature – that is the four-pilaster hall opening off a courtyard with a wide entrance – in the west court of the Northern Palace of Nebuchadnezzar (the *Hauptburg*) (Fig. 4; Gasche 2013: fig. 489, left) and in the west court of the Summer Palace (Fig. 5; Gasche 2013: fig. 489, right). He therefore concludes that there is evidence for Persian building or rebuilding in both these palaces.

---

13   Personal communication.

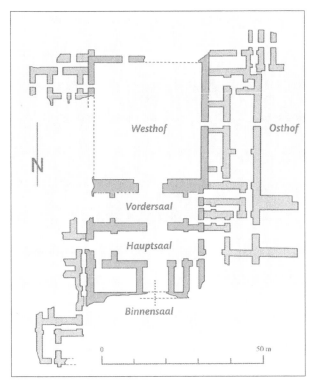

Fig. 4. Plan of the western part of the Northern Palace (from Gasche 2013: fig. 489, left).

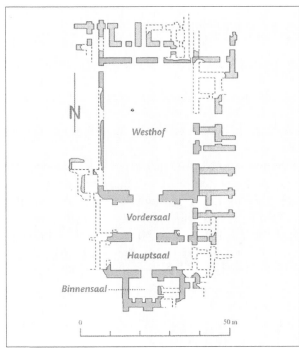

Fig. 5. Plan of the west court of the Summer Palace (from Gasche 2013: fig. 489, right).

Fig. 6. View of Tell Babil from the south. Photo J.E. Curtis.

If Gasche is correct – and his theory appears to be quite convincing – the west parts of the Southern Palace, the Northern Palace and the Summer Palace were all modified, or even built, in the Achaemenid period. However, would these palaces with their ostentatious decoration and close association with the former Babylonian regime, at least in the first two cases, have been suitable places of residence for the Persian king and his court? This seems unlikely, even with the addition of the so-called Persian building.

If we exclude the Southern and Northern Palaces of Nebuchadnezzar, there is no obvious location in the central area of Babylon, on either side of the Euphrates, where the Persian kings might have had a substantial palace of their own. This leaves us with Tell Babil (or Tell Mujelibè) often referred to as the Summer Palace of Nebuchadnezzar, in the most northerly point of the outer town, just within the outer city-wall and originally flanked on the west side by the River Euphrates (Fig. 6).

In his inscriptions, Nebuchadnezzar talks principally about the Southern and Northern Palaces (Beaulieu 2017: 9-10), particularly the latter, which is also described by the Babylonian priest Berossos writing at the beginning of the third century BC as follows:

He [Nebuchadnezzar] built in addition to his father's palace another palace adjoining it. It would perhaps take too long to describe its height and general opulence, except to say that, despite its extraordinary size and splendor, it was completed in fifteen days. In this palace he built high stone terraces and made them appear very similar to mountains, planting them with all kinds of trees, thus constructing and arranging the so-called Hanging Garden, because his wife, who had been raised in the regions of Media, longed for a mountainous scenery. (Rollinger 2013: 148)

Both Rollinger (*ibid.*) and Stronach (2018: 474-75) believe that this Northern Palace was also the likely site of the hanging gardens.[14] So, the two major palaces at Babylon are definitely associated with Nebuchadnezzar, but what about Tell Babil? In one inscription, a stone cylinder in the British Museum, Nebuchadnezzar refers to the building of a great palace in the north part of the city (Langdon 1905: no. XIV, col. 3, 11-29).[15] It is this reference that has led Koldewey and others to identify Tell Babil/Tell Mujelibè as 'the Summer Palace of Nebuchadnezzar'.[16] The case for this identification is certainly strong, but I submit that it is not quite proven. At least, the matter warrants further investigation. Let us now consider the archaeological evidence.

Tell Babil is described by Robert Koldewey as follows:

The mound rises with a steep slope to the height of 22 metres above the plain.[17] Its area forms a square of about 250 metres (i.e. 250m x 250m), and this hill, consisting of broken brick

---

14 For an alternative view, see Dalley 2013.

15 Langdon writes (1905: 19): 'No.14 is remarkable, because it contains the first mention of two new palaces built by the king, one between the inner and outer walls north of the old palace, and one north of the city on the hill now called Babil. . . . It is remarkable that we have no trace of this northern palace in the later inscription 15, nor as yet in any other inscription. Perhaps the scribes of no. 15, ever jealous of the glory of Marduk, chose to suppress all reference to a palace situated outside the sacred precincts and in [a] part of Babylon looking towards the ancient seat of Shamash of Sippar. At any rate, 14 is the sole source of information concerning this great palace and bulwark north of the city, which, like a phantom, appears in these few lines (col.3, 11-29) and then vanishes entirely from trustworthy history.'

16 See also Finkel and Seymour 2008: 67, and 99, n. 111; and Beaulieu 2017: 10.

17 On 27 February 2009, GPS coordinates at the highest point of the mound were noted as 140' ASL, N 32°33.950', EO 44°25.504'.

Fig. 7. An inspection of Tell Babil in February 2009. Photo J.E. Curtis.

or clayey earth, is pierced by deep ravines and tunnels, while on the north and south-west remains of walls of very considerable height are still standing, with courses of mud-brick held together by layers of well-preserved reed stems (Koldewey 1914: 10).

He comments (*ibid.*) on 'the astonishingly deep pits and galleries' occurring in places that 'owe their origin to the quarrying for brick that has been carried on extensively during the last decades'.

This extensive quarrying for bricks is still evident today,[18] although the quarrying no longer continues, and the mound is very much disturbed, to a considerable depth in places, so much so that on a brief inspection it is difficult to make much sense of the stratigraphy or of any building plans there might be (Fig. 7). Clearly visible, however, are, firstly, great blocks of brickwork with reeds or reed matting between the courses and, secondly, blocks of walling with pieces of brick (not complete bricks) set in gypsum mortar and with further gypsum mortar between the courses

18   I visited Tell Babil on 27 February 2009 as part of a UNESCO inspection of Babylon. There was rolled barbed wire all around the base of the site, and our party was told that no visitors or local people were allowed to access the site. It was protected by two guards. No recent damage was observed, and just one firing-point was noted, facing south-east on the crest of the mound. It was an oval trench, 2.40m x 1.20m, c. 0.70m deep. GPS coordinates were 113' ASL, N 32°33.936', EO 44°25.531'. See Van Ess and Curtis 2009.

Fig. 8. Inspecting brickwork at Tell Babil in February 2009. Photo J.E. Curtis.

Fig. 9. Brickwork at Tell Babil with reed matting between the courses in February 2009. Photo J.E. Curtis.

(Figs 8-9). These latter blocks of walling are faced with plaster. Around the site there is an abundance of glazed pottery in green or turquoise, either glazed on one surface or on both surfaces. There are also fragments of glass, kiln wasters, and fragments of monochrome glazed bricks.

The sites of ancient Babylon, in general, and Tell Babil, in particular, were visited by a number of early travellers, some of whom undertook limited excavations.[19] As many of these accounts are now difficult to access, and are relevant for our survey, we shall quote from them as appropriate.

19 For a summary of the various excavations undertaken in Tell Babil from the early nineteenth century onwards, see Reade 1999: 57-63.

Let us start with Claudius James Rich, who wrote in 1815:

> The summit (of Tell Mujelibè) is covered with heaps of
> rubbish, in digging into some of which, layers of broken burnt
> brick cemented with mortar are discovered, and whole bricks
> with inscriptions on them are here and there found: the whole
> is covered with innumerable fragments of pottery, brick,
> bitumen, pebbles, vitrified brick or scoria, and even shells,
> bits of glass and mother of pearl. (Rich 1815: 29, quoted in
> Seymour 2014: 136)

In the course of his excavations, Rich found a number of tunnels and
passages, and burials including a well-preserved skeleton in a wooden
coffin (Reade 1999: 59-61).

Robert Ker Porter (1821-22: II, 340-341) did not excavate here but
made some interesting and, as we shall see, prescient observations:

> The Mujelibè . . . is only second to the Birs Nimrood in being
> one of the most gigantic masses of brick-formed earth that
> ever was raised by the labour of man. It is composed of these
> sun-dried materials, to the present height of 140 feet. . . .
> Regular lines of clay brick-work are clearly discernible along
> each face. . . . From the general appearance of this piece of
> ruin, I scarcely think that its solid elevation has ever been
> much higher than it stands at present. I have no doubt of its
> having been a ground-work, or magnificent raised platform,
> (like that of Persepolis, though there it was of the native rock;)
> to sustain habitable buildings of consequence.

Layard, who excavated briefly at Tell Babil towards the end of 1850,
rediscovered the tunnels and passages investigated by Rich, and found
more coffins and inscribed stone slabs of Nebuchadnezzar (Layard 1853:
502). In addition,

> numerous deep trenches opened on the surface of the mound,
> and several tunnels carried into its sides at different levels,
> led to no other discovery than that of numerous relics of a
> doubtful period, such as are found in large numbers, in a more
> or less perfect state, amongst all Babylonian ruins, especially
> after heavy rains have washed away the loose soil, or have
> deepened the ravines. The most interesting were arrow-heads

in bronze and iron, small glass bottles, some colored, others ribbed and otherwise ornamented, and vases of earthenware of various forms and sizes, sometimes glazed with a rich blue color. (Layard 1853: 503)

Unable to make much sense of the ruins on the surface, however, Layard determined to attack the mound at its base. In his own words (Layard 1853: 504-5):

It was thus evident that the remains of the original edifice, if any still existed, were to be sought far beneath the surface and I accordingly opened tunnels at the very foot of the mound nearly on a level with the plain. A few days' labor enabled me to ascertain that we had at last found the ancient building. On the eastern side the workmen soon reached solid piers and walls of brick masonry, buried under an enormous mass of loose bricks, earth, and rubbish. We uncovered eight or ten piers and several walls branching in various directions, but I failed to trace any plan, or to discover any remains whatever of sculptured stone or painted plaster.

He further surmised (1853: 503) that above the 'enormous mass of loose bricks, earth, and rubbish' covering the original building was some kind of fortification which he dated to the Seleucid period:

Upon that great heap, over the fallen palace or temple, was probably raised one of those citadels, which formed the defences of a city built long after the destruction of the Babylonian empire and its magnificent capital, and which resisted the arms of Demetrius Poliorcetes. Of that stronghold the thick wall of sun-dried brick on the northern side is probably the remains.

He rightly recognised the graves as belonging to the Seleucid period or later (Layard 1853: 503).

J.P. Peters, the excavator of Nippur, who visited Babylon in 1885 and 1889, described Tell Babil as follows (1897: I, 208-210):

In one place I observed well-made columns of bricks, the spaces between which had been built up later, thus turning a construction resting upon piers into a solid mass. In another place I noticed a doorway which had been filled with rubble brick, after which a solid structure of brick had been erected in front of it. . . . Bitumen was used as a mortar in a portion, at least, of these brick structures; and the impressions in the bitumen showed that sometimes mats had been placed between the layers of brick. On top of the masses of baked brick was a mass of unbaked brick, about thirty feet of which I found in place. Between the layers of the unbaked bricks were thin mats. . . . There were occasionally palm beams thrust in among the unbaked bricks to strengthen the construction. Near the doorway, which I have described above, Hilprecht picked up a brick of Nabopolassar. All of the other bricks which we found here . . . bear the name of Nebuchadnezzar. . . . In the diggings on the mound, as well as on the surface, I found fragments of green glazed pottery, sometimes imbedded in bricks. . . . There were everywhere fragments of enamelled bricks, and these looked as though they had been exposed to the action of fire in a great conflagration.

These accounts, then, provide the background to the German excavations at Babylon between 1899 and 1917. What they discovered was an artificial platform about eighteen metres in height, that was 'so constructed that the building walls throughout are continuous and of the same thickness above and below, while the intermediate spaces are filled up to the height of the palace floor with earth and a packing of fragments of brick' (Koldewey 1914: 11). Layard was mistaken in believing that the original building was at ground level, and what he excavated was the artificial platform, with brick walls and piers with brick infill between them.

On top of the artificial platform was a monumental building with 'many courts and chambers, both small and large' (Koldewey 1914: 11). The published plan (Fig. 10; Koldewey 1932: pl. 32) shows part of a building, probably a palace, with two large courtyards (*Westhof* and *Osthof*) and on the east side of the east courtyard an intrusive burial chamber with alcoves, presumably of the Parthian period. Some small additions to the plan in the north-west part of the building were made by Iraqi excavations in the 1970s (Nasir 1979: 157, plan 3). Koldewey tells us that:

the floor consists of sandstone flags on the edge of which is inscribed 'Palace of Nebuchadnezzar, King of Babylon, son of Nabopolassar, King of Babylon'. There are also many portions

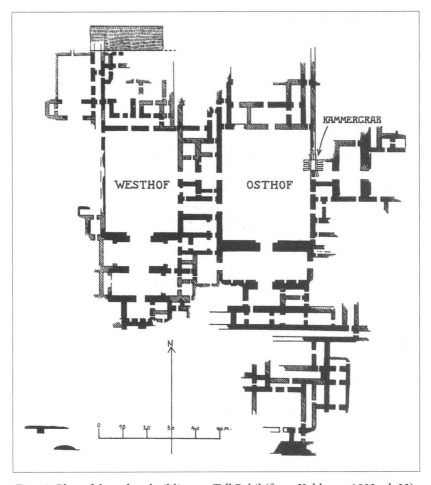

Fig. 10. Plan of the palace building on Tell Babil (from Koldewey 1932: pl. 32).

of a limestone pavement that consists of a thick rough under stratum, and a fine upper stratum half a centimetre thick, and coloured a fine red or yellow. . . . All the bricks stamped with the name of Nebuchadnezzar . . . were either laid in asphalt or in a grey lime mortar. (Koldewey 1914: 11)

Koldewey concluded (1914: 11) that it was 'impossible to doubt that Babil was a palace of Nebuchadnezzer's'. He based this on the presence of the sandstone flags and the bricks inscribed with the name of Nebuchadnezzar, and the reference in the Nebuchadnezzar inscription

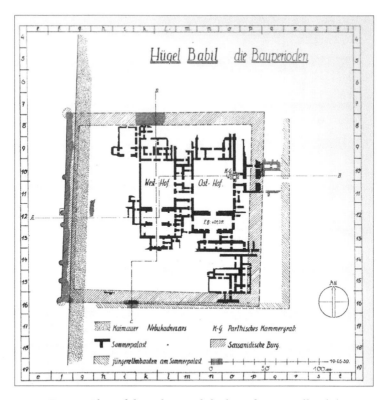

Fig. 11. Plan of the palace and the later fort on Tell Babil
(from Wetzel et al. 1957: pl. 13).

to his building a great palace in the north part of Babylon that we have
considered above. This identification is reflected in the modern name of
the building as 'the Summer Palace of Nebuchadnezzar'. But was it?

Before considering this, let is deal with the structure(s) above the
monumental palace building. This was a square fort-like building (Fig.
11; Wetzel, Schmidt and Mallwitz 1957: pl. 13), dated by Koldewey
(1914: 10) to the Sasanian or Islamic period, and by other scholars to
the Parthian period (for references, see Reade 1999: 62-63). My personal
preference, based on the form of the plan, would be for the Sasanian
period, but the date of this later structure does not concern us here.[20]
Our preoccupation is with the palatial building and its date.

---

20   We have already noted the presence of possible Parthian material. Architectural
      ornaments, including an antefix, may be of Hellenistic date (Wetzel et al. 1957:
      pls 23c and 23d; André-Salvini 2008: no 209 on p. 262).

As we have already noted, red cement-like floors are a feature of the Achaemenid period, and according to Koldewey many portions of the floor in the monumental building consisted of 'a thick rough under stratum, and a fine upper stratum half a centimetre thick, and coloured a fine red or yellow'.[21] There can be no doubt, then, that the palace was either built in the Achaemenid period or reused in the Achaemenid period. There are two further reasons for suggesting an Achaemenid association. The first is the plan of the building. As noted by Gasche, the room on the south side of the *Westhof* is a '*salle à quatre saillants*', which in his view is a hallmark of Achaemenid architecture. Secondly, there is the fact that the palace is built on an artificial mound eighteen metres in height.

Very often in the Achaemenid period, monumental buildings were constructed on an elevated platform, or *takht*, that might have been adapted from a natural feature (as at Persepolis), or built up artificially (as at Pasargadae, with the Tall-e Takht), or created by levelling and remodelling an existing mound (as at Susa), or by building a massive mud-brick platform on an existing mound (as at Tepe Sialk). At Persepolis, a raised terrace measuring about 455 metres by 300 metres was cut from the mountainside, while at Pasargadae a raised platform was created with an outer face of massive stone blocks and a central core of limestone chips (Stronach 1978: 11-23). This platform was apparently created by Cyrus as part of a building programme, probably for an elevated palace, that was aborted when attention switched to Persepolis and Susa. At Susa, the whole of the top of the Apadana Mound was leveled to create a *takht* on which to build the massive palace of Darius (Perrot 2013: fig. 100). It is possible that the massive brick platform uncovered by Ghirshman at Tepe Sialk (Ghirshman 1954: 83-84) (sometimes mistakenly thought to be a ziggurat) and the terrace at Masjid-e Soleiman (Ghirhman 1954: 122, fig. 49) were also both platforms (*takhts*) created in the Achaemenid period. There is, then, good evidence that in the Achaemenid period, royal palaces and other buildings were constructed on elevated platforms. Of course, this does not prove that the artificial mound of Tell Mujelibè dates from the Achaemenid period, but the similarity with Achaemenid platforms, as observed by Ker Porter, is striking.

Whatever the date of the platform, Babylonian or Achaemenid, it seems beyond doubt that there was an Achaemenid-period building on top of the artificial mound, but whether it was the original building

---

21   Koldewey remarks (1914: 128) that the red floors in the Persian building and in Tell Babil were 'made in exactly the same fashion'. Haerinck (1973: 113) also notes the presence of red floors in the Babil mound and sees it as a sign of Persian period occupation.

or whether it was on top of a Nebuchadnezzar building, or whether the Nebuchadnezzar building was modified and reoccupied in the Achaemenid period, are all matters for conjecture. It is worth noting, however, that bricks and fragments of brick with Nebuchadnezzar inscriptions were apparently found in the fill of the artificial mound. The implication must be that the debris used to build up the mound came from a disused Nebuchadnezzar building, which makes it rather unlikely – although not impossible – that the first building on top of the artificial mound also dates from the time of Nebuchadnezzar, although it could be from late in his reign. It is also possible that the inscribed sandstone flags and the Nebuchadnezzar bricks that were apparently found in association with the palace were also reused. Lastly, it might be argued that, if the original palace was of Achaemenid date, we might expect it to have been built in the Persian style, perhaps incorporating a column hall. However, the main part of Darius' palace at Susa is built in the Babylonian style, and like the North Palace it incorporates a 'salle à quatre saillants' that in the view of Gasche is an Achaemenid feature. It is tempting to agree with Gasche that because of the 'salle à quatre saillants' and the red floors the Summer Palace could be 'the work of one of the forebears of Artaxerxes II' (Gasche 2013: 448) but[22] the evidence at present remains inconclusive.

For the time being it does not seem possible to take this argument any further. The cuneiform evidence is strong, but not conclusive. Further excavation in the Tell Babil mound might clarify the matter but, as noted, the site is badly disturbed. Further study of the small finds from this area might also pay dividends. For example, it would be helpful to know whether the many fragments of glazed brick are made of clay in the Babylonian manner or of sintered quartz like the Achaemenid glazed bricks. It would be convenient for our hypothesis if it could be demonstrated that Persian kings, perhaps from the time of Darius onwards, spurned the great Babylonian palaces at ground level

---

22   The question of where Alexander might have stayed when he was in Babylon is also of interest but similarly unresolved. After the Battle of Gaugamela Alexander hastened to Babylon and stayed there for about a month before proceeding to Susa. After an eight-year absence he returned to Babylon following his Indian campaign and died there in 323 BC. Plutarch records (*Lives*, Alexander, LXXVI) that in the later stages of his last illness he was 'carried to the palace on the other side of the river', where he died. This account seems to be corroborated by Arrian (*Anabasis*, VII, 26) who states: 'Thence he was carried on his couch to the river, and embarking on a boat sailed across the river to the garden'; a few days later he 'was carried from the garden to the palace'. The problem with these accounts is that as far as is known the palaces are all on the east side of the river.

and preferred to live in a newly constructed palace on an elevated site to the north of the city, but this must remain conjecture for the time being. All we can definitely say at present is that the presence of red plaster floors and the '*salle à quatre saillants*' featuring in the Southern and Northern Palaces and the Summer Palace show that all these buildings were occupied or reoccupied in the Persian period. It would be gratifying to be able to conclude that the Summer Palace was a Persian-period construction on top of an artificial mound or *takht* but while this remains a possibility the evidence available at present is equivocal.

Bibliography

Altavilla, S., and C.B.F. Walker. 2016. *Late Babylonian Seal Impressions on Tablets in the British Museum, Part 2: Babylon and its Vicinity*, Messina: Arbor Sapientiae
André-Salvini, B. (ed.). 2008. *Babylone* (catalogue of exhibition), Paris: Musée du Louvre
Arrian. *Anabasis of Alexander*, Loeb Classical Library (1976), Cambridge, MA: Harvard University Press
Askari Chaverdi, A., and P. Callieri. 2014. 'Tol-e Ajori Monumental Building', *12th Annual Symposium on Iranian Archaeology*, Tehran: 39-40 (in Persian)
Askari Chaverdi, A., P. Callieri and E. Matin. 2017. 'The Monumental Gate at Tol-e Ajori, Persepolis (Fars): New Archaeological Data', *Iranica Antiqua* LII: 205-58
Basello, G.P. 2017. 'Two New Fragments of Cuneiform Inscriptions on Glazed Bricks from the Iranian-Italian Excavations at Tol-e Ajori (Fars)', *Iranica Antiqua* LII: 259-81
Beaulieu, P.-A. 2017. 'Palaces of Babylon and Palaces of Babylonian Kings', *Journal of the Canadian Society for Mesopotamian Studies* 11-12: 5-14
Briant, P. 2002. *From Cyrus to Alexander: A History of the Persian Empire*, Winona Lake, IN: Eisenbrauns
Dalley, S. 2013. *The Mystery of the Hanging Garden of Babylon*, Oxford: Oxford University Press
Ess, M. van, and J.E. Curtis (eds). 2009. *Final (UNESCO) Report on Damage Assessment in Babylon*, UNESCO
Finkel, I.L, and M.J. Seymour. 2008. *Babylon: Myth and Reality*, London: British Museum
Finkel, I.L. (ed.). 2013. *The Cyrus Cylinder: The King of Persia's Proclamation from Ancient Babylon*, London: I.B. Tauris
Fleming, D. 1989. 'Eggshell Ware in Achaemenid Mesopotamia', *Iraq* LI: 165-85
Gasche, H. 2013. 'The Achaemenid Persian Palaces of Babylon', in J. Perrot (ed.), *The Palace of Darius at Susa*, London: I.B. Tauris, 436-50
George, A.R. 1992. *Babylonian Topographical Texts*, Leuven: Peeters
George, A.R. 2010. 'Xerxes and the Tower of Babel', in J.E. Curtis and S.J. Simpson (eds), *The World of Achaemenid Persia*, London: 471-80
Ghirshman, R. 1954. *Iran*, Harmondsworth: Penguin
Haerinck, E. 1973. 'Le palais achéménide de Babylone', *Iranica Antiqua* X: 108-32

Haerinck, E. 1987. 'La neuvième satrapie: archéologie confronte histoire?', *Achaemenid History* 1: 139-45

Haerinck, E. 1997. 'Babylonia under Achaemenid Rule', in J.E. Curtis (ed.), *Mesopotamia and Iran in the Persian Period: Conquest and Imperialism 539-331 BC*, London: British Museum, 26-34

Herodotus. *Histories*, Loeb Classical Library (1989), Cambridge, MA: Harvard University Press

Karvonen-Kannas, K. 1995. *The Seleucid and Parthian Terracotta Figurines from Babylon*, Florence: Casa Editrice le Lettere

Koldewey, R. 1914. *The Excavations at Babylon*, London: Macmillan & Co

Koldewey, R. 1931. *Die Königsburgen von Babylon, Part 1: Die Südburg*, Leipzig, edited by F. Wetzel

Koldewey, R. 1932. *Die Königsburgen von Babylon, Part 2: Die Hauptburg und der Sommerpalast Nebukadnezars im Hügel Babil*, Leipzig, edited by F. Wetzel

Ker Porter, R. 1821-22. *Travels in Georgia, Persia, Armenia, Ancient Babylonia*, 2 vols, London: Longman, Hurst, Rees, Orme & Brown

Kuhrt, A. 2010. 'Xerxes and the Babylonian Temples: A Restatement of the Case', in J.E. Curtis and S.J. Simpson (eds), *The World of Achaemenid Persia*, London: Bloomsbury, 491-94

Langdon, S. 1905. *Building Inscriptions of the Neo-Babylonian Empire, Part 1: Nabopolassar and Nebuchadnezzar*, Paris: E. Leroux

Meadows, A.R. 2005. 'The Administration of the Achaemenid Empire', in J.E. Curtis and N. Tallis (eds). *Forgotten Empire: The World of Ancient Iran*, London: British Museum, 181-209

Mitchell, T.C., and A. Searight. 2008. *Catalogue of the Western Asiatic Seals in the British Museum: Stamp Seals III*, Leiden: Brill

Nasir, M. 1979. 'The So-called Summer Palace (Nebuchadnezzar's Life Palace)', *Sumer* XXXV: 152-59

Pedersén, O. 2011. 'Excavated and Unexcavated Libraries in Babylon', in Cancik-Kirschbaum, E., M. van Ess and J. Marzahn (eds), *Babylon: Wissenkultur in Orient und Okzident*, Topoi 1, Berlin: Walter de Gruyter, 47-67

Perrot, J. (ed.). 2013. *The Palace of Darius at Susa*, London: I.B. Tauris

Peters, J.P. 1897. *Nippur, or Explorations and Adventures on the Euphrates*, 2 vols, New York: G.P. Putnam's Sons

Reade, J.E. 1986a. 'Rassam's Babylonian Collection: The Excavations and the Archives', in E. Leichty. *Catalogue of the Babylonian Tablets in the British Museum* VI, London: British Museum, xiii-xxxvi

Reade, J.E. 1986b. 'A Hoard of Silver Currency from Achaemenid Babylonia', *Iran* XXIV: 79-87

Reade, J.E. 1999. 'Early British Excavations at Babylon', in J. Renger (ed.). *Babylon: Focus Mesopotamischer Geschichte, Wiege Früher Gelehrsamkeit, Mythos in der Moderne (2. Internationales Colloquium der Deutschen Orient-Gesellschaft 24.-26. März 1998 in Berlin)*, Saarbrücken: Harrassowitz Verlag, 47-65

Reade, J.E. 2000. 'Alexander the Great and the Hanging Gardens of Babylon', *Iraq* LXII: 195-217

Roaf, M.D. 1973. 'The Diffusion of the "*Salles à Quatre Saillants*"', *Iraq* XXXV: 83-91

Rollinger, R. 2013. 'Berossos and the Monuments: City Walls, Sanctuaries, Palaces and the Hanging Garden', in J. Haubold, G.B. Lanfranchi, R. Rollinger and

J. Steele (eds), *The World of Berossos*, Classica et Orientalia 5, Wiesbaden: Harrassowitz Verlag, 137-62

Schmidt, E.F. 1953. *Persepolis I: Structures, Reliefs, Inscriptions*, OIP 68, Chicago: University of Chicago Press

Seidl, U. 1976. 'Ein Relief Dareios' I in Babylon', *AMI* 9: 125-30

Seidl, U. 1999. 'Ein Monument Darius' I. aus Babylon', *Zeitschrift für Assyriologie* 89: 101-14

Strommenger, E. 1964. 'Grabformen in Babylon', *Baghdader Mitteilungen* III: 157-73

Stronach, D. 1978. *Pasargadae: A Report on the Excavations*, Oxford: Clarendon Press

Stronach, D. 1987. 'Apadana, ii: Building', *Encyclopaedia Iranica* II: 146-48

Stronach, D. 2018. 'Notes on Nineveh, Babylon and the Hanging Gardens', in S. Gondet and E. Haerinck (eds). *L'Orient est Son Jardin: Hommage à Remy Boucharlat*, Acta Iranica 58, Leuven: Peeters, 467-76

Waerzeggers, C., and M. Seire (eds). 2018. *Xerxes and Babylonia: The Cuneiform Evidence*, Leuven: Peeters

Wetzel, F., E. Schmidt and A. Mallwitz. 1957. *Das Babylon der Spätzeit*, WVDO-G 62, Berlin: Mann

Xenophon. *Cyropedia*, Loeb Classical Library (1914) Cambridge, MA: Harvard University Press

3

The Use of Seals in Babylonia under the Achaemenids

C.B.F. Walker

The study of seal impressions on late Babylonian tablets, for long neglected, has flourished in the last 30 years. Regrettably, T.G. Pinches, who was a master draftsman, was instructed by E.A.W. Budge not to draw the seal impressions on the tablets which he was copying, so his copies in the fifth Rawlinson volume (Pinches 1884: pls 67 and 68) are his last published drawings. For many decades it used to be customary just to note that a tablet was sealed, copy the accompanying captions and perhaps draw the outline of the seal impressions. Nowadays, while seals specialists have mostly concentrated on the surviving original seals, Assyriologists have become accustomed to drawing the seal impressions on tablets for themselves, and to look to see whether the same seal can be identified on more than one tablet. As a result we not only begin to get a much better idea of how seals were being used but also get a better basis for more precisely dating the surviving seals.

The following comments on seal usage under the Achaemenids are based primarily on tablets from northern Babylonia, particularly Sippar, Babylon, Borsippa, Dilbat and Kutha. The seal impressions on letter orders from Sippar were copied by John MacGinnis for his book (MacGinnis 1995), and those on tablets from Babylon, Borsippa and Kutha have been copied in numerous books and articles by Heather Baker, Michael Jursa, Caroline Waerzeggers and Cornelia Wunsch. Their work formed the starting point for the wider studies of late-Babylonian seal impressions published by Stefania Altavilla and Christopher Walker (Altavilla and

Walker 2009 and 2016). Much work has been done on tablets from Uruk by Erica Ehrenberg (Ehrenberg 1999), on the mid-Achaemenid archive of the Murašû family at Nippur by Linda Bregstein (Bregstein 1993) and, recently, on the late Achaemenid tablets from Uruk by Johannes Hackl and Joachim Oelsner (Hackl and Oelsner 2017; see also Oelsner 1978). Sadly, it is not possible to make any useful comments on the archives from Achaemenid Ur, since in the early 1950s the British Museum made the mistake of sending back almost all of the sealed Neo-Babylonian tablets copied by H.H. Figulla for *Ur Excavations Texts IV* (Figulla 1949) without making any drawings or photographs of the seal impressions.

Catalogues of the late Babylonian and Achaemenid cylinder seals in the British Museum have been published by Dominique Collon (Collon 2001) and Parvine Merrillees (Merrillees 2005), but unfortunately the equivalent catalogue of stamp seals (which might be as many as 600 in all) has made no progress. Terence Mitchell and Ann Searight's catalogue of stamp seal impressions in the British Museum (Mitchell and Searight 2007) is a useful source of illustrations but makes no attempt to discuss typology or context.

Discussion of seal usage must begin with two warnings. First, we have only a very partial view of what was happening in antiquity. From Sippar we have the archive of the Ebabbar temple but relatively few tablets from private archives. From Babylon, Borsippa, Dilbat and Kutha we have numerous private archives (Egibi etc.) down to the time of Xerxes but few such archives later (apart from the Murašû archive at Nippur), temple archives only from the late Achaemenid to Seleucid periods (the Esangila archives), and no archives from the central government (although this might partly be explained by a growing use of papyri). Second, the seal impressions on tablets are often disappointingly incomplete. In particular many cylinder seals were only partially rolled on the edges of tablets. Plainly what mattered was that the witness or contracting party was seen to have sealed the tablet, not that he sealed it well.

The tablets sealed may be divided into three groups, contracts, administrative texts and letters. The largest groups of sealed contracts are court records and property sales, and they have distinctive patterns of sealing. Court records are sealed by the judges and occasionally by other senior officials. The tablets have squared edges, and the judges and officials seal in order of seniority, the first sealing on the upper left edge, the next on the lower left edge, and others sealing on the upper and lower right edge, and finally on the lower and upper edges (Wunsch 2000: 564). Property sales (of land and houses) follow a similar pattern, with the distinct group of land-sale scribes sealing on the left and right edges.

Occasionally land sales are the result of legal disputes and in these cases the tablets are sealed by the judges in the same manner as court records. All seals on these tablets have captions identifying their owners.

On property sales the vendor does not seal, but instead impresses his fingernail with the accompanying caption, 'Fingernail of [Name], the vendor of the house/field, instead of his seal'. The fingernail is impressed in groups of three on the upper and lower edges, with the land-sale scribes sealing on the left and right edges. This practice goes back to the time of Assyrian rule over Babylonia and continues down to the time of Darius II. By contrast on ordinary contracts other than property sales when a party to the contract does not have a seal he impresses a single fingernail mark, and it may be impressed on any of the edges; this practice, rare in the Neo-Babylonian and early Achaemenid periods becomes common from the time of Artaxerxes I onwards.

On other categories of contracts, loans, receipts, dowry payments and so on, there are less clear patterns, and the smaller number of seals may be impressed on any of the edges or occasionally on the reverse since these contracts mostly did not have squared edges. The tablets may be sealed by parties to the contracts, by scribes, and by other witnesses, and the seals may not always be identified by captions.

With the suppression of Babylonia's revolt against Xerxes, while there is dispute about the extent of Xerxes' destructive activity in Babylon major social change seems to have occurred. The evidence for this has been discussed recently by Caroline Waerzeggers (Waerzeggers 2004 and 2018); in brief, almost all the known archives came to an end. But the change is also reflected in the patterns of sealing on contracts. The old order disappears to be replaced by disorder. There seems to be no common practice in terms of who seals where or in what sequence. Order returns only in the Macedonian and Seleucid periods when we observe that parties to contracts seal (or place their fingernails) on the right edges, while witnesses use the left, lower and upper edges (in that apparent order of priority); scribes rarely seal.

Administrative tablets are mostly 'pillow-shaped', lacking squared edges, so it is much commoner on them for the seals to be impressed on the reverse. Also since they were probably only written to be filed within an institution many of them have seal impressions without captions.

Letters sent though the post would almost always have been sealed on the clay envelope, but few such envelopes survive. By contrast the letters orders from Sippar studied by John MacGinnis (MacGinnis 1995) are all sealed in the blank space at the end of the letter and again, since they probably circulated only within the temple complex at Sippar and the sending officials were named, the seals are almost never captioned (there are only two exceptions). The same pattern applies in Babylon before the Macedonian era when captions start to appear on letter orders.

On all types of tablet the captions were written wholly above, below, or to one side of the seal impression until the time of Artaxerxes I, but from Darius II onwards the caption is mostly written around the seal impression in the format NA4.KIŠIB / seal / Name, although it can still sometimes be written to one side.

The types of seal used may also be divided into three groups, cylinder seals, stamp seals and ring seals (from the time of Artaxerxes I onwards). The choice of what type of seal to use probably depended on one's social or political status but, again, in most cases we do not have enough information to be clear about this – although cylinder seals were certainly the choice of judges and land-sale scribes.

Cylinder seals according to recent study (MacGinnis 1995; Altavilla and Walker 2009 and 2016) may again be divided into distinct groups. One may begin with the worship scenes, depicting a worshipper facing divine symbols placed on pillared pedestals. The worshipper might be shown as bald and clean shaven if he had the right to enter the inner parts of the local temple or hairy and bearded if he worked outside the temple. The divine symbols seem to have a clear order, with the moon god Sin in first place nearest the worshipper, with Shamash or Ea, Adad or Papsukkal, Ishtar or Gula, and occasionally Nergal following; that is the normal sequence although in practice there might be only two or three gods shown on a seal.

This leads to a point about how cautious we have to be about the evidence in front of us. We are accustomed to the story that the villain Nabonidus displaced Marduk from his position at the head of the pantheon and put Sin in his place, while the hero Cyrus, having defeated Nabonidus, restored Marduk to his rightful place. This is not in any way reflected in contemporary seals. The crescent of Sin occupies the first place on the worship scenes on cylinder seals from the time of Nebuchadnezzar II down to the end of the Achaemenid period, while the symbols of Marduk (the *marru* or spade) and Nabu (the stylus) are conspicuous by their relative rarity (Altavilla and Walker 2016: 115-16). By contrast on stamp seals the worship scenes overwhelmingly depict Marduk and Nabu. This must reflect something about the seal owners, but we cannot say what.

The second major group of cylinder seals are the contest scenes in which a hero fights animals. In some of the earlier seals the hero is a winged genius, but this type is better known in Assyria and does not

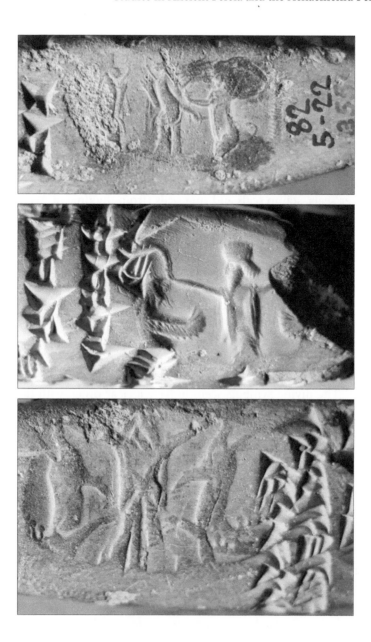

Fig. 1 (top) Cylinder seal impression showing a contest scene on tablet
British Museum 54205 (Photo by Stefania Altavilla, C117).

Fig. 2 (middle) Cylinder seal impression showing a contest scene on tablet
British Museum 54205 (Photo by Stefania Altavilla, C118).

Fig. 3 (bottom) Cylinder seal impression showing a contest scene on tablet
British Museum 54205 (Photo by Stefania Altavilla, C119).

Fig. 4 Cylinder seal impression showing a king, possibly Darius III,
between two sphinxes on tablet British Museum 36596
(Photo by Stefania Altavilla, C126).

survive in Babylonia beyond the reign of Darius I. In Neo-Babylonian
and Achaemenid seals the hero is a man, who may either stand between
two animals or face only a single animal. The animals may be natural or
fantastic (sphinxes, scorpion-men, lion-monsters) and may be winged,
and they may either rear up in front of the man or be held upside down.
For examples, see the seals on the tablet BM.54205 (Figs 1-3).

The man himself is the crucial point of interest for the historical
development of this seal type. Firstly, down to the time of Darius I he
always has bent arms, but from Darius I onwards he is commonly
depicted with straight arms. Secondly, from the time of Darius I he is
sometimes depicted wearing a crown, so is plainly intended to depict
the Achaemenid king. These are the only changes we observe in seal
design which can be directly attributed to Achaemenid influence, and
the depiction of the man as crowned only survives on one tablet possibly
datable to the Seleucid Era. The same story can be derived from contest
scenes on stamp seals, which almost always depict only a single animal.
It is on a stamp seal impression from Sippar that we have the earliest
example of a crowned man with two animals, dating to Darius I year 14
(Mitchell and Searight 2007: 144-45, no 416a), but on this seal he has bent
arms. A different picture is given by a seal on the tablet BM.36596 dated
to Darius II or III (Fig. 4); the king is depicted down on one knee in front
of two very tame looking sphinxes. One is tempted to date it to Darius
III and to say that the seal-cutter is showing the Achaemenid empire on
its last legs; that may seem cynical, but the seal is certainly very unusual.

Fig. 5 (above) Cylinder seal impression showing two men in 'Scythian' costume beneath a winged disc on British Museum tablet 46691 dating from the reign of Darius II (Photo by Stefania Altavilla, E105).

Fig. 6 (below) Cylinder seal impression showing a contest scene on a tablet dated to the reign of Darius I, British Museum 120024 (Photo by Jeanette Fincke, C123)

A third, much smaller, group of cylinder seals have hunting scenes or other narratives. It happens that the few we know all date to the Achaemenid period; there is no reason to suppose that that is significant, but one of them (on the tablet BM.46691, dated to Darius II year 10) (Fig. 5) shows two men wearing Scythian hats beneath a winged disk (of Ahura Mazda?).

As already indicated, stamp seals of the early Achaemenid period can have the same kinds of worship scenes and contest scenes as the contemporary cylinder seals. From the time of Xerxes onwards a greater variety develops, but that has to be discussed in the context of ring seals.

In the reign of Artaxerxes I, after years of war the Greeks and Achaemenid Persians finally made peace. The date of the supposed Peace of Callias is uncertain, but probably c. 449/8 BC. With the arrival of peace Greek traders seem to have sensed new opportunity and arrived in Babylonia offering a new type of seal with a quite new range of designs. The Babylonians were confronted with choices which they had never had before and seem to have taken to them with enthusiasm. Linda Bregstein's study of seal use in fifth century BC Nippur based on the Murašû archive shows that the first occurrences of ring seal impressions on Nippur tablets can be dated to Artaxerxes I years 26 (Bregstein 1993: 826, no 424) and 31 (Bregstein 1993: 983, no 578). The new style of seal becomes predominant at Nippur in the early years of Darius II. At Babylon our earliest evidence for the use of ring seals is on a tablet (BM.120024) (Fig. 6) dated to the accession year of Darius II (423 BC), and thereafter ring seal impressions become common, particularly on tablets from Borsippa.

Relatively few ring seals have survived in the Middle East, probably because gold and silver rings will have been recycled and copper or bronze rings will have disintegrated. The best examples are the ten rings found with the Oxus treasure (Dalton 1926: pl. XVI). These are all of the type which have an engraved metal bezel which may be circular or oval but may sometimes have a pointed appearance. Other rings had a stone bezel set in a metal mount and, while the mount may have disintegrated, the surviving bezels have yet to be fully distinguished in cataloguing from traditional style stamp seals.

In attempting to distinguish the impressions of stamp seals and ring seals on late Achaemenid tablets we have a particular problem with the way in which they were captioned. At Nippur the scribes conveniently captioned the ring seal impressions as *unqu* (ring), even adding notes that some were made of gold or silver. At Borsippa, Nippur, Larsa and Uruk the scribes seem to have fairly consistently captioned ring seal impressions, writing *un-qu* or *un-qa*. However, at Babylon, Dilbat and Kutha the scribes were traditionalists, and all but a few identifiable ring seal impressions are still captioned NA4.KIŠIB (*kunukku*), like the ordinary stamp seals. As a result, the ring seal impressions from Babylon can only be securely identified by their shape. Where the impression has pointed ends one may call it a ring seal but, if it is circular or oval, then it has to be called a stamp seal until one has more evidence. A very few ring seal impressions also show impressions of the ring mount.

A tablet from Babylon dated to the accession year of Darius (BM.120024) (Fig. 6), a private contract, has sixteen seals, only five of which are cylinder seals, while five of the eleven stamp seals are clearly identifiable as ring seals (Mitchell and Searight 2007: 136, no 381; Jursa and Stolper 2007: 280-81, Altavilla and Walker 2016: 65, no 532). The

Fig. 7 (above) Tablet dated from the reign of Darius I with cylinder
and stamp seal impressions, British Museum 120024
(Photo by Stefania Altavilla, F209 and C209).

Fig. 8 (below) Stamp seal impression showing a Greek soldier in short dress
with helmet and large circular shield on tablet British Museum 46691 on a tablet
dating from the reign of Artaxerxes I or Artaxerxes II
(Photo by Sarah Logan, J201).

most interesting is the first seal on the reverse (Fig. 7, F209), a ring
seal which belongs to Nādin, the *piḫātu* (governor) of Babylon, the
first witness. It shows a bull facing right. That's all; no self-portrait as a
worshipper, no picture of the king overpowering animals or monsters,

just a simple seal with a picture of an animal. The fact that a man of such status can officially use such a seal tells us all we need to know about the social and political acceptability of the new seal type. The second witness, Lâbâši, the *databaru* ('law-officer') also uses only a small stamp seal (Fig. 7, C209), although this one does show a royal contest scene. By contrast Iqīšaya, a *sepiru* (alphabet scribe), uses a cylinder seal with a full-size contest scene (Fig. 6).

The assemblage of late Achaemenid stamp seals and ring seals shows a much wider variety than was apparent in earlier periods. There are numerous pictures of normal animals, birds and fish, of *Mischwesen* (goat-fish, mermen, scorpion-men, winged animals, sphinxes and the *mušhuššu* of Marduk), and of men, both in worship scenes and in other contexts. A few of them are of plainly Greek origin or show clear Greek influence. The question how many of all these seals are Babylonian, how many are Greek and how many are of mixed influence requires much future work.

The seal on another fragmentary contract, BM.30136, unpublished but probably dating to the time of Artaxerxes I-II, is particularly surprising. It belongs to another *databaru* named Zammaspi, and shows a Greek soldier in short dress with a helmet and a large circular shield facing right (Fig. 8). Is it not remarkable that a man representing the Achaemenid king can use a seal proclaiming Greek military prowess only a short interval after the Greeks and Achaemenid Persians had been at war? One might think, 'What a slap in the face for his Persian masters.' But he apparently gets away with it, and that in turn may suggest a lack of close connection between the Achaemenid kings and their Babylonian subjects (compare the already mentioned seal on BM.36596).

All we have learned about the various changes in use and type of seals is of interest in itself, but it has also been of much use in determining the approximate dates of tablets which have lost their dates and in assembling archives. It is to be hoped that it will also be of use in the long-awaited task of cataloguing the British Museum's own collection of stamp seals.

Finally, as remarked above, it is sad that we cannot describe the seals impressed on tablets from Achaemenid Ur but there are still two points that one can make. Firstly, Woolley discovered a collection of 200 seal impressions in a coffin which he dates to the late Achaemenid period (Legrain 1951: 47-53 and pls 39-43); many of the seals were obviously Greek. That part of the collection which was allocated to the British Museum has been the subject of further study by Dominique Collon (Collon 1996) and was drawn by Ann Searight (Mitchell and Searight 2007: 168-81). Secondly, the sealed tablets of Achaemenid date have captions to the seal impressions most of which conform to the usual type with the seal described as KIŠIB or *un-qa*. However, two tablets (Figulla 1949, nos 2 and 25) have the impressions of seals described as NA4.ma-ka-nak-tu4 or NA4.ma-ak-nak-tu4, which should simply mean 'seal', but in both cases the seal belonged to a woman, raising the question what kind of seal the scribe wished to distinguish by this particular caption. We must wait for an answer when access to the tablets in Baghdad again becomes possible.

Bibliography

Altavilla, S., and C.B.F. Walker. 2009. *Late Babylonian Seal Impressions on Tablets in the British Museum, Part 1: Sippar*, Nisaba 20, Messina: Arbor Sapientiae

Altavilla, S., and C.B.F. Walker. 2016. *Late Babylonian Seal Impressions on Tablets in the British Museum, Part 2: Babylon and its Vicinity*, Nisaba 28, Messina: Arbor Sapientiae

Baker, H.D. 2004. *The Archive of the Nappāḫu Family* (Archiv für Orientforschung Beiheft 30), Vienna: Institut für Orientalistik der Universität Wien

Bregstein, L. 1993. *Seal Use in Fifth Century B.C. Nippur, Iraq: A Study of Seal Selection and Sealing Practices in the Murašû Archive*, PhD dissertation, Philadelphia

Collon, D. 1996. 'A Hoard of Sealings from Ur', *Bulletin de Correspondance Hellénique, Supplément* 29: 65-84 and pls 11-25.

Collon, D. 2001. *Catalogue of Western Asiatic Seals in the British Museum, Cylinder Seals V: Neo-Assyrian and Neo-Babylonian Periods*, London: British Museum

Dalton, O.M. 1926. *The Treasure of the Oxus*, Oxford: Oxford University Press

Ehrenberg, E. 1999. *Uruk: Late Babylonian Seal Impressions on Eanna Tablets*, Ausgrabungen in Uruk-Warka Endberichte 18, Mainz: Philipp von Zabern

Figulla, H.H. 1949. *Ur Excavations Texts, IV: Business Documents of the New-Babylonian Period*, London: British Museum

Hackl, J., and J. Oelsner. 2017. 'Additions to the Late Achaemenid Textual Record, Part I: Texts from Uruk', *Orientalia* 86: 42-96

Jursa, M. 2003. 'Spätachämenidische Texte aus Kutha', *Revue d'Assyriologie* 97: 43-140

Jursa, M., and M.W. Stolper. 2007. 'From the Tattannu Archive Fragment', *Wiener Zeitschrift für die Kunde des Morgenlandes* 97 (Festschrift für Hermann Hunger): 243-81

Legrain, L. 1951. *Ur Excavations Texts, X: Seal Cylinders*. London: British Museum.

MacGinnis, J. 1995. *Letter Orders from Sippar and the Administration of the Ebabbara in the Late-Babylonian Period*, Poznan: Bonami

Merrillees, P.H. 2005. *Catalogue of the Western Asiatic Seals in the British Museum, Cylinder Seals VI: Pre-Achaemenid and Achaemenid Periods*, London: British Museum

Mitchell, T.C., and A. Searight. 2007. *Catalogue of the Western Asiatic Seals in the British Museum, Stamp Seals III: Impressions of Stamp Seals on Cuneiform Tablets, Clay Bullae and Jar Handles*, Leiden: Brill

Oelsner, J. 1978. 'Zur Neu- und Spätbabylonischen Siegelpraxis', in B. Hruška and
    G. Komoróczy (eds.). *Festschrift Lubor Matouš*, Budapest: ELTE, Ókortörténeti
    Tanszék , 167-86
Pinches, T.G. 1884. *The Cuneiform Inscriptions of Western Asia, V*, London: R.E.
    Bowler
Wunsch, C. 2000. '*Die Richter des Nabonid*', in J. Marzahn and H. Neumann (eds).
    Assyriologica et Semitica: Festschrift für Joachim Oelsner, Alter Orient und
    Altes Testament 252, Münster: Ugarit Verlag, 557-97
Waerzeggers, C. 2004. 'The Babylonian revolts against Xerxes and the "End of
    Archives"', *Archiv für Orientforschung* 50: 150-73
Waerzeggers, C., and M. Seire (eds). 2018. *Xerxes and Babylonia, the Cuneiform
    Evidence*, Leuven: Peeters

4

An Iranian in the Court of King Nebuchadnezzar

Alan Millard

In his essay, 'Achaemenid History and the Book of Daniel',[1] Terence commented on the man to whom Nebuchadnezzar entrusted Daniel and his friends after they were deported from Jerusalem. This man bore the title *rab sārîsîm*, traditionally rendered 'chief eunuch', by most English translations, but now to be understood as 'chief of court officials' (*rab ša rēši*) from the evidence of extensive Babylonian sources.[2] In the 'ration lists' from Nebuchadnezzar's palace (see below) a *ša rēši* is responsible for issues to foreigners, while among the recipients are foreign *ša rēšis*. The highest officer was given the responsibility for the selected Hebrew youths.

Daniel 1:3 gives the officer's name as Ashpenaz. That, Terence wrote, 'seems to be an Iranian name, which would be unusual in the sixth century BC'. He proceeded to offer an interpretation of the name as a compound of the Median form of the word for 'horse', *aspa-*, appearing as *asa* in Old Persian, although the name is 'unknown in any ancient source', and

---

1. Terence C. Mitchell, 'Achaemenid History and the Book of Daniel', in John Curtis (ed.), *Mesopotamia and Iran in the Persian Period: Conquest and Imperialism 539-331 BC* (London: British Museum, 1997) pp. 68-78, see p. 77.

2. *Chicago Assyrian Dictionary* (Chicago Assyrian Dictionary) 14, R (1999) pp. 289-92; Michael Jursa, '"Höflinge" (*ša rēši, ša rēš šarri, ustarbaru*) in babylonischen Quellen des ersten Jahrtausends', in Josef Wiesehöfer, Robert Rollinger and Giovanni B. Lanfranchi (eds), *Ktesias' Welt* (Wiesbaden: Harrassowitz Verlag, 2011) pp. 159-73, see also p. 87.

the second element has not yet been explained. Earlier commentators had suggested the Old Persian form and some pointed to an '*spnz* occurring in an Aramaic magic bowl of much later date, the sixth century AD.[3] Noting 'many references to Media in the Assyrian inscriptions,' Terence continued, 'a Median at the court of Nebuchadnezzar would not be improbable.' His position can be strengthened by observing people with Iranian names present in documents of daily life in eighth- and seventh-century Assyria. Among them are: Abi-shtamba (an official of Sargon), Agnu-parna (a royal agent in Babylonia), Amakani (a Mede), Batānu (a cook at Kalhu), Paranshaka (a witness at Ashur), Partāma (a man at Nineveh).[4]

If there were Iranians among the inhabitants of Assyria, then it is likely there were also some in Babylonia. The Babylonian Chronicle reports Nebuchadnezzar had undertaken a campaign in Elam in his ninth year (596-595 BC)[5] and the ration lists from his palace record issues of oil to servants and house builders from Elam, to 800 Elamite guards for the governor's residence, to two messengers from Parsu and to one Mede.[6] Nebuchadnezzar's father, Nabopolassar, was allied with the Median ruler Cyaxares in his campaigns against the Assyrians, so he could well have taken a Mede to serve in the palace in Babylon who continued there early in Nebuchadnezzar's reign.[7]

Many of Nebuchadnezzar's officials are listed in a damaged text inscribed on a clay prism, a unique example for Babylonia, on which the king celebrates extensions made to the Old Palace in his capital during the early years of his reign.[8] He tells how he stored provisions

---

3.   James A. Montgomery, *The Book of Daniel*, International Critical Commentary (Edinburgh: T. & T. Clark, 1927) pp. 124.

4.   Karen Radner and Heather D. Baker (eds), *The Prosopography of the Neo-Assyrian Empire 1-3*, Neo-Assyrian Text Corpus Project (Helsinki: University of Helsinki, 1998-2011).

5.   A.K. Grayson, *Assyrian and Babylonian Chronicles*, Texts from Cuneiform Sources V (New York: J.J. Augustin, 1975) pp. 92-96; J.-J. Glassner, *Mesopotamian Chronicles*, Writings from the Ancient World 19 (Atlanta: Society of Biblical Literature, 2004) pp. 220-23.

6.   Ernst Weidner, 'Jojachin, König von Juda, in babylonischen Keilschrifttexten,' in Académie des inscriptions et belles-lettres, *Mélanges syriens offerts à Monsieur René Dussaud par ses amis et ses élèves*, Bibliothèque archéologique et historique 30 (Paris: Geuthner, 1939) pp. 923-35; Olof Pedersén, 'Foreign Professionals in Babylon: Evidence from the Archive in the Palace of Nebuchadnezzar II,' in W.H. van Soldt, R. Kalvelagen and D. Katz (eds), *Ethnicity in Ancient Mesopotamia* (Leiden: Nederlands Instituut voor het Nabije Oosten, 2005) pp. 267-71.

7.   Grayson, *op. cit.*, pp. 93-95; Glassner, *op. cit.*, pp. 230-31.

8.   First edited by Eckhardt Unger, *Babylon: Die heilige Stadt nach der Beschreibung*

inside Esangil in his seventh year, 598 BC (col. iv*. 26'), so the prism was made in that year or shortly thereafter. Its description of the magnificence of the building and its materials enumerates the officials and subject kings impressed to contribute to the work. The first six named were high-ranking courtiers (col. v*. 35'-40'), followed after a gap by sixteen other officials (col. vi*. 1'-18') and 2 3 prefects of southern and eastern Babylonia (col. vi*. 19'-32'), 22 other prefects (col. vii*. 1'-22') and seven kings of Levantine towns (col. vii*. 23'-29'). The list of high-ranking courtiers preserved gives the chief baker, the chief treasurer, the superintendent of the palace, the major-domo and the chief of the royal guard.

Absent from these lists is any *ša rēši* or *rab ša rēši*. However, as noted, the columns are damaged and there is no indication that the composition was intended to include every member of each group. In fact, the only cuneiform text mentioning a *rab ša rēši* under Nebuchadnezzar is the tablet dated in 594 BC on which Michael Jursa found the name *Nabû-šarrūssu-ukīn* with that title. His reading enabled Jursa to recognise the name as that hidden beneath *nbwšrskym* in Jeremiah 39:3, there entitled *rab sârîs*, and so to elucidate the names of Nebuchadnezzar's high officials at the fall of Bablyon in 586 BC as given there.[9] The Hebrew names and titles in that verse can now be rendered: Nergal-sharezer the Sin-magir (*smgr*; *simmāgir*) officer, Nebu-sarsekin the chief of court officials (*rab sârîs*; *rab ša rēši*), Nergal-sharezer the Rab-mag (*rab-māg*; *rab mu(n)gi*).

In the same chapter Nebu-zaradan, the captain of the guard (*rab ṭabbāḥim*; *rab ṭābiḥi*), appears in verses 9, 10, 11, then in 13 (cf. 2 Kings 24:8, 20) with Nebu- shazban the chief of court officials and Nergal-sharezer the rab-mag. In agreement with Jeremiah, the prism also has Nergal-sharru-usur, as the Sin-magir officer (col. vi*. 21'), who is generally agreed to be the later king Neriglissar, and the tablet BM 114789 has Nebu-sarsekin as chief of court officials. No rab-mag is named. The identical names for the Sin-magir officer and the rab-mag – Nergal-sharezer – may indicate a Hebrew scribe mistakenly wrote the

der Babylonier, Berlin/Leipzig: de Gruyter (1931) pp. 282-94; see now Rocio Da Riva, 'Nebuchadnezzar II's Prism (ES7834): A New Edition', *Zeitschrift für Assyriologie und Vorderasiatische Archäologie* 103.2 (2013), pp. 196-229.

9.   Michael Jursa, 'Nabû-šarrūssu-ukīn, *rab ša rēši*, und "Nebusarsekin" (Jer. 39:3)' N.A.B.U. (*Nouvelles Assyriologiques Brèves et Utilitaires*), no 1 (2008), p. 5; 'Der neubabylonische Hof', in Bruno Jacobs und Robert Rollinger (eds), *Der Achämenidenhof: Akten des 2. Internationalen Kolloquiums zum Thema «Vorderasien im Spannungsfeld klassischer und altorientalischer Überlieferungen» Landgut Castelen bei Basel, 23.-25. Mai 2007* (Wiesbaden: Harrassowitz Verlag, 2010) pp. 67-106.

same name twice, but the possibility should not be excluded that there were simultaneously two officials with the same name. That is evident in the prism which has a Bel-shum-ishkun as governor of Puqudu (col. vi*. 27') and a man with the same name as royal representative in a place with a lost name (col. vii*. 22'). Now, the prism differs from the biblical texts in naming one Nabû-zēr-iddin, which would be Hebrew Nabu-zaradan, as the chief baker (*rab nuḫatimmē*, col. v*. 36'), with Atkal-ana-mār-Esagil as chief of the guard (col. v*. 40').

However, the prism was probably written soon after 598 BC, so some of the courtiers, such as Nabu-zaradan, could have been promoted, or replaced, or died before the attack on Jerusalem in 587-586 BC. (Nabû-šarru-uṣur, an Assyrian rab-mag, rose to become *rab ša rēši* under Ashurbanipal. Unger noted the 'chief treasurer' [*rab kāṣirī*] named in the prism, Nabû-zēr-ibni [v'. 37'], had a predecessor Bēl-zēr-ibni in 605 BC.[10])

The question about Ashpenaz the *rab ša rēši* remains. The position clearly existed under Nebuchadnezzar but no document earlier than the tablet of 594 BC names the office or its holder. Does this mean there is no place for a *rab-sārîs* named Ashpenaz? Foreigners were employed in the court, for the prism lists 'the chief of the royal merchants' as Hanunu, which is a Phoenician name. Not infrequently such foreigners serving in Assyrian and Babylonian courts were given Babylonian names – Daniel and his three friends were not the only ones – so Ashpenaz may be concealed under a Babylonian name in local documents. The Mede who received rations bore the Babylonian name Kurbannu.[11]

When Michael Jursa studied the title *ša rēši*, he concluded that it fell out of use after Nabonidus' reign, apparently being replaced by the Persian term *ustarbaru*, which implies that Daniel 1 reflects the use in the Chaldean court, despite the use of Persian words in the same chapter (*paṯ-bag, part mîm*).[12]

At first sight, it seems unlikely to find an Iranian in the court of Nebuchadnezzar, but that is because we see forward to the subsequent events – the fall of Babylon to Iranian forces. Looking backward, an Iranian presence becomes feasible in the light of the alliance of Nabopolassar, and concomitantly his son Nebuchadnezzar,

10.   Raija Mattila, *The King's Magnates: A Study of the Highest Officials in the Neo-Assyrian Empire*, State Archives of Assyria Studies 11 (Helsinki: University of Helsinki, 2000) pp. 63-64; Unger, *op. cit.*, p. 289, n. 3.

11.   Weidner, *op. cit.*, p. 930.

12.   Mitchell, *op. cit.*, n.2, see p. 166.

with Cyaxares the Mede which led to the fall of Nineveh. While no independent witness reports an Ashpenaz, or any other Iranian, holding high rank in Babylonia at the end of the seventh century BC, no documents known exclude it. Other details in Daniel 1-6 show sound knowledge of the Neo-Babylonian and Achaemenid eras.[13] Nowadays, many commentators who date the production of the book in the mid-second-century BC accept that much older sources were available to the author. If research adopts Terence's attitude, 'in view of the considerable limitations to our knowledge ... it is sensible to treat it [the book] with respect and continue to study it with an open mind',[14] we may expect it to add more to knowledge of ancient history.

13. As Mitchell, *op. cit.*, has shown; cf. Alan Millard, 'Daniel in Babylon - an Accurate Record?' in J.K. Hoffmeier and D.R. Magary (eds), *Do Historical Matters Matter to Faith? A Critical Appraisal of Modern and Postmodern Approaches to Scripture* (Wheaton, IL: Crossway, 2012) pp. 263-80.

14. Mitchell, *op. cit.*, p. 78.

5

Biblical Archaeology in the Persian Period

T.C. Mitchell

There are various times in the history of Persia to which the designation 'Persian period' might be applied, but in this paper[1] I will be concerned with the time of the Achaemenid kings,[2] who ruled a very large empire between 539 BC when Cyrus conquered Babylon and 331 BC when Alexander the Great defeated Darius III, the last Achaemenid king, who was assassinated near Hecatompylos in the east, possibly by Bessos, the satrap of Bactria.[3]

---

1. The Anna Gray Noe Lecture in Biblical Archaeology, funded by Mrs Linda Noe Laine, given in the British Museum on 12 October 2005. Some of the wording may reflect the fact that the lecture was delivered before a non-specialist audience. I have dealt with some matters in more detail than was possible in the lecture, and, in some cases, I have pursued points which have interested me in even greater detail. I am indebted to Dr Mahnaz Moazami for helpful suggestions and for checking the parts of this paper dealing with Iranian philology.
2. Here I use the word Achaemenid to refer to members of the dynasty, the descendants of Achaemenes, and Achaemenian to the period and the culture.
3. A plausible account of the circumstances of the death of Darius III is given in Green 1991: 325-29 with 546 n. 22 (sources); see more briefly, Briant 2002: 864-66. An imaginary reconstruction of this event is given in the famous sixteenth-century painting by Paolo Veronese in the National Gallery in which the mother of Darius and others of his family bow before Alexander, reproduced, e.g., with discussion in H. Potterton, *The National Gallery, London* (London: Thames & Hudson, 1977) 85, and M. Wilson, *The National Gallery, London* (London: Charles Letts & Co., 1977) 80. In it the architecture and clothing are, of course, completely anachronistic.

The Achaemenian Empire stretched from India (Hinduš)[4] in the east to Egypt (Mudrāya)[5] and Ionia (Yauna) in the west. Ionia was part of the Empire for some years from the conquest of Cyrus until it was largely lost soon after the attempt at further westward expansion under Xerxes I, who was turned back by the Greeks in 480-479 BC at Thermopylae, Salamis, Plataea and Mycale.[6]

In this paper when I deal with the Persian period, I will be referring therefore to the roughly two centuries of Achaemenian power.[7]

Two basic questions arise, namely: what has Biblical archaeology got to do with this period and, indeed, what is Biblical archaeology?

Some writers limit the scope of Biblical archaeology to the area of Palestine,[8] but here I take it to embrace all aspects of the study of the ancient Near East as a whole – excavations, antiquities and inscriptions, and sometimes later texts – in so far as these illustrate the background of the Bible and individual points in the text. In some cases it will be instructive to consider evidence that is at one remove, so to speak, but which contributes to the general background. I will not give a systematic schoolbook essay but will aim, by selecting a number of individual samples of the kind of evidence we have, to give some glimpses of the field. Texts which are of interest for this period are written in a number of scripts, many with no representation of vowels, but there are standard ways of transliterating these into the Roman alphabet with diacritical marks on some letters to indicate sound values not known in English, and I will be including some of these. Some may feel that I have given too much attention to inscriptions rather than dirt archaeology, but the Old Testament consists of texts, and usually the clearest illumination comes from other texts.

---

4.   Old Persian Hiⁿdu- (written hⁱ-dᵘ-, the -n- being supplied on the basis of spellings in Avestan, Sanskrit, Greek etc. [Brandenstein and Mayrhofer 1964: 23, 145]) with the nominative singular termination -uš.

5.   A name which is not Persian or Egyptian (which would probably have been Kemē – kmt, 'Black (Land)' – the vowels supplied from Coptic) but Semitic, e.g. Akkadian muṣur, Hebrew miṣrayim, in Persian guise (see Brandenstein and Mayrhofer 1964: 133).

6.   For these events, see, e.g., Green 1996; for a handy brief summary from the Greek point of view, Andrews 1967: 60; and a useful collection of English translations of Greek historical texts and inscriptions bearing on these events, Dillon and Garland 1994: 179-214.

7.   This period was illustrated by the exhibition, 'The Forgotten Empire', which was held in the British Museum from September 2005 to January 2006 and accompanied by an illustrated catalogue, Curtis and Tallis 2005.

8.   E.g. K. Kenyon etc., on this see, briefly, Mitchell 1988: 8, 104 = 2004: 9, 124.

As far as the Bible is concerned and the 'People of the Book', who can reasonably be referred to as 'Jews' in this period,[9] the year 539 BC marked the end of their exile in Babylonia. Many of them had been taken there almost sixty years before by Nebuchadnezzar and now, under Cyrus, they were allowed to return to Palestine, though a good many remained in Babylonia and continued living there after the conquest by Alexander the Great in 331 BC, and subsequently into the Christian Era.

The Bible is made up of a number of books composed over a long period, and many of the events narrated in the Old Testament are concerned with the time before the Persian conquest of Babylon in 539 BC. Some of the Biblical books, however, notably Ezra, Nehemiah, Esther, Daniel, and the latest edition of Chronicles, as well as the prophetical books Haggai, Zechariah and probably Malachi, do relate to this time. The language of these books exhibits features of grammar and vocabulary characteristic of late Biblical, that is to say, post-exilic, Hebrew.[10] There are also passages in Aramaic in Ezra (4:8-6:18; 7:12-26) and Daniel (2.4-7:28) in a form of the language largely typical of this period.[11]

The accompanying chart lists the kings of the Achaemenid Persian dynasty, showing the forms of the names of those which are found in the Old Persian inscriptions, and the Hebrew or Aramaic transcriptions of those which occur in the Old Testament.

King	Dates	Persian Name	O.T. Spelling
Cyrus the Great	549-529 BC	kūru(š)	kôreš
Cambyses	529-522 BC	ka^mbūjiya	
Darius I the Great	521-486 BC	dārayavau(š)	dāryāweš
Xerxes I	486-465 BC	ḫšayāršā	'aḫašweroš
Artaxerxes I	465-425 BC	artaḫšaça	'artaḫšastě'
Xerxes II	425-424 BC		
Sogdianus	424 BC		
Darius II	425-405 BC	dārayavau(š)	
Artaxerxes II	405-359 BC	artaḫšaça	
Artaxerxes III	359-338 BC	artaḫšaça	

9.   See, e.g., Mitchell 1991: 419.
10. Characterised in Sáenz-Badillos 1993: 112-29; Kutscher 1982: 81-86.
11. Rosenthal 1961.

King	Dates	Persian Name	O.T. Spelling
Arses	338-336 BC		
Darius III	336-331 BC		

Concerning the beginning of this phase, there is a description in the book of Daniel of the experiences of some Hebrew exiles who were taken to Babylonia by Nebuchadnezzar shortly before 600 BC and who remained there until the conquest by Cyrus in 539 BC. Daniel is said to have prospered during the reign of Cyrus (Daniel 6:28), and to have lived into the reign of Darius, probably Darius I. There has been much discussion of the identity of a ruler referred to as Darius the Mede (*dārĕyāweš mādāyāʾ*) (Daniel 5:31; 11:1). This title is not found outside the Bible and, while it is not appropriate to go into this in detail here, it may be noted that one suggestion is to take it as another title of Cyrus.[12] The dating of the Book of Daniel is much debated but, again, this is not the place to enter into this question. Many would place its composition in the second century BC,[13] but it is not difficult to adduce linguistic arguments for placing the Aramaic passages (2:4b-7:28), which contain much of the historical material, in at least the fifth century BC.[14] A factor of relevance in considering the text of the Bible is that it has passed through the hands of scribal copyists who would sometimes revise the spellings and forms of words. On the basis of comparative material in the form of dated documents (on papyrus and leather) these passages have been characterised as Standard Literary Aramaic, with some scribal and editorial updating.[15] Hebrew inscriptions of the Achaemenian period are very limited, and there is not substantial comparative material until the Dead Sea Scrolls from Qumran, which date from the Hellenistic-Roman period (c. 200 BC-AD 100). The important Hebrew source the Mishna, Rabbinic traditions collected over several centuries and probably only written down by the second century AD, probably contains much that goes back to the colloquial speech of the Biblical period,[16] so deductions

---

12. See D.J. Wiseman in Wiseman 1965: 9-16; Bulman 1973: 247-67; Colless 1992: 113-26; and Mitchell 1997: 75-77.

13. E.g. Fohrer 1970: 477-78, but, though he cites opinions mostly favouring this late date, he includes, *passim*, references to those supporting earlier dates (471-79).

14. See, conveniently, Kitchen 2003: 520 n. 40 and, more generally, his chapter 3 with supporting endnotes; see also Dillard and Longman 1994: 329-52 arguing the case for a tentative sixth-century date.

15. E.g. J.C. Greenfield in Gershevitch (ed.) 1985a: 707; and in Geller, Greenfield and Weitzman (eds) 1995):5.

16. This was the conclusion of Segal 1927: 6-14 §§8-18, where (§19), on the

about the dating of Biblical Hebrew by comparison with Mishnaic Hebrew have limited validity. It is generally agreed that the language of the main body of the Old Testament can be described as Classical or pre-exilic Biblical Hebrew, and that, as mentioned above, Ezra, Nehemiah etc. are in post-exilic or late Biblical Hebrew.

An interesting reference to Cyrus is made in the Biblical book of the earlier prophet Isaiah where Cyrus is spoken of as in effect an agent of

---

basis of comparison with such books as Chronicles and Esther, he dated the colloquial forerunner tentatively to about the fourth century BC. Other views have been put forward on the dating of Chronicles, an earlier date having been proposed by Newsome 1975: 201-17, where, on the basis of consideration of its representation of the kingdom, of prophecy and of the cult, he argues for composition in the period between 538 (decree of Cyrus) and 515 (completion of the Temple), and a similar view, though proposing later completion, is taken by F.M. Cross 1975: 4-18 = 1998: 151-72 (revised and expanded), where he argues for three editions, Chr$_1$ shortly after 520 BC, Chr$_2$ after Ezra's mission in 458 BC, and Chr$_3$ in about 400 BC. These views are disputed by Williamson, who argues for some point within the fourth century BC (1977: 83-86) or about the middle of the fourth century BC (1982: 15-16). One point cited in support of a date in the fourth rather than the fifth century BC is the mention in 1 Chronicles 29:7 of the daric (*ădarkōnîm*), a coin first minted soon after 515 BC, but, since this passage refers to the time of Solomon (tenth century BC), reference to such a coin would have been the result of scribal updating (see n. 217 below), and Williamson suggests that 'sufficient time must be allowed for the anachronism to be tolerated' (1982: 15). It is possible, however, that such scribal updating was carried out on an earlier manuscript late in the Persian period, though Williamson rejects the idea that 'a later editor altered the original text of 1 Chronicles 29:7 to suit it to the currency of his own day' as too much like special pleading (1977: 126 n. 40). This is an understandable view, but it is not conclusive. Whatever the date, and even assuming a mid-fourth-century date for the forerunner of Mishnaic Hebrew, colloquial speech is likely to have been in use well before that time. Segal published a more thorough Hebrew version of his Grammar (*dqdwq lšwn hmšnh*) in 1936 in Tel Aviv but, in his Preface to a 1957 reprint of the 1926 English edition, he gave no indication that he considered his conclusions invalid. Further, it has been pointed out subsequently that manuscript discoveries have cast doubt on the reliability of the printed text of the Mishnah which was the basis of his work. This manuscript evidence shows that mediaeval copyists and printers tended to alter the Mishnaic text to bring it into line with Biblical Hebrew. On this see Kutscher 1982: 118-47; Sáenz-Badillos 1993: 163-201 (referring to it as Rabbinic Hebrew); and, briefly, B.A. Levine in Kaltner and McKenzie (eds) 2002: 158-59. Further work is needed on the manuscript evidence, but a tendency to correct the text towards the Biblical literary language could have diminished rather than increased indications of a colloquial forerunner to Mishnaic Hebrew, strengthening Segal's conclusions. See also, in relation to the Book of Ecclesiastes, Fredericks 1988: 51-52, 171-76.

the Hebrew god Yahweh (Jehovah) to release the Jews from captivity in Babylonia. Yahweh is quoted as saying of Cyrus, 'He is my shepherd and will accomplish all that I please; he will say of Jerusalem, "Let it be rebuilt"' (44:28).[17] The term used here, *rōʿeh*, 'shepherd', or perhaps 'one who causes to graze', has cognate forms in most Semitic languages and, apart from its basic agricultural meaning, was widely applied to rulers in the ancient Near East. In Mesopotamia this term and its Sumerian equivalent, SIPA, was used in reference to many Sumerian, Babylonian and Assyrian kings over the centuries,[18] Hammurabi, for instance, the king of Babylon in the early second millennium BC, is designated *rēʾû*, 'shepherd' (written *ri-iu-um*), in the introduction to his famous Law Code.[19] The passage in Isaiah continues:

> This is what Yahweh says to his anointed, to Cyrus (*kôreš*), whose right hand I take (*heḥĕzaqtî bîmînô* [*hḥzqty bymynw*], literally 'I take hold of his right') to subdue nations before him. (45:1)

Here the Hebrew word translated 'anointed' is *māšîăḥ*, literally 'anointed one' (Messiah), from the verb *māšaḥ*, 'anoint'. The word is already applied in the Old Testament to such figures as Saul and David, as well as to priests, who like kings received anointing with oil on assuming office.[20] In the New Testament *messias*, the Greek transcription of this title, is found only twice (John 1:41; 4:25),[21] normally being represented by the Greek equivalent *khristos* (from *khriō*, 'to anoint') with the same meaning,[22] and rendered 'Christ' in the English versions, but it would be anachronistic to apply to Cyrus the later particular range of meaning set out in the New Testament.[23]

17. Isaiah 40-55 is usually dated to the sixth century BC (e.g. Fohrer 1970: 374-77); see also discussion of the dating of parts of the book in Dillard and Longman 1994: 268-76.
18. CAD: R: 311-12; on the metaphorical use in Mesopotamia and Egypt, see G. Wallis in Botterweck, Ringgren and Fabry (eds) 1974-2006: XIII: 547-49; and J.W. Vancil, in Freedman (ed.) 1992: 5: 1188-89.
19. The phonetic spelling *ri-iu-um* occurs in column 1, line 51 (Driver and Miles 1955: 6-7, 120) but in other passages in the Code it is written with the Sumerogram SIPA. The root in question is *rʿh*, 'to tend' etc., not *rʾh*, 'to see', but the cuneiform script had only inadequate representation of the consonant *ʿayin*.
20. K. Seybold, '*māšaḥ*' in Botterweck, Ringgren and Fabry (eds) 1974-2006: IX: 43-54, and 49-53 on *māšîah*.
21. Danker 2010: 635.
22. Danker 2010: 1091; and F. Hesse in Kittel and Friedrich (eds) 1964-76: 9: 496-509.
23. On the transition from the Old to the New Testament understanding of the

The last Babylonian king, Nabonidus, had collected into Babylon the images of gods of subject peoples. Cyrus allowed these to be returned to their proper homes.[24] One of the familiar objects of Biblical archaeology is the Cyrus Cylinder (BM.90920),[25] a convex clay cylinder inscribed in cuneiform with an account of the conquest of Babylon by Cyrus, which was found at Babylon by Hormuzd Rassam in 1879.[26] The recent

---

role of the Messiah see Bruce 1971: 177-78.

24. This action is referred to in a letter found at Warka (Uruk): Clay 1919: no 86 (copy); Ebeling 1934: 72-73 (transliteration and translation) no C.86; and brief reference to other tablets referring to the return of deities under Cyrus in Cameron 1932: 304.

25. Here, and in what follows, cuneiform texts and other ancient Near Eastern objects in the British Museum will be cited by serial number preceded only by the abbreviation BM. This will be returning to the mode of reference used before 1955 (when the Department of Egyptian and Assyrian Antiquities was divided into [a] Egyptian Antiquities and [b] Western Asiatic Antiquities) following which the prefixes WAA, ANE and ME have been used in succession. These changes have led to some confusion and (apart from some objects from Egypt which are distinguished by the prefix BM.E.) the serial numbers used for departmental objects are not duplicated in any other department, so 'BM' is sufficient on its own.

26. BM.90920: Rawlinson and Pinches 1884: pl. 35; Weissbach 1911: xi, 2-9 (transliteration and German translation); A.L. Oppenheim in Pritchard 1955: 315-16 (translation); Berger 1974-75: 192-234 (transliteration and German translation, 194-203, with comments and discussion of new fragment, 202-34); M. Cogan 2000: 314-16, no 2.124 (English trans); Schaudig 2001: 550-56, no K2.1 (transliteration and translation); P. Michalowski in Chavalas 2006: 426-30 no 157 (English trans); Kuhrt 2007: I, 70-74 no 21 (English translation and notes); also Grayson in Grayson and Redford (eds) 1973: 124-26 (main extract with linking explanation); Lecoq 1997: 181-85 (French translation with annotations, and 75-77 [discussion]); Borger in Galling (ed.) 1968: 82-84 no 50 (German translation, selection); Ebeling in Gressmann (ed) 1926: 368-70 (German translation); and Rogers 1912: 380-84 (older transliteration and translation); Finkel and Seymour 2008: 171, fig. 161 (colour photograph with description); also Mitchell 1988: no 44 (brief account, with bibliography 106-7) = (2004), no 49 (with 128). I.L. Finkel gives a new translation of the cylinder (Finkel 2013: 4-7), with the restored passages in square brackets, and a transliteration of the surviving text (130-33, with the cylinder text marked A, and the parallel passages on the new fragments marked B_1 and B_2). Though the cylinder was found at Babylon, the records concerning its precise location are unclear (discussion by J. Taylor in Finkel 2013: 35-68), and there is greater uncertainty about the provenance of the new fragments (Finkel 2013: 18-20). It is probable that they also came from Babylon, though this cannot be certain, and that the complete flat tablet of which they were part was in effect a file copy of the text, available for public information, while the cylinder was buried, possibly at the same time as three other copies, at the corner(s) of an important

recognition of two fragments of a rectangular flat tablet (BM.47134 [81-8-30,656] and 47176 [81-8-30,698]), inscribed with the same text as that on the cylinder, suggests that they were part of what was in effect a file copy of the text, available for public information, while the cylinder was buried, very likely with other copies, at the corner or corners of an important building, in accordance with common practice. These fragments were acquired by the Museum in 1881, but identified only in 2009 and 2010 respectively. They preserve only minimal sections of the text, but each includes brief passages which have not survived on the cylinder, on which perhaps as much as 20 per cent is broken away, and to a very limited extent they therefore restore missing parts of the main text.[27]

The language of the inscription is Babylonian and not Persian, and the text follows the normal pattern of a Babylonian inscription, beginning, after a brief reference to the failures of the last Babylonian king (lines 3-8), by referring to Cyrus in the third person and attributing the success of his actions to the favour of Marduk, the God of Babylon (lines 9-19).[28] The text then changes to the first person and Cyrus is represented as describing his peaceful takeover of the land. He refers to areas and cities to the north and east of Babylonia and says that:

> (30) From (Shuanna [Babylon]) I sent back to their places to the city of Ashur and Susa, (31) Akkad, the land of Eshnunna, the city of Zamban, the city of Meturnu, Der, as far as the border of the land of Guti – the sanctuaries across the river Tigris – whose shrines had earlier become dilapidated, (32) the gods (*ilāni* [DINGIR.MEŠ]) who lived therein, and made permanent sanctuaries for them. I collected together all of their people and returned them to their settlements.[29]

---

building, in accordance with common practice.

27. Finkel's translation, see n. 27.

28. M. Dandamaev suggests that the text was composed by the priests of Marduk in Babylon, 1993.

29. Finkel's translation (2013: 6-7, lines 30-32). Previous renderings of this passage include: A.L. Oppenheim, '. . . (as to the region) from . . . as far as Ashur and Susa, Agade, Eshnunna, the town Zamban, Me-Turnu, Der as well as the region of the Gutians, I returned to (these) sacred cities on the other side of the Tigris, the sanctuaries of which have been ruins for a long time, the images which (used) to live therein and established for them permanent sanctuaries'. (Pritchard 1955: 316); and M. Cogan, 'From [Ninev]eh (?), Ashur and Susa, Agade, Eshnunna, Zamban, Meturnu, Der, as far as the region of Gutium, I returned the (images of) the gods to the sacred centers [on the other side of]

Though the areas referred to are mainly in Assyria and Iran, this document represents a policy which fits well with the account given in the Book of Ezra of the beginning of the reign of Cyrus. There the text, in Hebrew, quotes Cyrus as saying:

> Yahweh God of heaven (*yhwh ʾĕlōhê haššāmayim*) has given me all the kingdoms of the earth and he has appointed me to build a house (*bayit*) in Jerusalem which is in Judah. (Ezra 1:2)[30]

This declaration is repeated in the text of an Aramaic document quoted in Ezra which runs:

> Record (*dikrônâ*): In the first year of Cyrus the king, Cyrus the king issued a document (*ṭĕʿēm*). Concerning the house of God (*bêt-ʾĕlāhāʾ*) at Jerusalem: 'Let the house where sacrifices are offered be reconstructed and its foundations retained'. (Ezra 6:2-3)[31]

The word *ṭĕʿēm* has the senses 'understanding; command; report' in Old Testament Aramaic and is found regularly in Official Aramaic with the meaning 'order, decision' and the like.[32]

The passage goes on to give particulars of dimensions and materials. The injunction to retain the foundations of the temple, or in other words to rebuild it on its original foundations, follows a well-established Babylonian practice. This is a possible interpretation of a passage in the same document (Ezra 6:7) in which Cyrus says 'rebuild this house of God on its foundations' (*bêt-ʾĕlāhāʾ dēk yibnôn ʿal-ʾatrēh*, literally 'house of God this build on its foundations'), where the word *ʾatar*, 'place, location' and in this context 'foundation', is cognate with Akkadian *ašru*, 'place, site etc.', used similarly for instance in a building inscription of Nebuchadnezzar in the phrase concerning E-ur-imin-anki, a ziqqurat at Borsippa, 'I did not change its place (*ašru*) nor move its foundation (*temennu*).'[33]

---

the Tigris whose sanctuaries had been abandoned for a long time, and I let them dwell in eternal abodes. I gathered all their inhabitants and returned (to them) their dwellings'. (Hallo and Younger 2002: 2: 315).
30. It might have been expected that this passage, like Ezra 6:2-3, would have been in Aramaic rather than Hebrew. This point is discussed in Williamson 1987: 33-34.
31. On the background of this activity, see Mitchell 1991: 436-37.
32. Koehler and Baumgartner 2001: II: 1885-86; Hoftijzer and Jongeling 1995: 1: 427, *ṭʿm₂*
33. Langdon 1912: 98, Nebuchadnezzar no 11 (K.1685+), ii 7; see also CAD: A:

Another account of this, in Hebrew rather than Aramaic, is given at the
end of the Book of Chronicles (originally a single book, but divided into
two in the Septuagint), a composition also dating from the Achaemenian
period, which states:

> In the first year of Cyrus king of Persia in order to fulfil the
> word of Yahweh spoken by Jeremiah, Yahweh moved the
> heart of Cyrus king of Persia to make a proclamation (*qôl*)
> throughout his realm and to put it in writing (*běmiktāb*).
> (23) 'This is what Cyrus king of Persia says: "Yahweh, God of
> heaven (*ělōhê haššāmayim*), has given me all the kingdoms of
> the earth and he has appointed me to build a temple (*bayit*)
> for him at Jerusalem in Judah. Anyone of his people among
> you – may Yahweh his God be with him, and let him go up"'.
> (2 Chronicles 36:22-23)

The word *qôl*, which has the same role in this text as *ṭě'ēm* in the
Aramaic of Ezra (6:3), has the senses 'sound; noise; voice; report,
proclamation' in Old Testament Hebrew, and is found in the spelling *ql*
regularly in Phoenician and Punic, as well as a few times in Old and
Official Aramaic with the meanings 'voice; sound'.[34]

It may be thought unlikely that Cyrus would have invoked Yahweh, the
god of the Hebrews, as the instigator of this operation in Jerusalem, but
this simply follows the pattern found in the Cyrus Cylinder quoted above
where he invokes the Babylonian god Marduk. It does, however, raise the
question of the personal religion of Cyrus himself. In the Book of Isaiah
(45:4 and 5) the text represents Yahweh as saying to Cyrus, 'you have not
known me' (*lō' yěda'tānî*) (literally 'not' [*lō'*] 'you have known' (perfect
tense) 'me' [*-nî*]), using the common verb *yāda'*, 'to know', in other words
recognising that he did not have a monotheistic belief in Yahweh in the
way a Hebrew would. The New International Version translates this 'you
have not acknowledged me' in Isaiah 45:5 (and incorrectly in terms of
tense, 'you do not acknowledge me' in 45:4) but the more direct meaning
'know' is preferable.[35]

II: 456-60, this example cited under 1 (b) (456); and for the usage of *šr* in
early Aramaic, written *'tr* in Official Aramaic and later dialects, Hoftijzer and
Jongeling 1995: 2: 125-27, *šr₄*.

34. Koehler and Baumgartner 2001: II: 1083-85; Hoftijzer and Jongeling 1995: 2:
1010-11, *ql*.
35. The English Standard Version has 'you do not know me' in each of these
references, again incorrectly in terms of tense.

Outside the Bible, apart from the information given in the Cyrus Cylinder, the so-called Nabonidus Chronicle (BM.35382)[36] and a text known as 'A Persian Verse Account of Nabonidus' (BM.38229),[37] both, like the Cyrus Cylinder, in the Babylonian language, only three Old Persian monumental inscriptions in his name are known (referred to as C[yrus]M[urghab]a, CMb and CMc),[38] but it is possible that even these were not actually set up during his own reign. They are located in his palace at Pasargadae (modern Murghab), and it has been argued that they were not inscribed until the time of Darius.[39] Study of the building

36. Tablet BM.35382 (Sp.II.964): First published by Pinches 1882: 139-76; Smith 1924: 98-123, pls XI-XIV (transliteration, translation, full discussion and commentary); Grayson 1975: 21-22, 104-11 (Chronicle 7, transliteration and translation); A.L. Oppenheim in Pritchard 1955: 305-307 (English translations); and in Gershevitch (ed.) 1985a: 538-39 (English translation of ii:1-4 and iii:12-22); and B.T. Arnold in Chavalas 2006: 418-20 (English translation); Kuhrt 2007: 50-53 no 1 (English translation and notes); also E. Ebeling in Gressmann (ed.) 1926: 366-68 (German translation); R. Borger in Galling (ed.) 1968: 81-82, no 49 (German translation selection).

37. Tablet BM.38299: This text, which is only partially preserved, was given this designation by Smith 1924: 27-97, pls V-X (transliteration, translation, full discussion and commentary); Landsberger and Bauer 1926-27: 61-98, specifically 88-98, §5 (revised translation with comments); and A.L. Oppenheim, in Pritchard 1955: 312-14 (translation); Kuhrt 2007: 75-80, no 23 (translation and notes); also Finkel and Seymour 2008: 164 fig. 151 (colour photograph with description and translation of extracts). The text is in the Babylonian language but is 'Persian' in the sense that it was written in the Persian period and in the name of the Persian king. It criticises the activities of a Babylonian ruler (clearly Nabonidus though his name does not appear in the surviving part) and makes favourable reference to the restoration by Cyrus of the right ways in Babylon. The verse form is characterised by Smith as featuring the 'distich or double-line, in which the second line presents an opposition to, a complement or a continuation of, the first line. . . . Each line consists of two members which balance one another in construction, and probably in stress; . . .' (Smith 1924: 31-32).

38. Kent 1953: 107 (bibliography), 116 (transliteration and translation); also Herzfeld 1938: 2-4 nos 2 (= CMc) and 3 (= CMb) (copies, transliteration and translation), pls II and III (photos). Old Persian texts are cited in specialist literature according to the following conventions: *Kings*: A¹ = Artaxerxes I, A² = Artaxerxes II, A³ = Artaxerxes III, Am = Ariaramnes, As = Arsames, C = Cyrus the Great, D = Darius the Great, D² = Darius II, X = Xerxes I; *Locations*: B = Bisitun, H = Hamadan (Ecbatana), M = Murghab (Pasargadae), P = Persepolis, S = Susa.

39. Stronach 1990: 195-203; a view supported by Potts 2005: 7-28, specifically pp. 11, 20; It is probable also that later authorship applies to two inscriptions on gold tablets purporting to be of Cyrus' predecessors, Ariaramnes and Arsames, found respectively in 1930 and 1945 at Hamadan, ancient Ecbatana (Kent 1953: 107, 116, designated AmH and AsH; also G.G. Cameron in Dentan 1955: 96;

known as Palace P at Pasargadae, in which one copy of CMa is preserved,[40] suggests that the sculptured reliefs in the building had probably not been completed until about 510 BC, when Darius had been king for over ten years,[41] and therefore that the inscription was not carved until then. Classical authors quote differing versions of an inscription in his name, which they say was on his tomb at Pasargadae, but none actually survives there.[42] A further indication that these inscriptions may not have been made in the time of Cyrus is that the royal title in the principal trilingual inscription, C(yrus)M(urghab)a, has the simple form 'I, Cyrus the king, an Achaemenid', not using the title 'king of kings' and not naming his father. This is in contrast to the wording in the Cyrus Cylinder where he is designated 'king of kings', and his ancestry is given in full, namely:

> I am Cyrus, king of the world, great king, legitimate king, king of Babylon, king of Sumer and Akkad, king of the four quarters, son (*mār*) of Cambyses, great king, king of Anshan, grandson (*mār māri*) of Cyrus, great king, king of Anshan, descendant (*līpu* [ŠÀ.BAL.BAL]) of Teispes (*ši-iš-pi-iš*), great king, king of Anshan.[43]

This passage is more Babylonian in format than Persian, but such a conclusion would be in keeping with the suggestion that the earliest Old Persian cuneiform document was that of Darius in his trilingual inscription at Bisitun (Behistūn).[44] Analysis of the locations of the three

Brandenstein and Mayrhofer 1964: 90 no 10 [transliteration of the Ariaramnes inscription with comments]; and Lecoq 1997: 179-80, [French translations of both inscriptions, with notes, and general discussion, 124-26]).

40. The location in Palace P is marked in Lecoq 1997: fig. 1 at E (with locations of other lost copies marked '?'); and other copies surviving in Palaces S (three) and R (one), Lecoq 1997: fig. 1 at A-D. Colour photograph in J. Curtis (ed.) 1997: pl. VI.

41. Stronach 1978: 95-97, 103; and 1990: 195-96 and 197. Against this view, Lecoq argues that in the present state of knowledge it is best to assume that the inscriptions in the name of Cyrus the Great do belong to his own time (1997: 80-82, 185-86).

42. Summary in Lecoq 1997: 78-80, citing Arrian (*Anabasis* 6:29:4 and 8; translation of 6:29:4-7, Kuhrt 2007: 87 no 29), Strabo (*Geography* 15:3:7-8) and Plutarch (*Parallel Lives*, Alexander 69:4).

43. Mitchell 1988: no 44 = 2004: no 49; notably Weissbach 1911: 4-5, lines 20-21; Berger 1974-75: 196-97.

44. On the question of whether the Old Persian text at Bisitun was the earliest set up, see also Appendix I below. On the inscription, see Mitchell 1988: no 45 = 2004: no 50, with bibliography, 128; to which add Schmitt 1991. On spellings of

versions on the rock face there suggests that the text was inscribed: first, in Elamite (level with and to the right of the sculptures); second, in Babylonian (level with and to the left of the sculptures); third, in the principal Old Persian text (columns I-IV, mostly below the sculptures); fourth, in a second version in Elamite (below the Babylonian version); and, fifth, in a later addition to the Old Persian version (column V).[45] The wording of the inscription indicates that, apart from its permanent form on the rock face, it was intended as a proclamation for public reading and that this was affected mainly by the use of clay tablets (*pavastāyā*) and parchment (*čarmā*).[46] Fragments of an Aramaic version on papyrus found at Elephantine,[47] show that the document was also distributed in ways not mentioned in the text. There is no indication that the word *čarmā* included any reference to 'papyrus'.[48]

In Elam and Babylonia such dissemination might have been carried out through the medium of cuneiform on clay tablets, nevertheless, for most of the provinces of the Empire the material on which the text of the Bisitun inscription might have been circulated is more likely to have been parchment or papyrus, the Aramaic version on papyrus from Elephantine being an example. While copies going to Elamite-speaking areas and to Mesopotamia could have been on clay, in each case this would have required a large number of tablets. The Babylonian text runs to 112 long lines with roughly 65 cuneiform characters to the line, amounting to something like 7,280 characters;[49] and the Elamite text takes 260 lines (in three columns of 81+85+94 lines) with roughly 40 cuneiform characters to the line, amounting to as much as 10,400 characters;[50] neither version therefore being really practical for dissemination on clay tablets. Concerning the Old Persian text, in which, since the script is semi-alphabetic rather than logographic+syllabic, a word- rather than sign-count is appropriate, 414 lines (in five columns

---

the name Bisitun (Old Persian Bagastāna; Greek Bagistanon; Medieval Arabic Bihistân, Bîhistûn, Bîsutûn; modern Persian Bīsitūn, Bīsutūn), see Kent 1953: 108; le Strange 1905: 187.

45. Convenient summary of the probable sequence in Wiesehöfer 1996: 15-18; Hinz had outlined the same beginning elements in the sequence: first the sculptures; second [=1 above] Elamite to right of sculpture; third [=2] Babylonian to left of sculpture; fourth [=3] Old Persian below the sculpture (1973: 17).

46. On *pavastāyā* and *čarmā*, see Appendix I below.

47. Greenfield and Porten 1982; and already Cowley 1923: 248-71; also, Segert 1975: 507 no 33 (lines 1-3 in square script).

48. See Appendix I.

49. Von Voigtlander 1978: 11-48, with running notes.

50. Weissbach 1911: 8-74, transliteration, together with Old Persian.

of 96+98+92+92+36 lines) with an average of roughly eight words to a line,[51] amounts to over 3,000 words, something which, again, would have required a large number of tablets. In any case, it is unlikely that many people would have been able to read or understand Old Persian cuneiform.

Only a very limited number of clay tablets inscribed in Old Persian are known. Principal examples are the so-called Susa Foundation Charter (D[arius]S[usa]f), mentioned below,[52] which is known from fragments of many copies on clay and limestone tablets, as well as in a frieze on glazed tiles in the Palace at Susa;[53] and a limestone tablet of Xerxes clearly simulating a clay tablet (Xerxes Persepolis f), which was found under a corner of the Harem at Persepolis serving as a foundation text in the Babylonian tradition.[54] These show that such large clay tablets were sometimes inscribed for formal use. The Susa Foundation Charter (DSf) runs, however, to only 58 lines with an average of barely seven words to a line, amounting to little more than 400 words, a capacity far short of the more than 3,000 words of the Bisitun text.

Apart from tablets like these, the known evidence of Old Persian on clay consists of a single fragment of a tablet, acquired by the British Museum in 1893 (BM.82548 [93-5-13,7]), which has been identified as duplicating a short passage in an inscription of Darius (D[arius]S[usa] e), not part of the Bisitun text, but dealing with the re-establishment of order in the Empire.[55] The complete text (DSe) of which this is part would be a less improbable possibility for dissemination. It runs to only 52 lines with something like five words to a line, c.260 words, but it is possible that it was intended as a guide for the stonemasons who carved the text.

At present, only one other clay tablet inscribed in Old Persian cuneiform is known: Persepolis Fortification (PF) tablet: Fort.1208-101. This was found in a large archive of tablets and fragments (consisting of over 15,000 in Elamite and over 700 in Aramaic), which were excavated in 1933 in the Fortification Archive at Persepolis.[56] On this, the script is

---

51. Schmitt 1991: 27-48.
52. In Appendices IV and V below, with bibliography of text DSf in n. 414.
53. Scheil 1929: 3-34 no 1, 'Charte de Fondation du Palais'; Kent 1953: 110, 141-42.
54. Kent 1953: 112, 149-50.
55. Bezold 1911: 393-94; Weissbach 1911: xx, xxix, 99-101, 130 (unidentified at that time and therefore referred to as 'Inc[erta].b'); Weissbach 1937: 81-83 (identification of Inc.b with DSe); Hinz 1941: 227-33; Kent 1953: 110, 141-42; Steve 1974: 9 ('Dse 11'); Mayrhofer 1978: 47 ('Inc.b'); Lecoq 1997: 232-34 (French translation of the complete text with variants from the Elamite and Babylonian versions).
56. M.W. Stolper gives a preliminary publication of this text, with discussion of

clearly Old Persian, but only the right-hand portion survives, and not enough of the text remains to make the meaning fully clear. The last line, of a date formula, suggests that this was an administrative text. After virtually a century and a half of discovery and study only this example and the single Old Persian tablet fragment mentioned above have come to light, giving a reasonable indication of the rarity of such texts.[57]

It has been suggested that a group of inscribed clay bullae from Daskyleion in Asia Minor demonstrate that the Old Persian language and script were used for everyday purposes,[58] but the inscriptions on these are impressions of seals, and are not incised into the clay, so they do not provide evidence of the Old Persian script in daily use.[59]

Evidence from Babylonian and Assyrian sources indicates that, while in Mesopotamia there are no direct references in the texts to the use of leather (Akkadian *mašku*, sometimes written with the Sumerogram KUŠ) as a writing material,[60] there is extensive evidence of the use of

---

its context in the Persepolis archive, under the heading '1 ARTA 2007.001 Achemenet Juin 2007', on the Internet. (A copy kindly supplied to me by Professor A.R. Millard.) Stolper had also illustrated and described this tablet during a Symposium on the Cyrus Cylinder held at the British Museum in June 2010 (briefly summarised in Finkel 2013: 2-3). Though this is only one of a very large number of texts from Persepolis which are yet to be published, no other Old Persian example has been ecognized.

57. A second Old Persian fragment, shown in Constantinople to A.D. Mordtmann by Dr Konstantin Makridi (who was serving on a Persian-Turkish boundary commission) with other pieces in about 1859, and long believed to be part of a clay tablet, was published initially by him (Mordtmann 1860: 555-56), then included by Weissbach in 1911: xxix, 130, unidentified at that time and therefore referred to as 'Inc[erta].a', and described as a '*Tontafel*', but subsequently identified by him as part of the text Artaxerxes II Susa d/A²Sd (1937: 643-51) and recognised as 'Naturstein' (p. 646 n. 1). On the text A²Sd, see also Kent 1953: 114, 154-55; Mayrhofer 1978: 31 (§7.2) 45 (A²Sd) and 46 ('Inc.a'); Vallat 1970: 171; 205-206, 207; and Appendix IV below. Other stone fragments, parts of column bases, inscribed with this same text have been found more recently at the site of the Palace of Artaxerxes II at Susa (Vallat 1972: 203-11 with figs 63-65, specifically 205-206 with figs 65:1-2 and 64:2), so this fragment might well have been found on the surface there in the nineteenth century. Two other inscriptions on clay (Dsa and DSb) cited as tablets in some sources (Weissbach 1911: xx, 98-99 [*Tontafelfragment*]; Kent 1953: 109-10, 141 [clay tablet]; Hinz 1941: 222-26) are actually inscribed bricks, not clay tablets (Dieulafoy 1890-93: 309-10 figs 192 and 193 = Scheil 1929: 52 no 11 and 48-49 no 8 = Pezard and Pottier 1926: 205 nos 525-26).
58. Diakonoff 1970: 98-124, specifically, 119 n. 54.
59. Balkan 1959: 123-28.
60. CAD: M: I: 376-79.

papyrus (*niāru*),[61] occasionally in the form of a roll (*kirku*).[62] The word *niāru* occurs several times in a series of Assyrian divinatory cuneiform tablets of the seventh century BC which take the form of questions to the sun god. Some of these refer to themselves as 'this papyrus' (*niāru anniu*),[63] suggesting that they were originally written on papyrus. The word is also found in Babylonian texts in the combination *KUŠna-a-a-ri*, literally 'leather.papyrus', or ^{KUŠ}*na-a-a-ri*, '[leather]papyrus', taken by the Chicago Assyrian Dictionary to mean 'parchment',[64] but possibly 'flexible writing material' in general.[65] No actual examples of papyrus have survived from Mesopotamia, but there is physical evidence of its use in the Hellenistic period from impressions on the reverse of clay sealings from Babylonia.[66]

Another channel by which the Bisitun text might have been made public is perhaps to be seen in an inscribed basalt fragment found at Babylon (now in the Staatliche Museum, Berlin, VA Bab.1502), which carries a text partially matching lines 55-58 and 69-72 of the Babylonian version of the inscription.[67] This fragment, probably part of a large display inscription, was found in the area referred to by Robert Koldewey, the excavator, as the Principal Citadel (*Hauptburg*), to the west of the Processional Way and to the north of the Ishtar Gate.[68] A number of other objects were found in the same area, and this fragment (VA Bab.1502) is usually assumed to have been part of a collection deliberately kept together. Some of the pieces date from many centuries before the time of Nebuchadnezzar, and others derive from cultures outside Babylonia, so Koldewey suggested that these were 'treasures that Nebuchadnezzar and his successors heaped up in this portion of the palace',[69] and others have described them as war trophies, or as constituting a 'Castle Museum'.[70]

61. CAD: N, II: 200-201; see also Driver, 1976: 16-17 and n. 4.
62. CAD: K: 408-409, kirku B, 'roll'; and Parpola 1987: 36, no 34, reverse 19.
63. Starr 1990: 343 (index of occurrences).
64. CAD: N: II: 201, §2, citing Dougherty 1923: nos 54:8 and 92:5; see also Ebeling 1952: 213.
65. Millard 2003: 351.
66. Rostovtzeff 1932: 16.
67. Koldewey 1914: 166; a copy of this text is given in Weissbach 1903: no X, pl. 9 with transliteration, translation and comments 24-26; a transliteration is given in parallel with the Bisitun text in Voigtlander 1978: 63-65; and English translations of both are given, in parallel with the Aramaic version, in Greenfield and Porten 1982: 8-9.
68. Found in square r9, see schematic plan in Koldewey 1931: pl. 1.
69. Koldewey 1914: 160 (found in square r9 of the site, plan fig. 13); the group of objects is outlined in 156-69; see also Koldewey 1990: 161-69.
70. F. Wetzel in Koldewey 1932: 19-24 (Kriegstrophäen), specifically 23 no 22; and,

Nebuchadnezzar and Nabonidus, in particular, were interested in recovering the inscriptions of earlier kings, following ancient early tradition,[71] but Darius is unlikely to have had such a specific interest,[72] so, if this is a deliberate collection of antiquities, Nebuchadnezzar and Nabonidus are the kings most likely to have assembled it and this inscribed fragment would not originally have been part of it. There are, moreover, in this collection, a number of other basalt fragments, among them relief sculptures of part of a crowned head, of two raised hands, and of a star, which probably came originally from the same monument as the inscription.[73] These basalt fragments were therefore not part of the presumed collection of the Neo-Babylonian period. Possibly, by the time of the excavations, they had become mixed with the collection in the confusion of objects at the site.[74] A possible reconstruction (with wide gaps) of a monument made up of these fragments, together with the inscription, suggests a sculptured slab measuring some two feet (60cm) high by over eleven feet (3.54m) across.[75]

Official Achaemenian residence at Babylon is clearly demonstrated by a palace, possibly to be dated to the reign of Darius I,[76] located in the general palace area some distance (c.385 metres or c.420 yards) to the southwest of the find spot of the above collection of objects.[77] The presumed sculptured slab is unlikely to have been associated with this palace, but the fact that Darius chose to build it at Babylon makes it a plausible speculation that he would have placed some kind of version of

---

listed differently, Unger 1931: 224-28 (Schlossmuseum), specifically 225 no 23.

71. See Beaulieu 1989: 138-43; and more briefly E.A. Speiser in Dentan 1955: 46; Wiseman, 1991: 244; 1985: 65; Oates 1979: 162.

72. See Cameron in Dentan 1955: 93-94.

73. Seidl 1976: 125-30. She lists the possible component pieces in n. 4 (pp. 125-26), where her nos one and two = Wetzel's no 22; three = 18 (star); four = 14 (hands); five = eight (head); six to eight = 19q-s; nine = nine; ten = twelve; eleven = sixteen; twelve = 17ar; and thirteen = 17at. Not all of these pieces are today accessible but those that are can be identified as basalt. The whereabouts of two of the pieces (nos five [head] and nine) are unknown, so their material cannot be confirmed: they are recorded as 'Dolerit', a material different chemically but similar in appearance to basalt, so this may be no more than a first on-site unscientific description, in which case they may be basalt also. It is reasonable, therefore, to assume that they are also parts of the monument.

74. On later re-use of (suggesting hunting for) material from the site, see Koldewey 1914: 313-14.

75. Seidl 1976: 128, fig. 2, cross-section drawing at a scale of 1:30, measuring 2cm high (x 30 = 60cm = 1.97 feet) and 11.8cm across (x 30 = 3.54m = 11.65 feet).

76. Koldewey 1931: 120-25, pls 26-28; and Haerinck 1973: 108-32.

77. In square 25f of Koldewey's plan (see n. 63 above).

the Bisitun inscription on public display for the inhabitants of the city.[78] Such a monument might have stood near the north entrance to the main Palace, in the wall between it and the Processional Way.[79]

A different suggestion concerning the text of the Bisitun inscription is that it might have been circulated in Old Persian on parchment, either in the Aramaic script or in cuneiform written in ink,[80] though there is no direct evidence for the existence of such a document in Old Persian in either the Aramaic or the Old Persian script. A number of Middle Iranian (Parthian and Pahlavi) inscriptions in the Aramaic script are known, a few on ostraca and parchment, but none of these is earlier than the first century BC.[81] There is, however, a much damaged earlier inscription in the Aramaic script on the rock face of the tomb of Darius I at Naqsh-e Rustam.[82] It has been pointed out that in this inscription the phrase *ḥšyty wzrk* could represent Iranian *ḫšāyaṯiya vazraka*, 'Great King,'[83] and other surviving elements suggest that this entire text was in Persian.[84] Its date has been much debated. W.B. Henning saw the name Seleucus (*slwk*) in it and therefore dated it in the third century BC (though Seleucus I came to power in the late fourth century, 311 BC in Babylonia), and he designated it as either late Old Persian or early Middle Persian.[85] Henning

78. See the comments of Cameron (in Dentan 1955: 87-88) on the probable attitude of Darius to the use of public inscriptions.

79. Seidl 1976: 129.

80. Meissner 1925: 344; a suggestion supported by Dougherty 1928: 109-35, specifically 133-34; and Cameron 1948: 29 n. 24; see also Gershevitch 1971: in his Editor's Preface to a preliminary monograph publication of Hallock 1985 (suggesting that the stone-cutter would have copied Old Persian text from clay tablets). Hallock's chapter was published subsequently (without the Preface) as Chapter 11 in Gershevitch (ed.) 1985a: 588-609); see also Levy 1954: 182-88 (full reference in n. 303 below).

81. Convenient bibliography in Gignoux 1972: 9-14, 43-44.

82. Situated between two engaged columns to the right of the doorway to the tomb, below the Elamite version of the main inscription (DNb) (Schmidt 1970: pls 35 and 36A [with 12, 83] and a drawing of the façade of the tomb, fig. 32).

83. Copy of the inscription in Herzfeld 1938: fig. 6 (with 12) (the passage cited is in line 20 [line three of the area in the lower centre]); this is partially reproduced by Delaunay 1974: pl. V fig. 7 (line three in the block of text at lower left).

84. Frye 1982: 90.

85. Henning, 1958: 24-25, for other discussion of this inscription, see, previously, Herzfeld, 1926: 244; 1937: 12; Rosenthal 1939: 35-36; Cameron 1948: 29 and n. 21; and, subsequently, Schmidt 1970: 12, 83; Frye 1982: 85-90 (useful discussion of possible readings, with reasonably good photographs of the inscription, pls II-IX); Boyce and Grenet 1991: 118-20; and Wiesehöfer briefly in 1994: 390 (suggesting that by the time of the late Achaemenian period no one could read the cuneiform script [*unleserlich*]) and n. 4 (that the Darius tomb inscription is

was a highly respected Iranologist but it may be questioned whether he was correct in seeing *slwk*.[86] G.G. Cameron suggested that in the same line as ḫšyty wzrk it is possible to read the name [']*rtḫšš*, 'Artaxerxes',[87] in which case the inscription could have been placed there by one of the Achaemenid kings of that name, the latest being Artaxerxes III (359-338 BC), pointing to a date not greatly different from that proposed by Henning.[88] J. Naveh proposes, on the basis of palaeography, that it could be dated to the fifth century BC,[89] and Frye, in concluding that it is an Old Persian text in Aramaic script, suggests a date in the fourth or early third century BC,[90] though H. Humbach takes the inscription as an archaic form of Pahlavi, or 'Aramaeo-Iranian'.[91] It is possible, therefore, that this

---

late Achaemenian); cited by Hintze 1998: 147-61, specifically 152.

86. This name is not obvious in Herzfeld's copy – Henning may have had the second main surviving part of line four in mind – but Frye is doubtful, saying 'I have not found the word in the inscription' (1982: 87-88).

87. Cameron 1948: 29 and n. 22, referring to line 20 of the inscription; i.e. the first complete line, in the lower left-hand fragment in Herzfeld's copy (1938: 12); a reading supported by Frye (1982: 89).

88. An alternative possibility that [']*rtḫšš* might refer to Ardashir, the first Sasanian king in the third century AD, is ruled out both by palaeography (the form of the script in the Sasanian period was markedly different) and by the fact that the name of Ardashir (written *'rtḫštr*), as found in his rock inscription at Naqsh-e Rustam as well as on ostraca from Dura Europos (references in Gignoux 1972: 46.), shows a difference in the spelling (final -*štr* as against Achaemenian -*šsš* or -*šs*). Another suggested indication of date is to be found in the occurrence in the inscription of *m'hy spnd*[. . .] (Herzfeld 1938: 12, fig. 6, line nineteen [the first preserved line in the lower middle fragment], restored as *m'hy spnd*[*rmt*] by Frye 1982: 89), which is taken as the month name (*m'h* = 'month') Spandarmad (= February/March) in the Zoroastrian religious calendar, the equivalent of Viyaḫna in the Old Persian civil calendar. Gershevitch, following S.H. Taqizadeh, places the introduction of this Zoroastrian calendar and the replacement of Viyaḫna by Spandarmad, in 441BC (Gershevitch 1964: 12-38, specifically 20-22), but Boyce, following E.J. Bickerman, has dismissed this conclusion (1982: 244-45 n. 151). Moreover J. Duchesne-Guillemin considers *m'hy sndrm*(*t*), his reading from Herzfeld's hand-copy (1938: 12), as 'too uncertain' to be relied upon (in Yarshater 1983: 868 n. 4), so this point does not offer any secure dating. For parallel lists of month names, see Lecoq 1997: 171-73, with 174 on Spandarmad; and on the Zoroastrian calendar, see Boyce 1982: 243-51; and 1979: 70-74.

89. Naveh 1970: 42 n. 97 (on the basis of Herzfeld's hand-copy which 'shows a formal cursive of the fifth century BCE'. That Herzfeld's copy is a reasonable representation of the characters can be seen by comparison with the photographs published by Frye in 1982: pls II-IX.

90. Frye 1982: 90.

91. Humbach 1974: 237-43.

Naqsh-e Rustam inscription gives some indication of the appearance of
an Old Persian inscription in alphabetic script as it might have looked on
parchment or papyrus.

A considerable number of Aramaic papyri of the Achaemenian period
are known and a cache of Aramaic documents on leather, now in the
Bodleian Library, Oxford, came to light in 1933. These are of unknown
provenance but relate to Egypt and were probably found there; and a
single Aramaic leather fragment is known from Elephantine.[92] In the fifth
century BC Herodotus records that the Ionians 'called' (*kaleō*) 'papyrus'
(*bublos*) 'skins' (*diphtherā*), that is to say, they referred to papyrus as
skins, because:

> formerly for lack of papyrus (*bublos*) they used the skins of
> sheep and goats; and even to this day there are many foreigners
> who write (*graphō*) on such skins (*diphtherā*).[93]

In the context of Biblical archaeology it is worth noting that the
passage of the Bisitun text discussed above, by whatever means it was
disseminated, is somewhat comparable to an account found in the book
of Esther (3:12) which reports that:

> the royal secretaries (*sōpĕrê hammelek*) were summoned.
> They wrote out in the script (*kĕtāb*) of each province (*mĕdînâ*)
> and in the language (*lāšôn*) of each people (*'am*) all the
> orders of Haman[94] [the enemy of Esther] to the king's satraps

---

92. See Driver 1954; and rev. ed., abridged, without the plates, 1957), with summary
of other material, 1954: 1-2; 1957: 1-3; see also Rosenthal 1939: 37-38 and 295-
99, bibliography of ostraca, seals etc.

93. *The Histories* 5:58, quoting the translation of Godley 1971: 64-65. On
parchment, see Appendix II below.

94. Concerning Haman, it has been suggested that the name (*hāmān*) could reflect
that of the Elamite god Humban (Koehler and Baumgartner 2001: I: 251,
citing Altheim and Stiehl 1963: 203, who in turn cite Duchesne-Guillemin,
1953: 106 n. 3; see also K.D. Schunck in Reicke and Rost 1964: II: col.629
(suggesting Elamite Humman); Zadok 1976: 63 (different spellings of Elamite
Humban, Akkadian Ḫumban); and Hinz and Koch 1987: I: 695 (Humban
with references). If Haman is a form of Humban, it is possible that it was an
abbreviation of a name such as Humban-haltash, Humban-nikash or the like
(see, e.g., the names, usually written Huban-, in the index of Waters 2000:133-
34; and examples with Huban- as the first element in Hinz and Koch 1987: I:
677-81, and others in which -huban forms the second element (*ibid.*, p.677
under d.hu-ban). The occurrence of a name of this kind would have been quite
normal at Susa in the heart of Elam. Against the identification of the name

(*ăhašdarpān*), the governors (*pehāh*) of the various provinces and the nobles of the various peoples.[95] These were written in the name of king Xerxes (*ăhašwērôš*) and sealed with the royal ring (*nehtām bĕṭabba'at hammelek*).

While this passage does not indicate the medium on which the texts were written, and sealing with a ring (*ṭabba'at*) could imply impressions on tablets or clay sealings on either parchment or papyrus, the same situation could have applied as that appertaining to the Bisitun inscription. The passage in Esther does not mention public reading of the document, but that this was a familiar practice is shown by the action of Ezra when he read out the Book of the Law of Moses (*sēper tôrat mōšeh*) before the assembled Jews in Jerusalem at the time of the return from Babylonia (Nehemiah 8:1-9). It has been suggested that the Book in question was simply Deuteronomy but, since the reading is said to have taken from first light until midday (Nehemiah 8:3), it is possible that the entire Pentateuch was involved.[96] Such public reading of official documents was well known in the ancient Near East,[97] and earlier instances of the practice are referred to in the Old Testament (Deuteronomy 31:9-13; 2 Kings 23:1-2).

A common practice in the ancient Near East was the setting up of display inscriptions in which rulers named themselves and boasted about their achievements. There is some very limited evidence of this practice in the period of the Hebrew monarchy. The Mesha Stone from neighbouring Moab gives an idea of the form such a royal inscription might have taken, and the Hebrews readily adopted the practices of the

Hamam as Elamite is the statement that his father had the clearly Iranian name Hamadatha (Esther 3:1) (on which see Zadok 1986: 107 §6; and, conveniently, Gesenius 1987-2010: 2: 280; and on the termination –*dāta*, 'law, statute', also Mayrhofer 1978: 25 §4.4.3.1) and, perhaps less significantly, since a parent could be likely to name his children in keeping with the ruling culture, among his ten sons (Esther 9:7-8), five had Persian names – *'ăriday* (details conveniently in Gesenius 1987-2010: 1: 96; also Zadok 1986: 106 §2); *ărîdātā'* (Hinz and Koch 1987: I: 99); *ărîsay* (Hinz and Koch 1987: I: 99); *parmaštā'* (4 [2007]: 1079); *paršandātā'* (4: 1085; Zadok, 1986: 108-109 §9; also Mitchell 2004: no 52 [seal (BM.89152) inscribed *pršndt* and with a Persian image]) – and three others had probable Persian names: *ădalyā'* (1: 14); *'aspātā'* (1: 85; Zadok 1986: 107 §3); *pûrātā'* (4: 1045; Zadok 1986: 109 §10).

95. [These forms appear in the plural in the text.]
96. See discussion in Williamson 1987: 90-93.
97. See, e.g., briefly, Mitchell 2004: no 10, with bibliography, 125; also, Kitchen and Lawrence 2012: xxiii §4b (general) and, e.g., 560-61 (Hittite Treaty: Muwatallis with Alaksandu [BM.108569 a fragment of it]).

surrounding peoples, but it is possible that for them there was some hesitation to engage in the self-aggrandisement involved. The inscription in the Siloam tunnel is only partially on display (a reader would have to carry a light and wade through water to get to it)[98] but it may be significant that it does not name its author (probably Hezekiah). There is apparent reference in the Old Testament to the setting up (*nṣb*) of a monument (*yād*) by Saul for himself (*lô*), at Carmel (1 Samuel 15:12), and another passage states that Absalom, took a *maṣṣēbâ* and set it up (*nṣb*) for himself (*lô*), it being known as Absalom's monument (*yād 'abšālōm*), possibly though not certainly inscribed with his name (2 Samuel 18:18).[99] These actions took place when Saul was already behaving wrongly in general and when Absalom was rebelling against his father king David, so there is a marked element of disapproval in each.

It is worth noting that, while Darius chose to have his political statement put in writing, the early Zoroastrian attitude to committing the sacred book the *Avesta* to writing was rather different. The date of Zarathushtra, and therefore of the ancient nucleus of the *Avesta*, is disputed but Bailey considers it unlikely to have been later than c.600 BC.[100] For many centuries the text of the *Avesta* was passed down orally, particular stress being placed on accurate memory,[101] and it was probably not recorded in writing until the sixth century AD in the Sasanian period.[102]

When it comes to the Old Testament, though the early parts of Genesis were probably transmitted orally at first, the main corpus differs largely from the *Avesta* in indicating at many points that the religious and historical texts were regularly recorded in writing (e.g. Exodus 34:27; Deuteronomy 27:3; Joshua 8:32; 24:26; 1 Samuel 10:25; 2 Kings 17:37; Isaiah 30:8; Jeremiah 30:2; Habakkuk 2:2; Proverbs 22:20 etc.). An instance (relating to the ninth century BC) of the use of an official written text in Hebrew culture is found in 2 Chronicles (17:8-9) where it is recorded that priests (*kōhănîm*) went about (*yāsōbbû*) in all the cities

---

98. See, e.g., Cooke 1903: 15-16; or Gibson 1971: 21.
99. For this sense of the word *yād*, see Koehler and Baumgartner 2001: 1: 388 §6.a.; and P.R. Ackroyd in Botterweck, Ringgren and Fabry (eds) 1974-2006: V: 401. There is a possible occurrence of *yd* in a similar sense in a Ugaritic ritual text (Dietrich, Loretz and Sanmartín 1995: 122, no 1.106, line 17) where there is reference to the 'entrance' of a 'monument of the king' (*ptḥ yd mlk*); see del Olmo Lete and Sanmartín 2004: 2: 954 and 686; and discussion in del Olmo Lete 2004: 226-27.
100. See Bailey 1943: 172.
101. See, e.g., Boyce 1968: 35-36.
102. See Bailey 1943: 176; Boyce 1968: 33-35; also, more recently, Hintze 1998: 147-61, specifically 150-53. On this, see also Appendix III below.

of Judah with the Book of the Law of Yahweh (*sēper tôrat yhwh*) and taught (*yĕlammĕdû*) among the people (*bāʿām*). There is no indication that such a practice would have been known in early Iran.

Returning to the question of the religion of Cyrus, and the literary practice of the Iranians in the Achaemenian period, it should be pointed out that the view that the inscriptions in the name of Cyrus at Pasargadae (CMa, CMb and CMc) were carved in the time of Darius, and not of Cyrus himself, is not universally accepted, so it is best to treat it as a question still to be settled.[103] However, even assuming that they were of his own time, there is no indication in them, or in the inscriptions alleged to have been on his tomb, that he had any connection with Ahura Mazda.

Cyrus is said consistently in his inscriptions to have been from Anshan, the highland area of Elam, and his three immediate forebears are recorded in the Cyrus Cylinder each as 'Great King, King of Anshan', Anshan being the name of both the region and the capital city (modern Tall-e Malyan) in the Iranian highland a little over 30 miles (50 kilometres) west of Persepolis.[104] There is, however, no indication that his name itself was Elamite. Its etymology is disputed but it is of plausible Indo-European type, with a reasonable counterpart (Kuru-) in Sanskrit.[105] The basic Old Persian form *kūru-* always occurs (in the inscriptions of Darius) in the phrase 'son of Cyrus', and therefore with the genitive ending *-auš* > Kūrauš,[106] and in the, possibly later (nominally Cyrus), Pasargadae inscriptions, it is found with the nominative ending *-uš* > Kūruš (written *k-u-r-š*).[107] The name is found in Elamite as *ku-ráš* and in Babylonian as *ku-ra-aš*, in Biblical Hebrew and Aramaic as *kôreš*, and Greek as *koros* and *kuros*.

---

103. See, e.g., Kent 1953: 107, 116 (CMa, CMb and CMc implicitly of Cyrus the Great); Schmitt 1993: 526 (CMa of Cyrus the Great); Lecoq 1997: 80-82 (CMa and CMc of Cyrus the Great). Weissbach 1911: xxviii-xxix, lxvii-lxix, 126-27) assumes the possibility that CMa is a text of Cyrus 'the Younger', an ascription rejected, e.g., by Schmitt 1993: 526). 'Cyrus the Younger' (c.423-401 BC), a son of Darius II, was never king but mounted a campaign against his brother Artaxerxes II, during which he was killed at Cunaxa, leaving a contingent of Greek mercenaries to make their way back to Greece under Xenophon.

104. Reiner 1973: 57-62; with Sumner 1972: 176, and Reiner 1972: 177; and Stolper 1984.

105. See R. Schmitt in Yarshater (ed.) 1993: 515-16; Mayrhofer 1979: 23-24 §39; Kent 1953: 55 §164; Brandenstein and Mayrhofer 1964: 130; also, Hinz and Koch 1887: I: 519 (assuming an Old Persian origin). Eilers 1964: 180-236; also, briefly, Schmitt 1967: 119-45, specifically 121 and n. 15.

106. Brandenstein and Mayrhofer 1964: 130, 62-63, §72; Kent 1953: 180, 62 §181.

107. See also Mayrhofer 1973: 183 §8.864.

The name of Cyrus's earliest recorded ancestor, Achaemenes (Old Persian *haḫāmaniš*, written *h-ḫ-a-m-n-i-š*; Greek *'akʰaimenēs*), has a plausible Indo-Iranian etymology;[108] and a possible analysis of the name of his son Teispes (Old Persian *čišpiš*, written *č-i-š-p-i-*; Greek *teispēs*) as Indo-European has been proposed;[109] the name of the next king in his line of ancestors, Cyrus (I), is again plausibly Indo-Iranian; and, though disputed, that of his successor Cambyses (Old Persian *kaᵐbūjiya*, written *k-b-u-j-y*; Greek *kambusēs*), the father of Cyrus the Great (II), has a possible Indo-Iranian etymology.[110] It is thus reasonable to see the Achaemenids as Iranian rather than Elamite, but as people who must have had contact with Elamite religion in Anshan.[111]

It is appropriate here to refer to the account of Cyrus given in the *Cyropaedia* of Xenophon, which includes reference to his religion. This, a composition of Xenophon's old age,[112] which has been characterised as an 'historical novel, centred around Cyrus, on the education of statesmen',[113] and as 'an imaginary and instructive account of the education of the ideal ruler',[114] was not intended primarily as a contribution to the writing of history, but to serve as a vehicle for Xenophon's civic views. He had had contact with Persians when he took part in the expedition of Cyrus the Younger, the pretender against Artaxerxes II but this was in 401 BC, over a century and a quarter after the time of Cyrus the Great, and, though it is clear from the *Anabasis* that he had first-hand knowledge of Mesopotamia, and from the *Cyropaedia* that he 'evidently drew . . . on his own memories of the younger Cyrus and his companions',[115] the value of the evidence it supplies is limited. According to the *Cyropaedia*, Cyrus followed the practices of the Magi (7:5:35, 57; 8:3:11, 24),[116] which included sacrificing to 'gods' (plural, *theois*: 8:1:23, also 1:5:6) and praying 'to ancestral Hestia (*hestia patrō*$_i$*a*$_i$), ancestral Zeus (*dii patrō*$_i$*ō*$_i$),

---

108. Mayrhofer 1979: II: 22 §36; Brandenstein and Mayrhofer 1964: 122; Schmitt 1967: 119-45, specifically 120 and n. 8.
109. Mayrhofer 1979: II: 17-18 §23; Brandenstein and Mayrhofer 1964: 112-13; Eilers 1964: 205-206; Schmitt 1967: 121-22 and ns 23, 24. A suggested connection with the name of the Hurrian deity Tešub has received little acceptance.
110. Kent 1953: 178-79; Mayrhofer 1979: II: 23 §38; Brandenstein and Mayrhofer 1964: 128; Eilers 1964: 210-13; Schmitt 1967: 121 and n. 13. A suggested pre-Iranian etymology (see, e.g., Frye 1962: 87 and 266 n. 52) has not been widely accepted.
111. On Elamite religion, see, e.g., Hinz 1972: 41-67.
112. Anderson 1974: 2-3, 195-96.
113. Easterling and Knox (eds) 1985: 789 (sub-edited by M. Drury).
114. Bowra 1933: 148.
115. Boyce 1982: 211, and 211-16 in general on Xenophon and the Persians.
116. On the Magi, see also below.

and the rest of the gods (*tois allois theois*)' (1:6:1; also 7:5:57). While the name of Hestia (the hearth goddess, connected in the Greek world with fire)[117] is here possibly a 'translation' of Iranian Ātar, the god of fire,[118] and the name Zeus (the supreme god), was perhaps a 'translation' of Ahura Mazda,[119] these indications could be merely a reflection of the time of Cyrus the Younger, who is likely to have followed such practices himself,[120] and they provide rather thin evidence for a Zoroastrian faith on the part of Cyrus the Great.

There are no known Old Persian inscriptions in the name of Cambyses, Cyrus's successor, but Ahura Mazda is mentioned frequently in the inscriptions of Darius I,[121] the third ruler of the dynasty, showing that he at least had some association with Zoroastrianism. In the main sculptured relief on his tomb at Naqsh-e Rustam he is shown worshipping at a fire altar,[122] thereby demonstrating his adherence to that aspect of Zoroastrianism.[123] That this element played a part in the religious practices at Persepolis is shown by some of the Elamite texts which refer to the 'Fire-watcher' (*ha-tur-ma-ak-šá* < Old Persian *ātar-vahš*), a functionary known in Avestan literature.[124] Concerning Cyrus, parts of stepped

---

117. Burkert 1985: 61 (60-64, fire rituals), 170.
118. As suggested by Boyce 1982: 298, with 215-16; the identification by W. Miller of Hestia as 'the Persian goddess of primal fire (the nurturing Anahita)' (Xenophon, *Cyropaedia*, II [Loeb 52], 1914: 472) reflects an outdated view.
119. Suggested by Boyce 1982: 165, 214, 297; the assumption already of Miller 1950: 478.
120. Cf. Boyce 1982: II: 200-201.
121. Kent 1953: 107-12, 116-47, and the references to Ahura Mazda listed, 164-65; Weissbach 1911: xi-xxiii, 8-107, and the references to Ahura Mazda in all three versions, 137. It is appropriate to mention that the body of monumental Old Persian text in the name of Darius is far more extensive than that of all the other Achaemenid kings combined (in Kent 1953 the inscriptions of Darius [transliteration and English translation] occupy 30 pages [116-47] as against ten [147-57] for all the others).
122. Schmidt 1970: frontispiece (whole façade), pl. 19 (main upper relief). See, also, on this, Boyce 1979: 57, with discussion of other Zoroastrian elements, 57-59; and, more fully, 1982: 112-16.
123. Concerning the place of fire in Zoroastrianism, Dr Mahnaz Moazami writes: 'The sacred fire is a major symbol of the religious marks of the Zoroastrian tradition. The great fires of victory (*atash wahram*) consecrated in temple sanctuaries are theologically understood as exemplifications of the infinite light of Ahura Mazda. These fires are thought of as warriors fighting the dark forces of decay, deceit, ignorance and death, and thus serve as icons of the good creation's victory over the forces of evil.' (Personal communication)
124. Hinz and Koch 1987: I: 650; and Cameron 1948: 7-8, referring to texts subsequently published in Hallock 1969, references there on 695 Persepolis Fortification tablet (PF) 761 (a text cited by Cameron as Fort.3126); Avestan

fire-holders, as well as parts of stepped plinths, probably intended to take portable fire-holders, all found at or near his capital Pasargadae,[125] and therefore assumed to date from his reign, might be thought to suggest that both he and Cambyses were Zoroastrians,[126] but fire was involved in Indo-Iranian religion quite apart from Zoroastrianism. It is clear from the extensive Sanskrit written sources that fire played an important part in ancient Indian religion.[127] There is also archaeological evidence from Central Asia of buildings already associated with a fire cult in the second millennium BC, in ancient Margiana, Bactria and probably Khorasmia (roughly in modern Turkmenistan and Uzbekistan);[128] and more generally in the Indo-European context the equally extensive Latin sources indicate that fire played a significant part in Roman religion.[129] It is a reasonable possibility therefore that the religion of Cyrus and Cambyses contained traditional pre-Zoroastrian Indo-Iranian beliefs, involving fire worship, and possibly such deities as Mithra[130] and Varuna, and that it was Darius who introduced Zoroastrianism, or more properly Zarathushtrianism, to the Empire.[131]

---

    references in Bartholomae 1904: cols 318-19. On fire in ancient Iranian religion, see Duchesne-Guillemin 1962: 77-95, 179-80, and on fire altars 153-54; on the Iranian fire deity Ātar, see references in Bartholomae 1904: cols 312-16; for a convenient summary on Ātar see Malandra 1983: 159-61; also on Ātar and the Indian counterpart Agni, Widengren 1968: 51 (pre-Zoroastrian), 101 (Achaemenian period).

125. Stronach 1978: 138-42, fig. 72, and pls 103-107.

126. See, e.g., Boyce 1982: 51-53; and in Davies and Finkelstein (eds) 1984: 285-86; Duchesne-Guillemin 1962: 153-54; and Cameron 1948: 7-8 (on Ātar-vaḫs, 'Fire watcher').

127. See, e.g., Eliade 1979: 208-10, with bibliography, 438; Chaudhuri, 1979: 72-74; Geldner 1951(translation, which begins with hymn to Agni); Macdonell 1917: 1-10 (introductory comments, text of first hymn to Agni, with notes); O'Flaherty 1975: 97-115 (on the fire god Agni); and see Winternitz 1910: 207-10 (references in Sacred Books of the East volumes to fire-worship in India). On other Indo-European cognates (Latvian, Lithuanian, Old Church Slavonic and Russian) of Agni and Latin ignis, see Mallory and Adams 2006: 122-23.

128. See Betts and Yagodin 2007: 435-53, specifically 437-44 (on Tash-k'irman Tepe) and 445-51 (summary of other evidence).

129. See Dumézil 1970: 1: 311-26. On the element of fire in Greek religion, see, conveniently, Burkert 1985: 60-64.

130. On fire in connection with Mithra, see Gershevitch 1959: 7, 30, 59, 60-61, 136-37, 278-79.

131. E.g. Gershevitch assumes that neither Cyrus nor Cambyses was a Zarathuštrian since there is no mention of Ahura Mazda in their inscriptions, and he characterizes the religion of Darius as 'a monotheism centred in Ahura Mazdā' (1964: 16-19). At a symposium on Ancient Persia held at the British

On the other hand, Boyce argues that Cyrus was a Zarathushtrian, citing, in addition to the fire-holders at Pasargadae, the fact that his cousin Arsames (grandfather of Darius the Great)[132] had already given his son the name Hystaspes (*vištāspa*), possibly showing respect for Vishtaspa, the eastern ruler who had been the patron of Zarathushtra,[133] and that he, Cyrus, had named his eldest daughter Atossa, possibly after Hutaosa, Vishtaspa's queen,[134] both suggesting a hereditary and personal adherence to Zarathushtrianism, and that this, with similar evidence of personal names in the dynasty, points to the conclusion that the Achaemenid family had accepted Zarathushtrianism in the early sixth century BC.[135] There are thus arguments on both sides.

There is indirect reference in the inscriptions of Darius to one basic element of Iranian religion, the role of the Magus.[136] This word (Old Persian *maguš*; Elamite *makuš*; Babylonian *magušu*; Aramaic *mgwš*) is found in the Bisitun inscription, but there solely in reference to Gaumata, a Magian priest who claimed falsely to be Bardia (Greek Smerdis)[137] the brother of Cambyses and therefore heir to the throne.[138] Several individuals with the title Magus are mentioned in the Elamite tablets from Persepolis, however, as recipients of rations.[139] The Magi were priests of the pre-Zoroastrian Iranian religion, who adopted and modified the

---

Museum in 2005 R.N. Frye also argued that neither Cyrus nor Cambyses was a Zoroastrian.

132. On whom, see, e.g., Bresciani 1987: 546.

133. On the name, see Mayrhofer 1977b: 97 no 379.

134. See Mayrhofer 1977b: 52 no 179; also, Schmitt 1989: 13-14.

135. Boyce 1984a: 281.

136. On which, see Schwartz in Gershevitch (ed.) 1985a: 696-97; and a dated (from a 1942 German original) but useful account, Delling 1967.

137. The form Smerdis is given by Herodotus (c.484-c.425 BC) (*The Histories*, 3:61-79), but Aeschylus (525/4-456 BC) has Mardos (*Persai*, 774) and Aeschylus lived nearer in time to the original than Herodotus and had indeed fought in the Persian wars. The sound change *b->m-* is well attested in Persian > Greek personal names (examples in Schmitt 1967: 129-30, 134, see, also, 126 with n. 61, and, on the name Smerdis, 121-22 with ns 21, 22), as well as in Old Persian *bandaka*, 'subject, servant' (from **banda*, 'bond, fetter') > Greek *mandakēs*, 'bundle' (suggested by E. Tucker in Christides [ed.] 2007: 778). For a sound change (*b->)m->sm*, i.e. from Bardia to Smerdis, Lecoq (1997: 294) suggests influence from Greek *mikros*, 'small', which occurs frequently in the spelling *smikros* from Homer onwards and regularly in Herodotus; and Cook suggests the change might have resulted from 'attraction to the existing Greek names Smerdes and Smerdios' (Cook 1983: 237 n. 6).

138. References in Kent 1953: 182.

139. References in Hallock 1969: 723, under Makuš I.

system introduced by Zarathushtra.[140] According to Herodotus they were a Median tribe (*The Histories* 1:101), some of whom interpreted dreams (1:107, 120, 128) and participated in animal sacrifice (1:132, 140), suggesting perhaps a situation analogous to the priestly role of the tribe of Levi in ancient Israel.[141] In the Biblical context it may be noted that the word *magos* occurs in the Septuagint (the Greek translation of the Old Testament) as the translation of Hebrew *'aššāp* at Daniel 2:2 etc., *'aššāp* being Babylonian-Assyrian *āšipu*, 'sorcerer, incantation-priest'. The word is best known, however, in the New Testament in reference to the so-called Wise Men (*magoi*) at the birth of Jesus (Matthew 2:1, 7, 16), and in a derived meaning 'magician' in reference to a man named Elymas, who is described as *magon pseudoprophētēs*, 'magician false prophet', encountered by the Apostle Paul at Paphos in Cyprus (Acts 13:6, 8).[142]

Whether or not Cyrus or Cambyses were Zoroastrians, or were simply adherents of pre-Zoroastrian Iranian religion or influenced by Elamite beliefs, as realists, they and later Persian kings saw the value of supporting the local deities in their subject territories. Evidence for this is found in the heart of the Empire at Persepolis where the Elamite cuneiform tablets of the time of Darius I and Artaxerxes I record rations issued for use in religious ceremonies involving not only Ahura Mazda and Mithra but also such other deities as the Elamite Humban, Babylonian Adad and several other little-known gods who had no connection with Zoroastrianism.[143] This attitude is clear also from the Nabonidus Chronicle, which records the reign of Nabonidus, the last king of Babylon, and concludes with an account of the conquest by Cyrus, and states that 'there was no interruption of offering in Esagila or the (other) temples, and no time was missed' (3:17-18: *baṭ-la ša mimma ina é-sag-gíl u ēkurrāti*[É.KUR]^meš DIŠ *ul iš-šá-kin* | *ù si-ma-nu ul innitiq*[DIB]^iq),[144] literally, 'interruption (*baṭla*) which (*ša*) anything

---

140. Gershevitch 1964: 24-26; see also Brandenstein and Mayrhofer 1964: 130-31 on the word *magu-*.

141. See comments of Lecoq 1997: 161.

142. Danker 2010: 608-609 with useful bibliography. For later usage of the word, see Butler 1948.

143. Hallock 1969: 18-19 and 770 (Uramasda), 732 and 19 n. 11 (Mišebaka), 768 (Umban, Hupan), 665 (Addad); Boyce 1982: 139-41.

144. BM.35382: Smith 1924: 98-123, pls XI-XIV, (introduction, text, transliteration, translation and commentary), specifically 113, 117, 121, pl. XIII; Grayson 1975: 104-11, specifically 110, iii.17-18 (transliteration and translation). English translations also: Oppenheim in Pritchard 1955: 305-307, specifically 306, col. 2; and in Gershevitch (ed.) 1985a: 539 (translation of 3:12-22); Arnold

(*mimma*) in (*ina*) Esagil and temples (*ēkurrāti*) offering (DIŠ = *ginû*) not (*ul*) was placed (*iš-šá-kin/ iššakin* < *šakānu*, passive [N = IV stem], "to be put" etc.) | and (*ù*) time (*simānu*) not (*ul*) was missed (*innitiq* < *etēqu*, "to go past" etc.)'. Taking *baṭla* (interruption) as referring forward to *ginû* (regular contribution),[145] in other words, the religious rituals in the temple of Marduk the chief god of Babylon, and in other temples, continued without interruption under Cyrus.

Similar evidence in the time of Cambyses is found in Egypt. Cambyses established the twenty-seventh Egyptian Dynasty in 525 BC, beginning a period of Persian rule which, with the exception of 60 years of native control (402-343 BC; Dynasties 29-30), continued (thirty-first Dynasty) until the death of Darius III in 332 BC.[146] In this period an inscription on the statue of an official named Uje-Ḥar-resnet (*wḏ3-ḥr-rs-n.t*), who was involved with the temple of the goddess Neith at Sais in the Delta and who retained his post after the Persian conquest, says concerning Cambyses:

> His Majesty commanded that the temple of Neith should be cleansed and all its people placed in it, together with the priesthood of the temple. And his majesty commanded that the revenues should be given to Neith the great, the god's mother, and to the great gods who are in Sais as they were in former times. And His Majesty caused all their festivals and their processions to be made as they were in former times.[147]

It is reasonable to see this as further evidence that the Achaemenid kings were, so to speak, hedging their bets when it came to religion. Some will question the accuracy of the Biblical text, but it is quite plausible to see the invocation of Yahweh as merely another instance of the same policy.

A basic point to note about the Achaemenian period is the fact that,

---

in Chavalas 2006: 418-20, specifically 420. For this passage Grayson has 'there was no interruption (of rites) in Esagila or the (other) temples, and no date (for a performance) was missed'; and other translations are offered in CAD: B: 177 (*baṭlu*) and CAD: S: 270 (*simanu*). Smith reads *baṭ-la* as *be-la*, which he takes as 'weapon', with 'no one's weapon was set up'.

145. Smith and Grayson, however, both pass over the sign DIŠ in the text, considering it 'superfluous' (Smith 1924: 121) or 'a scribal error' (Grayson 1975: 110).

146. On the Persian occupation of Egypt, see E. Bresciani in Gershevitch (ed.) 1985a: 502-28; and, for the dynasties in question, Gardiner 1961: 452-53.

147. Vatican Museum I.31: Grenier 1993: 17-18, pl. 5; translation with discussion in Gardiner 1961: 366-68.

though in the different parts of the Empire the local languages continued to be spoken, Aramaic, which had already been widely used in the Assyrian and Neo-Babylonian Empires, was adopted together with its alphabet as the official medium of communication, the *lingua franca*, throughout the Empire. It is therefore generally referred to as Official or Imperial Aramaic (*Reichsaramäische*).[148] The archives of Elamite cuneiform tablets found at Persepolis show that the Persian bureaucracy there was in the hands of Elamite scribes, most of whom would have been at least bilingual in Elamite and Persian. That those scribes who were Persian were themselves heirs to the Median bureaucracy is suggested by what can be deduced from the Old Persian vocabulary and the forms of proper names.[149] With this scribal system at his disposal, the king, if he wished to communicate with officials in the area formerly under Elamite rule, would have dictated his message in Persian, it would have been written down in Elamite, and the local scribe at the destination would have read it out to his superior in his own language.[150] In the same way the evidence of widespread use of Aramaic throughout the Empire,[151] together with the discovery at Persepolis of over 700 tablets inscribed in Aramaic,[152] and the fact that some of the Elamite tablets found there have Aramaic endorsements in ink,[153] shows that in the capital there were also Aramaic scribes and that, just as the Elamite scribes provided the means of communication within the former Elamite areas, so the Aramaic scribes would have been used for communication with the outer Empire. If, for instance, the Great King in Susa wished to send a message to an official in Sardis in western Asia Minor, he would have dictated in Persian, the scribe would probably have written in Aramaic, and his counterpart the scribe in the Lydian court would read the message out in Persian or Lydian.

It will be appropriate here to select a few instances where outside

---

148. On Official Aramaic, see useful summaries by J. Naveh and J.C. Greenfield in Davies and Finkelstein 1984: 115-29; and Greenfield in Gershevitch (ed.) 1985a: 698-713; and, in more detail, Folmer 1995.

149. Lecoq 1997: 46-49.

150. See analysis by I. Gershevitch in his Editor's Preface to the preliminary monograph publication of Hallock, 'The Evidence of the Persepolis Tablets' (see n. 81 above): 5. Hallock's chapter was published subsequently (without the Preface) as Chapter 11 in Gershevitch (ed.) 1985a: 588-609.

151. Good survey up to 1939 in Rosenthal 1939: 24-38; a limited selection of texts (in the Hebrew script with English translations and notes) is given in Gibson 1975: 23-37.

152. See n. 57 above.

153. E.g. Hallock 1969: nos 693 (*twrn*, 'oxen'), 1798 (*mgwš*, 'the Magus'), 1819 (*bšnt 23 byrḥ 'b 20*, 'in year 23, in month Ab, [in day] 20') and personal names.

evidence has some bearing on the Biblical text. Starting in the Persian homeland, Persis, at the great site of Persepolis, the ceremonial capital of the Achaemenid kings, there are, as already mentioned, monumental inscriptions in cuneiform on the buildings in the three main languages of the Empire, Old Persian, Elamite and Babylonian, but also a large number of clay tablets inscribed in Elamite cuneiform.[154] For example, in ration records there is frequent mention of recipients who are referred to by the Elamite word *puhu*, 'boy', but individuals designated in this way often received the same rations as adult men, including wine, and it is clear that they did men's work, so it is probable that they were often men junior in status rather than age.[155] The usage of this word is analogous to that of Hebrew *na'ar* which often means 'young boy' in the Old Testament (e.g. in Isaiah 3:4) but this meaning is not appropriate in the account of Nehemiah's activities in Jerusalem where it is stated (Nehemiah 5:15), that 'even their boys lorded it over the people'.[156] This inappropriateness was recognised in the Authorised (King James) Version which translates the word as 'servants', while the more recent New International Version renders it 'assistants' and the more popular, but linguistically based, Good News Bible (today's English Version) returns to 'servants'.

Another discovery made during the excavation of the Treasury Building in the palace at Persepolis consisted of a collection of stone mortars, pestles and platters, made of a material described as green chert.[157] Many of these bear Aramaic inscriptions in ink, in which the language contains elements which have parallels in the Aramaic portion of the Biblical book of Ezra. There, in the account of the finding at Ecbatana of a scroll (*mĕgillâ*) of Cyrus authorising the rebuilding of the Jerusalem Temple (Ezra 6:2), the Biblical text says it was 'in the city of Ecbatana', '*bĕaḥmĕtā* *bîrtā*', that is, literally, 'in (*bĕ*-) Ecbatana (*'aḥmĕtā*) the city (*bîrtā*)'. *Bîrtā* (*byrt*) is usually translated 'fortress', but examination of its use in other contexts suggests that in texts of the Persian period it is better translated 'city', or 'fortified town',[158] and this interpretation is followed here as a working hypothesis.

---

154. Cameron 1948; Hallock 1969.
155. Hinz and Koch 1987: I: 229-32 (the word in various combinations).
156. This analogy is pointed out by Williamson 2004: 219-20.
157. Bowman 1970, a publication which has generated a number of discussions and reviews, including P. Bernard 1972: 165-76; Naveh and Shaked 1973: 445-57; Delaunay 1974: 193-217; Hinz 1975: 371-85; and others cited by Hinz, 371-72, 384-85.
158. See Lemaire and Lozachmeur 1987: 261-66, in which they cite texts where this word is applied to such site names as Samaria, Susa, Ecbatana, Elephantine, Syene, Sardis and Xanthos. As mentioned below, the trilingual inscription from Xanthos indicates that this place was referred to as *bryt* in Aramaic but *polis* in Greek (1987:

Several of the inscriptions on the chert objects begin with a similar frame of words, the first line reading either *bsrk byrt'*, *bprkn byrt'* or *bhst byrt'*,[159] that is 'in *srk* the city', 'in *prkn* the city' or 'in *hst* the city'. The similarity of this wording can be seen in the transliterations set out below, where, for clarity of comparison, the Biblical text is given without the vowels supplied to the text by later Rabbinic scholars.

Persepolis	b-srk	byrt'	in *srk* the city
Persepolis	b-prkn	byrt'	in *prkn* the city
Persepolis	b-hst	byrt'	in *hst* the city
Ezra 6:2	b-'ḥmt'	byrt'	in *Ecbatana* the city

The same pattern can be seen, incidentally, in the Hebrew counterpart found at the beginning of Nehemiah (1:1) where the author writes that he was 'in the city of Susa' (*bĕ-šûšan habbîrâ*, i.e. unvocalised, *b-šwšn hbyrh*), or as the Authorised Version puts it 'in Shushan the Palace'.

After the introductory passages ('In *srk/prkn/hst* the city') in these Aramaic inscriptions, the texts continue 'under the authority of (*lyd*) N[a] the governor (*sgn*), N[b] made this mortar/pestle/plate under the authority of N[c] the treasurer (*gnzbr*), in front of N[d] the sub-treasurer (*'pgnzbr*), a gift (*'skr*)', where N[a], N[b], N[c] and N[d] are different personal names. The senior man, the 'governor' (*sgn*, a loanword from Akkadian *šaknu*),[160] had a title which is found also, with others, in the book of Daniel (3:2, 3, 27; 6:8). The title of the official below him, *gnzbr*, 'treasurer' (literally 'treasure'[*gnz*]-'bearer'[*br*]), is an Iranian loanword and, again, is mentioned in the same passage in Daniel (3:2, 3) in the spelling *gdbr*, and this word is found also in the spelling *gzbr* in Ezra (7:21-22).[161] The variant spellings *gdbr* and *gzbr* may reflect borrowings from Old Persian and Median respectively, *gdbr* being a Persianised form of Median *gzbr*.[162] The *'pgnzbr*, 'sub-treasurer',

---

263, 264); again, Samaria is referred to in date formulae of the Wadi Daliyeh papyri in one instance as *byrt'*, 'the byrt', but otherwise regularly as *qryt'*, 'the city' (1987: 263, 264; see also Dušek 2007: 173); similarly, concerning Susa, the Old Testament uses *bîrâ*, the Hebrew counterpart of Aramaic *byrt*, in the phrase *šûšan habbîrâ*, 'Susa the bîrâ' (Esther 1:2 etc.), while in one instance it is referred to in the phrase *hā'îr šûšān*, 'the city of Susa' (Esther 8:15), where *'îr* has the meaning 'city', again supporting the interpretation of *bîrâ* as 'city' (1987: 264); the Persepolis inscriptions are also mentioned in 1987: 262-63. See also, briefly, Lemaire in 1995: 424. This conclusion is not accepted by all however, see, e.g., Hoftijzer and Jongeling 1995: 1: 155-56.

159. Bowman 1970: e.g. 76, text four line one, the first clearly preserved reading, and many others, indexed on 192.

160. See Brinkman 1968: 297-98; Dušek 2007: 510-11.

161. Conveniently set out in Naveh and Shaked 1973: 450-51.

162. Hinz 1975: 102, **ganzabara-* (Median) and **ganδabara-* (Persianised

the official junior to the *gnzbr*, has a designation not mentioned in the Old Testament. At the beginning of these phrases, the word *lyd*, literally 'to' or 'into' (*l*) '(the) hand' (*yd*), 'into the hand of' is plausibly rendered 'under the authority of' by Naveh and Shaked.[163]

These Aramaic inscriptions from Persepolis illustrate a point familiar in the study of ancient texts that interpretations change and further study often leaves questions open. R.A. Bowman, the first editor of *Aramaic Ritual Texts from Persepolis*, influenced by the fact that many of the stone objects were mortars and pestles, took the word *prkn* to mean 'crushing ceremony' which he associated with the sacred haoma plant,[164] the juice of which played a part in the Iranian religious cult,[165] and he translated the phrase *bprkn byrt'* 'In the (*haoma*-) crushing ceremony of the fortress'.[166] The analogy of the comparable Biblical phrase (Ezra 6:2), however, suggests that *prkn* was more likely to have been a location than a ceremony, something considered but rejected by Bowman,[167] and that *srk* and *hst* were likewise locations.

Several of the inscriptions indicate that these green chert objects came to Persepolis from Arachosia (*hrḥwty* < Old Persian *harauvatī*)[168] in modern Afghanistan, the capital city of which, also named Arachosia, was probably on the site of modern Kandahar.[169] This could suggest that, if these three words are place-names, they might have been located further out in the Empire and, in that case, most probably in the east within reasonable travelling distance of Kandahar.[170]

---

transcription of Median *ganzabara-); on this see also Mayrhofer 1968: 1-22, specifically 13-14. The related Greek form, *gaza*, 'treasury', occurs in the New Testament in the passage identifying the Ethiopian official in charge of the treasury of Queen Candace (Acts 8:27).

163. Naveh and Shaked 1973: 451.

164. He takes *prk* as a verb 'to rub, grind down, pulverise' (Bowman 1970: 74), a meaning finding rather thin support in a single occurrence, a Lydian-Aramaic bilingual grave inscription from Sardis, in which it has the sense 'to break, damage' in a passage warning against vandalism of the tomb (Hoftijzer and Jongeling 1995: 2: 939, *prk₁*; citing Donner and Röllig 1964: 260:6).

165. On 'Haoma', see M. Boyce 2003: 659-67; also, conveniently, Cameron 1948: 5-6; and, briefly, Schwartz in Gershevitch (ed.) 1985a: 676-77; and Boyce 1979: 5.

166. Bowman 1970: 22.

167. Bowman 1970: 20-22; Williamson 2004: 214 n. 9.

168. Kent 1953: 213-14; Brandenstein and Mayrhofer 1964: 124; Bowman cites the spelling *hrwḥty* in the Aramaic version of the Bisitun inscription, the counterpart of Babylonian *a-ru-ḫa-at-ti* (Bowman 1970: 82).

169. See Schmitt 1987: 246-47; see also Lecoq 1997: 138-39. The modern name is possibly derived from Macedonian Alexandropolis (|ø<l|k<x|n|d|h<ø|r|ø<p|ø<l|ø<s|).

170. On possible identifications of *srk*, *prkn* and *hst*, and related trade routes, see

When the Jews returned to Palestine in the years following 538 BC, a considerable number remained in Babylonia, as is indicated by the statement in the book of Ezra (1:5-6) that the neighbours of those who went contributed silver, gold, livestock and valuable gifts, implying therefore that they were prosperous and chose not to make the journey themselves.[171] This is confirmed by the Murashu documents, the archives of a prominent Babylonian family of this name, which was based in Nippur, the ancient Sumerian city in southern Babylonia. These archives, which are largely concerned with agricultural matters, deal with the business activities of members of the family and its agents in the area around Nippur.[172] The tablets are dated in the reigns of Artaxerxes I and Darius II and the beginning of Artaxerxes II, mainly from about 440-416 BC, probably partly at the time when Nehemiah was governor in Judah. The personal names of those who were involved in business transactions show that Babylonians made up about two thirds of the number, those bearing Aramaic names comprised about a quarter and of the remainder roughly a tenth consisted of people from other areas. Their places of origin are usually indicated by geographical names with the ending -a-a (-aia/aya), the equivalent of English '-ian' and show the widespread contacts of Babylonia in the Achaemenian period. They included men from Sardis (sapardaia, 'Sardian'), the capital of Lydia in western Asia Minor;[173] Cimmerians (gimiraaia) (Biblical Gomer), people known to live to the north of the Black Sea and then in the seventh century BC in Asia Minor;[174] men from Melid (miliduaia) (Classical Melitene, modern Malatya), north of the Taurus mountains in eastern Asia Minor;[175] men from Urartu (uraštaia) (Biblical Ararat) in Armenia;[176] men from Tyre (ṣuraia) in Phoenicia;[177] as well as Arabians (arbaia), that is to say, men from the part

Appendix V below.

171. Much is known from cuneiform sources about Babylonia in the Achaemenian period, on which see Oppenheim 1985: 529-87.
172. Cardascia 1951; Stolper 1985) with review by Van Driel, 1989; useful summary with bibliography in Stolper 1992: 4: 927-28; and, for the general historical background, Stolper 1994.
173. Zadok 1985: 265 (at this reference and in the following notes, publications dealing with the Murašu texts are those cited under BE 8, BE 9, BE 10, MPLAB and PBS 2/1).
174. Zadok 1985: 139-40 (and see n. 164 above) (written gi-mir-ra-a-a etc.); see also Diakonoff, 1981: 103-40; Bouzek, 1997: 11-12; and a handy summary in Andrews, 1967: 56 = 1971: 60-61.
175. Zadok 1985: 228-29 (and see n. 174 above); on the kingdom, see, e.g., Burney, 1971: 134-36; and, on the site of the capital city, modern Arslan Tepe, Garstang, 1929: 198-209 and pl. XXXVIII, figs 14-17 (carved reliefs from the site).
176. Zadok 1985: 320-21 (and see n. 174 above).
177. Zadok 1985: 281 (and see n. 174 above).

of the Arabian peninsula adjacent to Mesopotamia in the south;[178] and even men from the Indus Valley (*indumaia*) further east.[179] The particular interest of the archive for the present topic lies, however, in the fact that a number of the people involved in the business, and in contact with these other groups,[180] can be identified by their personal names as Jews. This is clear from the fact that many of them are compounded with the divine element Yahweh.[181] One tablet from Nippur in the British Museum (BM.12957), acquired in 1896, is a receipt for silver paid for land occupied by a man called Hananiah.[182] In this name, written *ḫa-na-ni-'-ia-a-ma* in the cuneiform script, the final character which is most frequently read as *ma* could also in the late period have the value *wa* (conventionally represented as wa_6), in other words the ending *-ia-a-ma* could be read *-ia-a-wa* (or *-ia-a-wa_6*),[183] that is to say, *-yawa*, representing *-yahu*. The name Hananiah was common in this period. According to the Old Testament, where it is written *ḥănānyahû*, it was the name of one of the sons of Zerubbabel, and of six other individuals who are mentioned in Ezra and Nehemiah (Ezra 10:28; Nehemiah 3:8; 3:30; 7:2; 10:24; 12:12, 41). It was also the name of one of the three young Jews (*bĕnê yĕhûdâ*) named with Daniel as active in Babylon in the time of Nebuchadnezzar (Daniel 1:6 etc.).[184] Another instance of cuneiform *m* as the counterpart of Hebrew *w* can be seen in the name of Ionia, Old Persian *yauna*, Greek *'iōnia* (< hypothetical early Greek **'iāwones*) and Biblical Hebrew *yāwān*, where it referred to Greece (Isaiah 66:19; Daniel 8:21; 10:20; 11:2; and elsewhere), while this name is written *ia-ma-nu* in the Babylonian version of the Bisitun inscription, and in similar spellings in other texts.[185]

---

178. Zadok 1985: 26 (and see n. 174 above).
179. Zadok 1985: 181 (and see n. 174 above).
180. The Jews had, of course, wide contact in the Hellenistic and Roman period with other societies in the Diaspora, in several cases in settlements begun earlier than that period. See summary of this dispersion in Mesopotamia, Syria, Arabia, Asia Minor, Egypt, north Africa, Greece, the Balkans, Italy and other parts of western Europe in Schürer 1986: 1-86.
181. Coogan 1976: 52-53.
182. Stolper 1985: 248 no 34, dated to 4/7/7 of Darius II = 417BC.
183. See von Soden and Röllig 1967: 37 no 193 (Spätbabylonische Zeit); Brinkman 1969: 297 cites evidence for this usage already in the late eighth century BC; see also Borger 2003: 361-62 no 552; and evidence cited by Coogan 1976: 63 n. 69; and also Stolper 1976: 22-25 and, specifically, 26-27 on final *-ia-a-ma*.
184. Several personal seals inscribed with this name are known (references in Fowler 1988: 345). This name continued to be current in New Testament times in the form *ananias* – Ananias, two of them known in the New Testament: (a) the early believer who welcomed the Apostle Paul into the Christian community in Damascus (Acts 9:10-17); and (b) the High Priest in Jerusalem who opposed Paul (Acts 23:2-5).
185. Brinkman 1989: 53-71; Brandenstein and Mayrhofer 1964: 156; Zadok 1985: 186-88.

Hananiah and his fellow Jews are never referred to as such in the
Murashu documents and are treated as though they were fully assimilated
into the Babylonian population. Indeed, in some cases elsewhere in
Mesopotamia men with Jewish names gave Babylonian names to their
children.[186] Another British Museum text (BM.13264) concerns a payment
of silver by a man named *pi-li-ia-a-ma*.[187] This name, the equivalent of
Hebrew *pĕlāyāh* (Pelaiah in the English Versions), is known in the Old
Testament as that of a descendant of King David living in the time of the
exile (1 Chronicles 3:24). This tablet has the added interest that incised on
it, probably after baking and therefore rather crudely done, is the Aramaic
note *šṭr plyh*, 'document of Pelaiah',[188] where *šṭr* is a loanword in Aramaic
from Babylonian *šaṭāru*, 'document', and is found incised on other tablets
as well as in ink in the Aramaic papyri of the fifth-fourth centuries BC,[189]
including the Samaria papyri, on which see below.

Many of the tablets are precisely dated, and it is possible to see from
this that these Jews seldom conducted business on what for them would
have been the sabbath day, suggesting that they still observed their
religion.[190] In the book of Zechariah there is implied criticism of the
fact that many Jews remained in Babylonia rather than returning to
Palestine (Zechariah 2:6-7; 9:12). The Jewish community continued to
thrive there, and was indeed ancestral to the Rabbinic school which in
the Christian Era produced the Babylonian Talmud.[191] It is reasonable
to assume that the area in which they were settled in the Persian period
was much the same as that indicated by the later Talmudic sources,
which show that they lived largely in central Babylonia, with one of their
particular centres at Sura only about six miles north of Babylon. Nippur
was outside this area, a little to the south.[192]

186. See, e.g., Mitchell 1991: 419-20.
187. Stolper 1985: 272 no 94, dated to 26/5/37 of Artaxerxes I = 428 BC.
188. The /p/ is rather high and angular and separated from the /l/; the /y/ is
    possibly comparable to some examples of the fifth/fourth centuries BC from
    documents in ink included by Gibson 1975: 188; but the /h/ (not /ḥ/) is clear.
    This reading is already proposed by Coogan (1976: 33), who gives *plyw/h*,
    but h is the most likely final character. The inscription is incised, indeed
    almost scratched (and not in ink as stated by Stolper in the doctoral thesis
    which preceded his book), so some strokes may be accidental. See also Zadok
    2002: 36-37 no 65.
189. Kaufman 1974: 101 and n. 352; Hoftijzer and Jongeling 1995: 2: 1124.
190. Stolper 1992: 928, 'They rarely did business on sabbaths or feast days.' On adherence
    to the Sabbath in the later Diaspora, see Schürer 1973-87: III:1: 141-42.
191. See, e.g., Strack and Stemberger 1991: 208-44; Neusner 1994: 182-90, 203-207.
192. Newman 1932: 6-7, with map at the front; Obermeyer 1929: 215-318, with map
    at the end; Oppenheimer 1983: 417-422 on Sura, and map at the end. On the

Turning again to Egypt, it is appropriate to look at an important series of discoveries made there in the late nineteenth and early twentieth centuries. These consist of a number of Aramaic papyri, mainly from a Jewish colony at Elephantine near Aswan on the upper Nile,[193] as well as the collection of leather documents mentioned above, also probably from Egypt, all of the fifth century BC.[194]

Elephantine Island lies in the middle of the Nile, just downstream from the modern Aswan dam, and the town of Aswan lies on the east bank of the river opposite the island.[195] The island had the ancient Egyptian name *3bw* (or *'bw*), a word which had the basic meanings 'elephant; ivory',[196] perhaps signifying here something like 'Elephant place', probably because it was there that the Egyptians traded for ivory and perhaps encountered elephants. This name was transcribed by the Aramaic scribes as *yb*, and in the Ptolemaic period it was known by the Greek equivalent *elephantine*. At the same time, the settlement on the east bank was referred to by the Egyptians as *swnw*, presumably since it was a place of 'trade' (*swn*).[197] This was transcribed in Aramaic as *swn* and by the Greeks as *Suene*, a name which has come over into Arabic as Aswan. *Suene* is often quoted as 'Syene', because the Greek vowel *u* (upsilon) came to be pronounced as 'i' in the Graeco-Roman period.[198]

The Greek form *Suene* suggests that Aramaic *swn* would have been pronounced something like 'sewen', and this illuminates some references in the Old Testament. In Ezekiel's prophecy of the sixth century BC against Egypt (29:10) and in his lament for Egypt (30:6), there is the phrase 'from Migdol to Sewen', referring to the northern and southern limits of Egypt. In these verses 'to Sewen' represents Hebrew *sĕwēnēh*,

---

Jews in Babylonia in Sassanian and Islamic times, see Morony 1984: 306-31, with bibliography 613-20.

193. Porten 1968; Grelot 1972, with useful general survey 33-69 and annotated translations of texts.

194. Driver, 1954 (see n. 87 above).

195. Plan of the area c.1800 in *Description de l'Égypte publié par les ordres de sa majesté l'Empereur Napoléon le Grand*, I (Paris, 1809; miniature reprint, Cologne, 1994) pl. 21, reproduced in Porten 1968: pl. 3; simplified plan in Grelot 1972: fig. 2 (41).

196. Erman and Grapow 1961 (3rd ed.): 7, the three meanings represented by different spellings.

197. Faulkner 1962: 217; and Hannig 1995: 678, 1379 (the place-name).

198. A. Malikouti-Drachman in Christides (ed.) 2007: 530 (the change /u/ > /y/ by about the end of the fifth century BC); Palmer 1980: 205-207. This transference is found regularly in Greek words borrowed into English, as for example 'crypt', 'hypocrite', 'psychology' etc., in all of which the 'y' represents 'u' (upsilon) in the Greek forerunner. (See also n. 9 above.)

which can be analysed as *sĕwēn-ēh*, or perhaps better *sĕwēn-āh*, with the Hebrew ending *-āh*, 'to'.[199] This interpretation of 'Sewen' as 'Syene' is strongly supported by the phrase that follows in Ezekiel 29:10, which runs 'and to the border of Kush', where Kush was the area south of Aswan, modern Nubia. *Sewen* in these passages is now generally acknowledged to refer to Suene/Syene. The Authorised Version gave it as 'Seveneh' but the Revised (1885), the Revised Standard (1952) and the English Standard (2001) Versions have 'Syene', and the New International Version gives the modern form 'Aswan'. The Migdol in Ezekiel's phrase was very likely a place of that name in the east Delta, modern Tell el-Ḥer, which is mentioned in the Egyptian inscriptions,[200] as well as in the Biblical account of the Exodus (Exodus 14:2).[201]

This is the background of the Elephantine papyri and other related Aramaic texts of the Persian period. They exhibit language very similar to that found in Ezra (4:8-6:18; 7:12-26) and Daniel (2:4-7:28). The people who wrote the Elephantine texts were a colony of Jews living in southern Egypt. That they were Jews is clear from their personal names, many of them, like those in the Murashu archives, compounded with elements of the name Yahweh. That they were Jews is further clear from references to a Temple of Yahu in the settlement. The Jerusalem Temple is referred to in the Hebrew Old Testament as the *hêkāl yhwh*, whereas references to the Elephantine temple are written *'gwr' yhw* (i.e. *'egōrā' yhw*), but the meaning was virtually the same. Both terms are actually Sumerian in origin, borrowed probably via Akkadian (Babylonian-Assyrian).[202] To have such a building, rivalling, so to speak, the Temple at Jerusalem, was contrary to strict Judaism.[203] It is probable that the institution of the Synagogue was established during the exile in Babylonia[204] and, since the earliest papyrus in the Elephantine archive is dated to 495 BC, the time of Darius I, it is likely that the colonists would have known what was going on elsewhere in the Diaspora, and should have followed a similar practice.

199. Speiser 1954: 108-115 = 1967: 494-505.
200. Oren 1973: 7-44; and, briefly (with plan of the site), in Stern (ed.) 1993: 4: 1392-93.
201. For another aspect of the name Suene, see Appendix VI below.
202. *Hêkāl* < Akkadian: *ekallu* < Sumerian: *é.gal* = 'great house'; *'egōrā'* < Akkadian: *ekurru* < Sumerian: *é.kur* = 'mountain house'.
203. On the centralisation of worship in ancient Israel, see de Vaux 1961: 331-40, with 340-41 on the Elephantine temple, and bibliography on 542-43; a different treatment is given in Jacob 1958: 258-62; see, also, on a basic Biblical text concerning this matter (Deuteronomy 12:1-31), e.g., Craigie 1976: 49, 213-20; and Haran 1978: 132-40.
204. See, e.g., Mitchell 1991: 424-25.

A further possible indication of the religious practices of the colony is a much-damaged papyrus letter in the archive which suggests that the Passover was celebrated by the community.[205] A restoration of the text includes the passage (lines 3-7):

> Now this year, the fifth year of Darius (*drywhwš*), it has been sent from the king to Arsh[am the prince, saying: 'Keep away from the Jew]ish [garrison.]' Now count four[teen days from the first of Nisan and the Passover ke]ep. From the 15th day until the 21st day of [Nisan keep the festival of Unleavened Bread. . . . You] be pure and take heed. Work do no[t perform on the 15th day or on the 21st day. Beer do no]t drink and anything unleavened do no[t eat].

The extensive restorations (in square brackets) depend on comparison with such Biblical passages as Leviticus 23:15-16, Numbers 28:16-18 and Deuteronomy 16:9-10, the words for Passover (*psḥ*) and Unleavened Bread (*pṭyrn* [Aramaic counterpart of Hebrew *mṣh/mṣwt*]) not surviving in the original. That the restoration of *psḥ* is reasonable is demonstrated by an Aramaic ostracon said to have been found at Elephantine which clearly does refer to it.[206] The fifth year of Darius II was 419 BC, so this gives some illustration of part of the Jewish diaspora after the period covered by the Old Testament, Nehemiah again still possibly being governor of Judah. The Arsham mentioned was the satrap of Egypt. The position of the writer of the letter, a man named Hananiah, is not clear from the sources.

Arsham is known also from the group of letters already mentioned, directed to him in Aramaic on leather, which were contained in a leather bag, possibly part of the equipment of an official courier.[207] Their place

---

205. Cowley 1923: 60-65 no 21 and pp.xxiv-xxv (discussion); Gressmann in Gressmann (ed.) 1926: 453 no 4; Porten and Yardeni 1986: 54-55 no A4.1 (copy [with restorations], transliteration and translation); Porten 1968: 128-33 (discussion with translation of restored text), 311-14, (restored text in square script with commentary); Segert 1975: 502 no 28 (restored text in square script); H.L. Ginsberg in Pritchard 1955: 491 (translation); E. Lipinski in Beyerlin (ed.) 1978: 254-55 no 22; Grelot 1972: 378-86 no 96 (introduction, translation and comments); also Gressmann in Gressmann (ed.) 1926: 453 no.4 (German translation); Soggin 2001) 96-97 (translation and brief discussion); Porten in Hallo and Younger (eds) 2002: 116-17 no 3.46 (introduction , translation and notes); also Kuhrt 2007: 854-55 no 31 (doubting the passover interpretation).
206. Répertoire d'épigraphie Sémitique, Paris, 1916-1918: III: no 1793; and other references in Porten 1968: 131 n. 60.
207. Driver 1954: pl. XXIV.

of origin is unknown, but their contents suggest that it might have been
Susa or Babylon. One of the letters is an instruction to various officers
situated on the route from Babylonia to Damascus to supply rations to
the bearer and ten men in his party while in their jurisdiction.[208] This
letter therefore almost amounts to a passport, since care of the travellers
is implied. This episode is paralleled by the precaution Nehemiah is
described as taking when he travelled from Babylonia to Palestine. The
Biblical text (Nehemiah 2:4-7) reads:

> The king (Artaxerxes) said to me, 'What is it you want?' Then . . .
> I answered the king, 'If it pleases the king . . ., let him send me to
> the city of Judah where my fathers are buried so I can rebuild it.'
> Then the king . . . asked me, 'How long will your journey take,
> and when will you get back?' It pleased the king to send me; so
> I set a time. I also said to him, 'If it please the king, may I have
> letters to the governors of Trans-Euphrates (*ʿēber hannāhār*), so
> that they will provide me safe-conduct until I arrive in Judah?'[209]

In this passage, 'letter' is *ʾiggeret*,[210] possibly a loanword from Akkadian
egirtu with the same meaning,[211] and used in much the same sense as
sēper;[212] and *ʿēber hannāhār* is the Hebrew form of the Babylonian

208. Driver 1954: 20-23, pl. VIII; 1957: 27-28 (text and translation), 56-62
(commentary).

209. This analogy has been pointed out by Williamson 2004: 228-29. A related
aspect of travel in the Achaemenian period is seen in a group of Elamite
texts from Persepolis which record the issue of rations to travellers who
carry a *halmi*, 'sealed document', of authorisation from the king or an official
(Hallock 1969: 6 and 365-440 (transliteration and translation of these texts),
688 (variant spellings)); Greenfield refers to this point in his paper 1981: 110-
30, specifically 126 n. 51. That Elamite *hal-mi* was the equivalent of Aramaic
ḥtm, 'seal', is demonstrated by a Persepolis Fortification tablet (PF 2067) which
includes the statement (lines 10-14) 'the seal (*hal-mi*) that formerly (was) mine
has been replaced. Now this seal (*hal-mi*) (is) mine that has been applied to
this tablet' (Hallock 1969: 639) and the seal referred to, which is impressed on
it, has the Aramaic inscription 'seal (*ḥtm*) of Parnaka son of Arsham (*prnk br
ʾršm*)' (Garrison and Cool Root 2001: 92-94 no 22 (PFs 16*); 2, *Plates*, pl. 15,);
a drawing of the seal impression in Kuhrt 2007: II: 782 fig. 16.3(b); Cameron
draws attention to this tablet (citing it as Fort.7096) in a discussion of the form
hal-mi (Cameron 1948: 53-54); for the meaning 'sealed document' for *hal-mi*,
see also Hinz and Koch 1987: I: 604, 'Siegel, gesiegelte Urkunde'.

210. Found frequently in Official Aramaic (Hoftijzer and Jongeling 1995: 1: 12).

211. Kaufman 1974: 48; Iranian or Hittite origins have also been suggested (Koehler
and Baumgartner 2001: I: 11.

212. G.R. Driver suggests that the two words are used virtually interchangeably in

designation Eber-Nāri, 'across the river', that is to say 'west of the Euphrates'. This geographical designation occurs in Aramaic passages in the Old Testament (e.g. Ezra 4:10 etc.) in the form *'ăbar-nahărā*[213] The phrase 'safe-conduct' is expressed by the verb form *ya'ăbîrûnî* (literally 'they will allow – or cause – me to pass over').[214]

Moving now to Asia Minor, modern Turkey, it is appropriate to mention an element in Achaemenian culture which varied throughout the Empire, namely the currency.[215] Soon after 515 BC, Darius I introduced a new coin, the gold daric, probably named after him, which shows a king, running to the right and holding a spear and bow. A fine example in the British Museum (CM 1919-0516-15), which probably dates from late in his reign or possibly early in the time of Xerxes I, weighs 8.37 grammes,[216] the normal standard probably being about 8.35 grammes,[217] presumably following the standard of the Babylonian šiqlu or shekel, which weighed about 8.4 grammes.[218] The Achaemenian silver coin known as the siglos (< *šiqlu* or *šeqel*[219]), however, represented a normal standard of about 5.6 grammes,[220] a good example in the British Museum of the same date (CM 1845-1217-272) for instance, weighing 5.37 grammes.[221] The weight of 5.6 grammes amounts to about two thirds of 8.35 (67.06 per cent), probably reflecting the sexagesimal system of numeration which was widely used in Babylonia and Greece. In this case a siglos evidently represented four sixths of a daric.[222] These coins were minted in western Asia Minor,[223] responding economically to the use of coins in the Greek

---

Esther (1976: 83 n. 11); *sēper* occurs in most phases of the Biblical text while *'iggeret* is used only in Late Biblical Hebrew texts, see Young, Rezetco and Ehrensvärd 2008: 1: 38, 72, 114 etc.

213. On this geographical designation, see, e.g., Leuze 1935: 183-184 (27-28).
214. *Ya'ăbîrû* (Hip'il [causative] imperfect) of the verb *'br*, 'to go over, cross over') +*-nî* ('me').
215. See Robinson 1958: 187-93; and A.D.H. Bivar in Gershevitch (ed.) 1985a: 610-25.
216. Hill 1922: 153 no 40, pl. XXIV.24; Curtis and Tallis 2005: no 321.
217. Hill 1922: cxxi (based on an analysis published in 1914, but still reasonable).
218. Meissner 1920: 357 (8.4 'gr'); Borger cites the weight as 8⅓ (i.e. 8.33) grammes (2003: 434 no 836).
219. This etymological derivation of the word does not mean, however, that it was equivalent to the Babylonian *šiqlu* (on this point, see A.D.H. Bivar in Gershevitch [ed.] 1985a: 617).
220. Hill 1922: cxxii.
221. Hill 1922: 158 no 74; Curtis and Tallis 2005: no 322.
222. On the relationships of these two weights and their materials, see Bivar in Gershevitch (ed.) 1985a: 617-18.
223. A.R. Meadows in Curtis and Tallis 2005: 200.

world, and the daric was used mainly in the countries bordering the Mediterranean, while elsewhere in the Empire the ancient method of weighing precious metals seems to have continued.[224] The daric, which is referred to in Greek sources as the *dareikos*, is probably mentioned in the Old Testament, in the plural form *ădarkōnîm*, in the account of the return of Ezra from Babylonia to Judah in 458 BC (Ezra 7:15-16). There, permission is quoted from Artaxerxes I to transport the silver and gold which the king and his advisers have contributed voluntarily for the God of Israel (*ĕlāh yiśrāēl*) whose dwelling place is at Jerusalem, together with all the silver and gold which you get from the entire province of Babylon (*mĕdînat bābel*) and the voluntary offerings of the people and the priests, freely contributed for the house of their God at Jerusalem.[225]

In carrying this out Ezra says:

> I weighed out the silver, the gold, and the vessels, the contributions for the house of our God which the king, his advisors, and all Israel there present had made. I weighed out into their hand 650 talents of silver, 100 silver vessels weighing [probable gap in the text] talents, 100 talents of gold, 20 gold bowls valued at 1000 darics. (Ezra 8:25-27)[226]

A talent, probably on the Babylonian standard (there the *biltu*), weighed about 30 kilograms, or something over 66 pounds, so, if the figures are correct, and numbers are particularly vulnerable to scribal errors, large quantities of gold and silver were involved.

An example of an actual talent weight is provided by a fine bronze lion in the British Museum (BM.E.32625) from Abydos near Troy,[227] in what would have been the satrapy of Yauna in the north west of the Persian Empire. This has a Greek *alpha* at the base of the spine and an Aramaic inscription on the side of the base which runs *'sprn' lqbl stry' ksp*, 'exact according to the staters of silver', taking *str* as a defective writing of *sttr*, 'stater'. In this the word translated 'exact' or 'correct' (*'sprn'*), probably another Persian loanword, occurs several times (*āsparnā*) in Ezra, as for example in the decree of Darius authorising the building work in Jerusalem which ends

---

224. See, e.g., Bivar 1971.

225. For a group of typical gold and silver vessels, see Curtis and Tallis 2005: fig. 45.

226. The word daric (*ădarkōnîm*) occurs also in 1 Chronicles 29:7, referring to the time of Solomon, probably reflecting a scribal updating of the text (on this, see also n. 17 above). The different form *darkĕmōnîm*, which occurs in Ezra 2:69 and Nehemiah 7:69-71, is probably a loanword from Greek *drakʰmē* (drachma). On these forms, see Williamson 1977: 123-26; also, Polzin 1976: 133 no 21.

227. Mitchell 2004: no 53; Curtis and Tallis 2005: no 302.

with the command 'I, Darius have decreed it. Let it be carried out exactly' (Ezra 6:12). The association of the word here with the use on the weight supports the meaning 'exact'. This was unknown to the translators of the Authorised Version, who gave the phrase as 'Let it be carried out speedily', and in fact some other modern versions follow the older tradition, e.g. the New International Version renders it 'with diligence'. The word 'stater', a loan from Greek *statēr* ('weigher'),[228] which referred to the principal denomination in use in any particular area and period, is a further demonstration of Greek influence in this part of the Empire.

I have already mentioned the multilingual nature of the Persian Empire, and the wide use of Aramaic for communication, which meant that it was known and used by the educated throughout the Empire. A formal illustration of this situation is provided by an inscribed stela of the time of Artaxerxes found in 1973 at Letôon, a temple about two and a half miles (four kilometres) southwest of Xanthos, the capital of Lycia in southwestern Turkey.[229] According to Herodotus Lycia was part of the satrapy which included Ionia (Yauna) (*The Histories* 3:90).[230] (There is a fine collection of sculptures including bilingual inscriptions in Greek and Lycian from Xanthos in the British Museum, excavated by Charles Fellows in the years from 1839 to 1844.[231]) This newly discovered inscribed stela, which was set up by the satrap of the area and deals with

---

228. Andrews 1967: 127 = 1971: 139. *Statēr*, 'a weight . . . then a coin of various values' (conveniently, Liddell, Scott and Jones 1940: 742), from the root STA (ΣΤΑ), *'istemi/'istēmi*, 'place, set, stand' (*idem.*, 384).

229. Metzger, Laroche, Dupont-Sommer and Mayrhofer 1979 presents the three versions in transliteration, with translation and commentary, and gives a comparative analysis with transliterations of the Lycian version with interlinear Greek and Aramaic (58-60), and a French translation in three parallel columns; the Greek text also in Pleket and Stroud 1980: 245-46 no 942 (with introductory remarks, slightly favouring 337BC against 358BC); also translation with introduction, bibliography and notes, Lycian and Greek in parallel columns, Aramaic separately, by I. Kottsieper with I. Hajnal in Dietrich et al.., 2001: 194-99; English translations of the Greek and Aramaic texts in Davies 1978: 237-39 = 1993: 244-46; and translations of all three versions in Kuhrt 2007: II: 859-63, with reproduction from the initial publication of drawing showing the distribution of the versions, fig. 17.7; see also Teixidor 1978: 181-85; and Lemaire 1995: 423-32, with transliteration (423-24) and translation (430).

230. Herodotus's list of satrapies was probably derived from that given in the *Periēgēsis* of Hecataeus, an explanatory text to his map of the world (see, e.g., Herzfeld 1968: 288). See also Armayor 1978: 1-9, specifically 8; also, Usher 1969: 2-3; and Grant 1970: 39-40; and a convenient summary in Howatson 1989: 261.

231. For a useful account of Lycian material from Xanthos in the British Museum, see Jenkins 2006: 151-85.

the cult of a local deity and arrangements for offerings, gives the text in
Lycian on what was presumably the face, in Greek on the reverse, and
Aramaic on the narrow right face. The stela was found lying with the
Greek text uppermost but it would have stood where all sides could be
seen. It is clear that the text in the local language, Lycian, and that in
Greek, which was widely spoken in the area, were the principal versions,
while that in Aramaic, the official imperial language, was less prominent
on a narrower edge. The Aramaic text begins (commas supplied) 'In
the month Siwan, year one, Artaxerxes the king, in 'Orna the city' (*byrḥ
sywn šnt ḥd 'rtḥšsš mlk' b'wrn byrt'*), that is, with the date, the name
of the Persian king, and the name of the local capital. The Lycian and
Greek versions of the text do not begin with this passage, but they show
elsewhere that *'wrn* was a transcription of the Lycian placename *arñna*
and that *xantʰos* was the Greek equivalent. In the introductory passage
the Aramaic text defines *'wrn* (*Arñna* = Xanthos) as a *byrt*, a word
usually taken to mean 'fortress', as discussed above,[232] but though this
passage is not paralleled in the Greek or Lycian text, it is clear from other
passages in those versions that the Greek designation of the site (line12)
was *polis*, 'city', and this may well have been the meaning of *teteri*, the
Lycian equivalent (lines12-13).[233]

The Lycian and Greek versions open with the name of the local satrap
Pixōdaros of Caria (Aramaic *krk*) and Lycia (Aramaic *trmyl*; Lycian
trmmisñ; 'Termil'; Greek *lukias*),[234] whose Greek name Pixōdaros[235] is
recorded in the Lycian version as *pigesere* and in Aramaic as *pgswdr*.
Characteristic of this multilingual situation is the borrowing of the
Iranian word *ḫšaçapavān*, 'satrap', which appears on this monument in
Lycian as *ñssathrapazate*, in Greek as *zadrapēs* (rather than *satrapēs*)[236]

232. See n. 128 above.
233. As assumed by Laroche in Metzger, Laroche, Dupont-Sommer and Mayrhofer
    1979: 121. My colleague Ian Jenkins of the British Museum, who has knowledge
    of the site, comments, however, that 'fortress' would be an appropriate
    description of Xanthos in the fifth century BC, a view consonant with the
    meaning 'fortified city'.
234. For the relation of the terms Lycia (Lukka) and Termilai, see the convenient
    summary by Mellink in 1991: 2: 656-57.
235. See J. Miller, 'Pixodaros' in Pauly-Wissowa, *Realencyclopädie der classischen
    Altertumswissenschaft* (Stuttgart), XX₂ = XL (1950), cols 1893-94, (3), (not
    the same as [2] who is mentioned by Herodotus [5:118]); and on the Carians
    see Bockisch 1969: 117-75; S. Hornblower in Lewis et al. 1994: 215-16; and
    in Hornblower and Spawforth (eds) 2003: 1187; for a convenient outline of
    the history of the Carian dynasty in the fourth century BC, with a table of the
    rulers, see Jenkins 2006: 203-205.
236. Metzger in Metzger et al. 1979: 32, transcription, line 1, and pl. XIII, photograph

and in Aramaic as *ḥštrpn*.[237] It is likely that the Greek version, which is of a reasonable standard, was a translation from the Lycian text, elements of which are reflected in it.[238] There are a number of scribal errors in the Aramaic version, possibly having arisen from miscopying of a text supplied to the stonemason in ink on leather or papyrus.[239] It is probable that there were scribes in the Persian capital who were competent in the languages of the provinces, and this gives further background to the statement at Esther 3:12, mentioned above. The king named in the Aramaic version could have been either Artaxerxes III (358-337 BC) or Artaxerxes IV (337-336 BC), and since Pixōdaros the local satrap ruled from 341-336 BC, the date of the monument could have been either 358 or 337 BC. Both dates have been advocated,[240] but there are substantial arguments in favour of 358.[241] This is late in the Achaemenian period, but the evidence is still illustrative of the situation.

Greek has, of course, been studied for generations in modern times, but the Lycian language, which only became known in the nineteenth century from inscriptions such as those found by Fellows at Xanthos,[242] is closely related to Luwian which, with Hittite, belongs to the Anatolian branch of the Indo-European group of languages. Fellows had concentrated his excavations at Xanthos but he visited the Letôon site in 1842-43, and it is interesting to reflect that, if he had found this stela at that date, the evidence it supplies of the Aramaic language and script in the fourth century BC would have been of great value to scholars. At that time there was very little early Aramaic material for Semitists to work on, as is shown by a small number of Aramaic inscriptions which had been included five years earlier by the great German Hebraist Wilhelm Gesenius in his Phoenician grammar.[243]

---

of the text. The spelling *satrapēs* is found, e.g., in Xenophon, *Cyropaedia*, 8:1:11 and 8:6:1 etc.

237. This Aramaic spelling (on which see Dupont-Sommer in Metzger et al. 1979: 141) may be compared with *'ḥšdrpn* in both Biblical Aramaic (Daniel 3:2-27; 6:2-7) and Hebrew (Esther 3:12).

238. Blomqvist1982: 11-20, particularly 14, 19-20.

239. Lemaire 1995: 423-32, specifically 431-32.

240. On the date and its bearing on other sources, see Dupont-Sommer in Metzger et al. 1979: 165-69; and reference to those favouring identification with Artaxerxes IV, and 337BC as the date of the inscription, in Blomqvist 1982: 14 n. 23.

241. Dupont-Sommer in Metzger et al. 1979: 166 n. 1.

242. On these, see Kalinka 1901: 32-52 nos 36-51 (copies, transliteration and notes); and Friedrich 1932: 61-70 (transliteration and notes); those in the British Museum being nos 40 (GR.950), 41 (ANE.135846), 44 (ANE.135847-49) and 45 (ANE.135850).

243. Gesenius 1837: the Aramaic inscriptions in this are identified in Lidzbarski 1898: I: 17-18 under no 135, one example being the so-called Bar Punesh

Mention of the word 'satrap' raises an interesting point about the Biblical books of this period. In them there are a number of Persian loanwords, some already mentioned, mostly in the Aramaic passages and a smaller number in the Hebrew, in most cases probably borrowed into Hebrew via Aramaic.[244] Among these are words involved in government administration including such offices as 'satrap' (*'aḥašdarpan*), 'counsellor' (*'ădargāzar*), 'police chief' (*tiptāy*), 'judge' (*dĕtābar*) and 'treasurer' (*gĕdābar*), and items such as 'decree' (*dāt*) and 'treasure' (*gĕnaz*). It is not surprising that such words should be borrowed since many of them apply to things introduced by the new Persian regime.

Also among these is *'appaden* (Daniel 11:45), from Old Persian *apadāna*, which probably had some such meaning as 'columned hall'.[245] This word occurs only once in the Old Testament, in an unusual context in the book of Daniel (11:45), which runs, literally, 'he will pitch the tents of his appaden (*wĕyiṭṭa' 'āhŏlê 'appadĕnô*) between seas to glorious holy mountain'. In this, the phrase 'between seas (*yammîm*) to glorious holy mountain' probably refers to Jerusalem, between the Mediterranean, 'the great sea' (*yām haggādôl*, e.g. Joshua 1:4), and the Dead Sea, 'the salt sea' (*yām hammelaḥ*, e.g. Genesis 14:3), but the passage, 'pitch the tents of his appaden' needs explanation. In this the verb *nāṭah* means 'to reach out; spread out' or the like, and *'ōhel* is the normal word for 'tent',[246] so the general sense seems to be to spread or pitch a tent. In this context *'ōhel* is in the plural, where the literal meaning of *'āhŏlê* is 'tents of', so, in view of the association of the word *apadāna* with columns, it might be suggested that this passage refers to a widespread series of tents with vertical supports or poles. It is a commonplace of linguistics that words change their meaning with changing times and circumstances,[247] so this may be simply an instance of this process, Palestine where large buildings with numerous columns are unlikely, being different from Iran.

A different aspect of the multilingual nature of the Achaemenid Empire can be seen in an alabaster alabastron (BM.132114) found by Charles Newton with fragments of others during his excavations at Halicarnassos in western Asia Minor, which bears the inscription 'Xerxes great king' in four languages: cuneiform Old Persian (*ḥšayāršā ḥšāyaṭiya*

---

papyrus now in the British Library, BL.Or.106 (Mitchell 2004: no 51).
244. Those in Aramaic set out in Rosenthal 1961: 558-59 §189; those in Hebrew in Wagner 1966: 152-53.
245. On *apadana*, see Appendix IV below.
246. For a survey of the usage of *'ōhel*, see K. Koch in Botterweck, Ringgren and Fabry (eds) 1974-2006: I: 118-30.
247. E.g. Lehman 1992: 254-78.

vazraka [*ḫ-š-y-a-r-š-a ḫšayaṯiya v-z-r-k*]), Elamite (ⱽ*ik-še-ir-šá* ⱽ*sunkik ir-šá-ir*) and Babylonian (ᵐ*ḫi-ši-'a-ar-šá-'a šarru rabū*ᵘ̆), and hieroglyphic Egyptian (*ši3rwš3 prꜥ p3ꜥ3*).²⁴⁸ This alabastron, from the time of Xerxes I (486-465 BC), was found on the steps leading to the tomb chamber of Mausolos (ruler of Caria, 377-353 BC), having probably been handed down as an heirloom.²⁴⁹ A large number of fragments of other stone vases with this same inscription were found by W.K. Loftus during his excavations at Susa in 1851-52. He selected five of these for the British Museum (BM.91453-6, 91459),²⁵⁰ and it may be that other fragments in Paris, and Philadelphia, acquired at different times, were from the same deposit.²⁵¹

A significant area from the point of view of Biblical studies is of course Palestine, and it is appropriate now to turn attention to that province. When the Jews received permission to return there in 538 BC and to rebuild the Temple, a large contingent made the journey under Sheshbazzar, who is described as the *nāśi' lihûdāh* (*nśy' lyhwdh*), 'elected chief of Judah' or the like (Ezra 1:8), the word *nāśi'* probably being a passive participle of the verb *nāśā'*, 'to lift, raise (high)', and therefore reasonably interpreted as 'one raised high (by election)'. It is a term found in reference to tribal leaders in the period before the monarchy (e.g. Genesis 17:20; Numbers 1:16; 3:32; 7:2; 16:2; Joshua 22:14; 1 Samuel 9:21 etc.) but in the time of the kings it was applied only to such individuals as heads of families (1 Kings 8:1) or of tribes (1 Chronicles 5:2).²⁵²

---

248. Newton 1862: pl. VII; and S. Birch in *idem*. II.2: 667-70; Weissbach 1911: xxvi, 118-19; Kent 1953: 115, 157, XVs; Searight, Reade and Finkel 2008: no 269; Curtis and Tallis (eds) 2005: no 140 (damaged parts restored); Jenkins 2006: 303, fig. 197 (restored); also Kuhrt 2007: I: 295 fig. 7.4 (without restoration). In the Elamite text the raised ⱽ indicates a single vertical wedge (equivalent to ᵐ before the personal name in the Babylonian text) though in Elamite it is used also before nouns. The name Xerxes is spelled *ḫšyrš* in other Egyptian sources (e.g. von Beckerath 1984: 220-21), while here the name is spelled without the initial guttural (*ḫ*). The vase is on display in Gallery 15, Case 3 in the British Museum (2011).
249. Jenkins 2006: 203. Incidentally, Pliny (*Natural History* 36:30), who categorises the tomb as one of the Seven Wonders (*septem miracula*), provides the date of the death of Mausolos as the second year of the 107ᵗʰ Olympiad = 351/350 BC (the relevant passage with translation and notes in Stuart Jones 1895: 177-80).
250. Loftus 1857: 409-10, with lengthy discussion of these and related matters by S. Birch, 410-13; see also Curtis 1993: 1-55, specifically 14, 26-27 nos 78-82, pls 11b (original drawings), 19a; and Walker 1980: 75-81, specifically 81; Searight, Reade and Finkel 2008: nos 271-76; Curtis and Tallis 2005: nos 141-45, selection of some fragmentary pieces with photographs.
251. Weissbach 1911: xxvi; Kent 1953: 115; Curtis and Tallis 2005: nos 141-45.
252. See Speiser 1963: 111-17, and n. 10 on analysis of the passive participle. On

It is appropriate to outline the events following this first return as they are described in the Books of Ezra and Nehemiah.[253] The two men after whom these books are named were resident in the heart of the Persian Empire, Ezra probably in Babylon and Nehemiah in Susa. The exact sequence of their arrival in Palestine is not certain, but one possible outline can be set out in the accompanying chart.

Nearly 20 years after Sheshbazzar, in 520 BC, in the time of Darius I, a larger number returned to Palestine under Zerubbabel who in his turn was appointed governor (*peḥâ*) of the Persian province of Judah. At this time work was resumed on the Temple. On this occasion Tattenai, the satrap of the province Eber-Nāri, in which Judah lay, questioned the legality of the work and wrote to Darius for confirmation. Permission was given for the work to continue when the authorisation previously issued by Cyrus was found in the archives at Ecbatana, and the Temple was completed in 515 BC.

The number of those who returned is given in both the books of Ezra (2) and Nehemiah (7) as well as in the Apocryphal book 1 Esdras (5) as nearly 50,000, but the mathematical total of the various contingents which are listed in these sources amounts only to something under 39,000. It may be that the larger figure represents the total of two main returns, and that the figure of 39,000 indicates the number who returned on the second occasion in 520 BC.

There is little written information bearing on the next half century, until in 458 BC, in the time of Artaxerxes I, Ezra the Scribe returned to Palestine together with about 1,500 more people (Ezra 7:1-10). He was well qualified as a priest (*kōhēn*) and a scribe (*sōpēr*) (Nehemiah 12:26), both Hebrew titles, which gave him authority with the population in Jerusalem. There he concentrated on legal and religious matters but he may have made an effort to rebuild the city wall (Ezra 4:12), probably in about 448 BC.[254] As a result of this some of the surrounding people wrote a letter to Artaxerxes objecting to the building work by the Jews. The text of this letter, which is in Aramaic, is given in Ezra (4:11-16) together with the king's reply (4:17-22) in which he says that he had had the matter looked into and that Jerusalem was found to be a rebellious city. This brought an end to the work.

this title, see also Williamson 1987: 85, suggesting that its later use might have been a recollection of the lists of 'princes' of the tribes of Israel in the book of Numbers (2:3-31; 7:1-83; 34:18-28).

253. For a convenient account of the material in Ezra and Nehemiah with useful bibliography, see H.G.M. Williamson 1987, with a summary of the history (48-76). See also an outline of the situation in Palestine in the early Persian period in Mitchell 1991: 430-40.

254. Williamson comments that in this passage the Jews referred to as rebuilding the city 'can be most naturally understood as Ezra's caravan' (1987: 75).

Persia	Old Testament	Judah
559-529 Cyrus 539 Capture of Babylon	*Kôreš*	538-522 Jews return under Sheshbazzar 538/537(?) dedication of the altar
529-522 Cambyses		
522-486 Darius I	*dāryāweš*	520 Jews return under Zerubbabel 520-515 Building of the Second Temple
486-465 Xerxes I	*aḥašweroš*	[Esther]
465-425 Artaxerxes I	*artaḥšastĕʾ*	458 Ezra to Jerusalem 448 (?) Attempt to rebuild walls 445-433 Nehemiah governor (1) 430 (?) Nehemiah governor (2)
425-424 Xerxes II 424 Sogdianus 424-405 Darius II 405-359 Artaxerxes II 359-338 Artaxerxes III 338-336 Arses 336-331 Darius III		

The next development was instigated by Nehemiah, a Jew living in Persia, who is described as a cup-bearer (*mašqeh*) to Artaxerxes. Visitors from Judah told him about the situation in Palestine, so he obtained permission from the king to go there himself. In Judah he held the office of governor (*peḥâ*) (Nehemiah 12:26), a title taken from Assyrian *bēl pīḥātu*, 'provincial governor' (lord of a province), which gave him authority and good access to the administration in Susa. In Palestine he set about rebuilding the walls of Jerusalem. This was again seen as a threatening act by some of the neighbouring people, particularly Sanballat, the governor of Samaria (Nehemiah 4:1-2; 6:1), Tobiah, an official in Ammon across the Jordan (Nehemiah 4:3; 6:1), and an Arab named Geshem in the south (Nehemiah 6:1). These men are known in non-Biblical sources: Sanballat in one of the Elephantine papyri where he is described as governor of Samaria (*snʾblṭ pḥt šmryn*);[255] Tobiah as a

255. Porten and Yardeni 1986: 1: 68-75, no A4.7 = A4.8 (copy [with restorations], transliteration and translation), line 29 = 28; Cowley 1923: no 30 = 31; Segert 1975: 496-98 no 23 (text in square script); Gressmann in Gressmann (ed.) 1926:

member of a well attested family,[256] the name of a later member of the
family (*ṭwbyh*) being prominently displayed, for instance, on the façade
of the stone tomb known as the Qaṣr el-ʿAbd at ʿArâq ʾal-Emîr in Jordan,
probably dating from the early third century BC;[257] and Geshem (*gšm*)
in an inscription on the rim of a decorated silver bowl found in the
Egyptian Delta.[258] It is interesting to note concerning the word *pḥt* in the
Elephantine papyrus that the original text gives only *pt* with the *ḥ* written
above the line, showing that the scribe had omitted it by mistake, and
inserted it later.[259] This is an example of the kind of textual error found
in handwritten texts. If the scribe had not noticed his mistake himself,
and added the correction, it would have been necessary for the modern
scholar to make a conjectural emendation. The Biblical text describes
the completion of the rebuilding of the wall by workers under armed
protection (Nehemiah 4:13-23: 6:15-16).

As indicated on the chronological chart, the evidence is sparse for the
last century of the Persian period in Palestine, and it is not appropriate
to discuss this limited evidence here.

In fact, when the Jews returned, they were confined to a very limited
territory in the Judaean hills, centring on Jerusalem.[260] According to
Nehemiah (11:1) the leaders settled down in Jerusalem and others in the
surrounding towns and villages. Though various excavations have been
carried out at Jerusalem for nearly a century and a half, relatively little has
been found which can be dated to this period.[261] The area of the Temple is
completely covered by the Haram ash-Sharif, the walled and paved area in
which stand the Dome of the Rock and the Aqsa Mosque, both of Islamic
date. A stretch of the retaining wall on the east side shows a junction of
two styles of masonry. That to the south (on the left as viewed from the

450-52 no 1 (translation); Galling in Galling (ed.) 1968: 84-87 no 51 (translation).

256. Mazar 1957: 137-45, 229-38; and, briefly, Mitchell 1991: 333 and 436.

257. Illustrated, e.g., in Vincent 1923: 55 (photograph), 63 (copy); Mazar 1957: 141-
    42 (sixth-fifth century BC); on the date, see preferably Cross 2003: 15 n. 77.

258. Rabinowitz 1956: 1-9, specifically 2 and pl. VII, Inscription C, and 6-7 on
    Gešem; also, Gibson 1975: 122-23 no 25; and B. Porten in Hallo and Younger
    (eds) 2000: 176, no 2.51D; and Hoyland 2001: 63 and pl. 10 (photograph).

259. This can be seen in the hand-copy in Porten and Yardeni 1986: 1, near end of
    penultimate line (29) on copy (69), near end of line 29 in transliteration (68),
    and indication, 'govnor' with supralinear 'er' (gov[er]nor), in translation (71); a
    number of other supralinear additions to this text are also clear, indicating,
    perhaps, a careless scribe.

260. Maps of Judaean territory in Aharoni 1979: map 34 (417), with 411-19; Stern
    2001: map III.6 (375); Weippert 1988: fig. 5.2 (p.691) (marking sites mentioned
    in Ezra and Nehemiah).

261. Good survey in Stern 2001: 353-82; and his earlier volume, Stern 1982.

east) dates from the time of Herod in the Roman period; and at one time it was thought that the part to the north (right), which is obviously earlier, belongs to the time of Zerubbabel in the late sixth century BC. This dating depends to a considerable extent on the similarity of the masonry with that of Achaemenian date found at Byblos and Pasargadae,[262] and it is now probably best to leave the question of the date undecided.[263]

No substantial architecture of this period has been excavated in the limited area of Judah, but a fine public building was found at Lachish, modern Tell ed-Duweir, in northern Idumea,[264] the administrative area just to the south of Judah. This building, usually referred to as a Residency, has a large court and what appear to be two audience chambers in sequence. It has no clear parallels elsewhere and on present evidence seems to be of local design.

Examples of antiquities from inside the territory of Judah, include a group of Achaemenian silver vessels, found before World War I by R.A.S. Macalister in a tomb group at Gezer.[265] From outside Judah, a glimpse of gracious living was found by W.M. Flinders Petrie at Tell el-Far'ah in the south west, in the administrative area of Philistia. There he excavated an Achaemenian burial which contained a silver bowl and dipper,[266] and the bronze components of a couch and a stool, with iron tie-rods.[267] Petrie assumed that these elements were parts of a single couch, but J.H. Iliffe has demonstrated that they made up both a couch and a stool. At the same time he was able to observe that, though the surfaces are much corroded, there had been single alphabetic characters on the upper surface of each corner of the couch. Only two of these characters remain legible, but these, *b* and *š*, are standard Aramaic forms

262. E.g. Kenyon 1974: 175-78, pls 35-36; and summary of the evidence, Mitchell 1991: 437-39 (with speculation that it might be ascribed to Nehemiah).
263. See the cautious summary of H. Geva in Stern (ed) 1993: 2: 743.
264. Tufnell 1953: *Text*, 131-35; *Plates*, 118-20 (plan and isometric reconstruction); and Ussishkin in Stern (ed.) 1993: 3: 910 and plan 911; see also Amiran 1967: 3017-23, specifically 3020 with fig. 1082; Stern 1973: 42, 57.
265. Macalister 1912: 292-97, with figs 154 and 157 (Graves 4 and 5 respectively). Macalister believed these to be Philistine, but they have long been recognised as Achaemenian, see Stern 1973: 39, 147 and figs 89-90 (74) 240-44 with material from other sites (146); also, Amiran 1967: figs 1088a and b, with 3020.
266. Flinders Petrie 1930: 14, pls XLIV.3-5, XLV.1-4; and Iliffe 1935: 182-86, specifically 183-86; pls XC-XCI; and R. Gophna in Stern 1993: 2: 444 fig.; also, Amiran 1967: fig. 1089 (bowl), with 3022. This site was thought by Petrie to be Biblical Beth-Pelet, but it was more probably ancient Sharuhen.
267. Flinders Petrie 1930: I: 14, pls XLV.5-6, XLVI; also, Stern 1973: 143-44, fig. 236; Stern 1993: 524 fig. (restoration); and Amiran 1967: fig. 1091 (bed and stool) with 3022.

of the Achaemenian period.[268] It is tempting to speculate that if these two characters had been at opposite corners, the four might have been marked [m]š[k]b, i.e. mškb, 'couch, bed', well attested in Phoenician, and Hebrew (e.g. at 1 Kings 1:47; 2 Kings 6:12; Isaiah 57:8) but only in late Aramaic (Nabataean).[269] Such markings could have indicated the relative locations of the different components. From further north, another chance find was made in the course of building work at Khirbet Ibsan to the west of the Sea of Galilee. This consists of a bronze censer with duck's head terminal on the handle, the bronze handle of a strainer with a cruder duck's head terminal, and a bronze bowl, giving an indication of life in northern Palestine.[270] Another illustration of Persian culture in this period is a bronze chair-foot in the form of a lion's paw, and a ringed cylindrical bronze member which probably decorated the leg above such a foot, both said to be from Samaria. This provenance is supported by part of a clay mould for a similar ringed cylindrical piece which was found during the excavations at Samaria in 1908-10. These components, together with a second bronze foot obtained from a dealer, can be reconstructed as parts of a throne very similar to examples represented in scultures at Persepolis.[271]

The Persian province of Samaria was an important neighbour to Judah, and valuable light has been thrown on it by a find made in 1962 in a cave in the Wadi ed-Daliyeh, a deep defile on the west side of the Jordan valley about eight miles north of Jericho, and within the province of Samaria.[272] This included a number of skeletons together with coins and jewellery, but particularly papyrus documents secured by clay bullae stamped with seal impressions, some of which are clearly Achaemenian

---

268. Iliffe 1935: 182-83, who, following consultation with E.L. Sukenik, takes the characters as b and h ('which has lost its lowest horizontal bar'), but the latter is clearly š and both are normal Aramaic forms (not Phoenician as suggested by Stern 1973: 143), pl. LXXXIX, 1-2 (reconstructions), 3-4 (inscribed components).

269. See, e.g., Mitchell 1996: 49-60, specifically 56-57; and Hoftijzer and Jongeling 1995: 2: 701. It is conceivable that the stool might have been marked k-r-s-' at the corners, a form well attested in Aramaic, though usually in contexts where its meaning was 'throne' (see, e.g., Mitchell 1996: 54-55; and Hoftijzer and Jongeling 1995: 1: 536-37.), but this would be to venture further into speculation.

270. Amiran 1972: 135-38, pls XIII-XIV.

271. Tadmor 1974: 37-43, pls 3 (bronze lion's paw), 4 (purchased paw), 5A (ringed cylinder), 7A (clay mould), 7B (paw and cylinder together), 7CF (Persepolis relief), fig. 1 (suggested reconstruction); Stern 1973: 143, fig. 237 (paw and cylinder together).

272. Summary by N.L. Lapp in Stern (ed.) 1993: 1: 320-23.

in style.[273]. The papyri, many in a fragmentary condition, are inscribed in Aramaic[274] and are mostly concerned with the sale of slaves. In them, the transactions involved are referred to by the word *'sr'*, which has the meaning 'bond', that is, basically, 'something bound', and in this context can be reasonably translated 'agreement' or 'covenant'. This same word (*'ĕsārā'*) is found in the Aramaic portion of the book of Daniel (6:8-9, 10, 13-14, 16) in the well-known passage in which Daniel is thrown into the lions' den. This punishment is described as the consequence of his refusal to obey a written decree (*'ĕsārā'*) of Darius (I) that people should pray only to him and not each man to his own god. This is another example of the way in which the vocabulary of the Aramaic passages in the Old Testament is found to be part of the surrounding world of the Persian Period.

According to the Old Testament, when the Jews planned to rebuild the Temple in Jerusalem under Nehemiah, they were obstructed by Sanballat, evidently the ruler of Samaria, though he is never given an official title in the Biblical text (Nehemiah 4:1-2, 7-8 etc.). His name appears in a seriously damaged papyrus from the Wadi Daliyeh, recording the sale of a slave.[275] Near the end of this document it is possible to read, [. . .]*w' br sn'blṭ ḥnn sgn'*, '[. . .]u'a son of Sanballat, Ḥanan the Governor', where '[. . .]u'a', possibly to be restored as Yaddu'a or Yešu'a,[276] and Ḥanan were probably acting as witnesses to the transaction.[277] The date on this

---

273. Leith 1997: pls XVIII and XX (seal impressions), XXII (papyrus with clay sealings).

274. The most complete publication of these papyri is Dušek 2007, which has (37-38) a concordance of his publication numbers with those (sometimes different) of previous publications: namely Cross 1963: 110-21 [Dušek: Cross 1963a]; Cross 1969: 41-62 [Cross 1971]; Cross 1974: 17-29 [Cross 1974a]; Cross 1985 [N. Avigad Volume] [Cross 1985]: 7*-17*; Cross with P.W. Lapp 1974; and Gropp 2001 [Gropp 2001]; and summary in Gropp 1992: 931-32. It will be simplest here to make all references to Dušek 2007, whose numbering of the papyri differs from that of Cross, and whose readings sometimes differ from those of both Gropp and Cross, but nevertheless to refer to the papyri by the system used by Gropp, namely WDSP (W[adi] D[aliyeh] S[amaria] P[apyrus]) followed by the number, with obverse (for his r = recto = front) and reverse (for his v = verso = back), and the line number.

275. Papyrus (WDSP) 11, front, line 13: Dušek 2007: 248-65 (discussion, transliteration, translation and commentary), pl. XI (front); Gropp 2001: WDSPpapDeed of Slave Sale J? ar, pls. XI-XII (no analysis of this document in the text).

276. See Dušek 2007: 261-62.

277. Dušek 2007: 254 (transliteration and translation), 261-264 (comment on line 13); Cross 1969: 43 n. 4 no 1 [Papyrus 14] = Cross and Lapp 1974: 18 n. 10 no 1 [Papyrus 14]; Gropp 2001: pl. XI, second line from the bottom. Gropp does

document (on the line which follows the names) is badly damaged but, on the basis of the probable occurrence of the name Artaxerxes on the back of the same papyrus, again very badly damaged,[278] together with more complete dates on other documents, this may probably be restored as:

> [In day X month Y of year Z of Artaxerxes the king in] Samaria
> this document (*šṭr*) [has been writ]ten.[279]

The form of the script shows that the obverse (front) and reverse (back) of the papyrus were probably written by the same scribe though not necessarily at precisely the same time, and that a date before c.350 BC is likely, pointing to a time late in the reign of Artaxerxes II (405-359 BC) or early in that of Artaxerxes III (359-338 BC).[280]

A study of the names of the High Priests in Jerusalem who are referred to in Ezra and Nehemiah,[281] and are known also in Josephus, *Antiquities of the Jews*,[282] and some also in the Elephantine papyri,[283] shows that, if a possible Yaddu'a or Yešu'a is to be dated to this time, it is a reasonable possibility that he is to be identified with the High Priest Yaddua (*yaddû'a*) mentioned in Nehemiah (12:10-11, 22).[284] This would mean that his father, Sanballat, could be dated in the time of Artaxerxes I (465-425 BC),[285] and therefore identified with the man encountered by Nehemiah.[286]

---

not mention this in the text or the concordance of the volume, and only refers to it as 'WDSP 11 front 13' in Schiffman and VanderKam (eds) 2000: II: 824.

278. Papyrus WDSP 11, back, line 1: Dušek 2007: 266 (text and translation), pl. XII, with discussion 267-68; Gropp 2001: pl. XII, but with no mention of this in the text or the concordance.

279. I.e.: [*bX lY šntZ 'rtḫšsš mlk' b*]*šmrn šṭr' znh*[*k*]*tyb*, where X, Y and Z represent the day (a number), month (a word) and year (a number) respectively, which, on the basis of the narrow spaces available in the text, Dušek speculates could have been: day (X) 1, 10 or 20 [each only a single character], month (Y) Ab [only two characters, *'b*], and year (Z) 1, 10 or 20 (2007: 254, 264-65).

280. Dušek 2007: 474-75.

281. Listed by Dušek in 2007: 550-52.

282. Dušek 2007: 554-58.

283. Dušek 2007: 553-54.

284. See chronological chart, Dušek 2007: 590.

285. As concluded by Dušek in 2007: 549 (chronological chart).

286. This view of J. Dušek (2007: 590) adopted here, who gives a thorough discussion of the evidence, with a chronological chart. This view differs from that of F.M. Cross who has done important work on this material. He has proposed that the king be identified as Artaxerxes II (405-359 BC) and therefore that the Sanballat in the Wadi Daliyeh papyri would have been a Sanballat II,

Another papyrus in this archive was secured by a clay sealing with an impression consisting mainly of a damaged Hebrew inscription in two lines which reads, [. . .]*yhw bn* [*sn'*] | *blṭ pḥt šmr*[*n*], '. . .iah son of [Sin'u]|balliṭ governor of Samar[ia]'.[287] The date in the first line of the papyrus is largely missing, but the surviving part has [. . .]*š mlk'*, '[. . .]sh the king'. In this the king's name could be either Artaxerxes ('*rtḥšsš*) or Darius (*dryhwš*),[288] but the form of the script on this papyrus suggests a date in the first half of the fourth century BC (i.e. c.400-350 BC)[289] and that there is a good case for identifying him as Artaxerxes II (404-358 BC),[290] and therefore that Sin'uballiṭ the father of . . .iah, in the seal impression, could again have been the Sanballat (*sanballaṭ*) who was contemporary with Nehemiah (Nehemiah 2:10, 19; 3:33; 4:1; 6:1, 2, 5, 12, 14; 13:28).

This opens the further possibility that . . .iah (. . .*yhw*), the son of Sin'uballiṭ, named on the seal impression, was Delaiah, the successor of Sin'uballiṭ. He is known from the Elephantine papyri, where, in a letter to Bagohi,[291] the Persian governor of Judaea, dated to 407 BC, the Jewish

---

Nehemiah's contemporary therefore being Sanballat I (his definitive view in 'A Reconstruction of the Judaean Restoration' in Cross 1998: 151-202; charts of his conclusions in Dušek 2007: 562 and 563).

287. Clay bulla W(adi) D(aliyeh) 22 on Papyrus WDSP 16: Dušek 2007: 321-31, pl. XL upper; only mentioned by Leith in a footnote (1997: 3 n. 2) and not by Gropp, though visible at the bottom of the papyrus (Gropp 2001: pl. XVII); previous discussions by Cross 1974: 18, with pl. 61 (Papyrus 5); also 1969: 42-43, with figs 34-35 (Papyrus 5); and N.L. Lapp in Stern 1993: 322 fig. (The -'- in the reconstruction *sn'blṭ*, also found in the Elephantine Papyrus mentioned above [see Porten and Yardeni 1986: 1: 68-71 no A4.7, line 29, just preceding p^ḥḥt], reflects the fact that the name is Babylonian Sin-uballiṭ).

288. Papyrus WDSP 16: Dušek 2007: 315-20, pl. XVII; (Gropp 2001: WDSP papDeed of Pledge of Vinyard? Ar, pl. XVII, not mentioned in the text [the sealing can be seen at bottom of the photo]).

289. Dušek 2007: 480.

290. Dušek 2007: 316-17.

291. Probably to be identified with Bagoses mentioned by Josephus (*Antiquities* 11:297: *bagōsēs ho stratēgos tou allou 'artaxerxou*, 'Bagōsēs the general of the other Artaxerxes' [most likely Artaxerxes II (405-359BC)], and also in *Antiquities* 11:300)) in the late fifth century BC, and not with Bagoas, mentioned by Diodorus Siculus, *Library of History* 17:5: *bagōas ho k^ʰiliark^ʰos*, 'Bagoas the Chiliarch' (Welles 1963: 130-31) – Chiliarch, being 'commander of a thousand' (from *k^ʰiliark^ʰ*, 'thousand', on which, see, briefly, Bar-Kochva 1976: 92; and the possibility that Greek *k^ʰiliark^ʰos* was a translation [calque] of an Iranian equivalent *hazahra-pati*, *hazārbad*, see Benveniste 1966: 67-71); also, Diodorus, *Library of History* 16:47-51, indicating that he was a man so involved in administration of the affairs of Artaxerxes [most likely Artaxerxes III (c.344BC)] that he was *tēs basileias kurion*, 'master of the kingdom' (C.L. Sherman, *Diodorus Siculus*, VII, Books XV.20-

priests ask for support for the rebuilding of the temple there, mentioning that 'Delaiah and Shelamiah the sons of Sanballat governor of Samaria' (*dlyh wšlmyh bny sn'blṭ pḥt šmryn*) had failed to respond to an earlier request.[292] If Sanballat in this passage is to be identified with the man of Nehemiah's time, this text provides the information, not found in the Old Testament, that his official title was 'Governor [*pḥt*] of Samaria'. The word *pḥt* is a loan from Babylonian *pīḫatu*, which had the basic meaning 'district, province'. The official in charge of such a district was referred to as the *bēl pīḫati*, 'provincial governor', literally 'lord of the district', a title found in Babylonian texts from the second millennium BC onwards, but in some instances in the Achaemenian period a shortened form *pīḫatu* was used on its own as the title 'governor', the equivalent of the Persian word, satrap.[293] In the Old Testament the title is found in the spelling *peḥāh* in both Hebrew and Aramaic passages: in reference to Tattenai, the governor of the Persian satrapy Eber-Nāri, 'across the river', which included Palestine (Ezra 5:3, 6; 6:6, 13); as well as to Sheshbazzar (Ezra 5:14) and Zerubbabel (Haggai 2:21), the Jewish governors of Judaea. Other references in the Old Testament include its use in reference to an unspecified Assyrian official mentioned in the speech of Sennacherib's general at the siege of Hezekiah's Jerusalem (2 Kings 18:24) and to provincial governors in the time of Nebuchadnezzar (Daniel 3:2-3, 27). It is also used of an unnamed Aramaean officer in the time of Solomon (1 Kings 10:15), a usage perhaps reflecting scribal updating of the vocabulary.

Returning to Delaiah, the appeal from the Elephantine priests received a reply, probably recorded by the messenger, in which he is associated with the governor, 'Memorandum (*zkrn*) of what Bagohi (*bgwhy*) and Delaiah (*dlyh*) said', which authorised the rebuilding of the temple.[294] In this, the word *zkrn* is related to the verb *zkr*, 'to remember', which

---

XVI.65 [Loeb 389] [1952]: 380-81); see Dušek 2007: 527, 593-98. This is contrary to the view of F.M. Cross who favoured the identification of Bagoses with Bagoas (e.g. 1975: 4-18, specifically 5 and n. 10; also 1998: 153 and n. 12).

292. Lines 29-30: Porten and Yardeni 1986: 1: 68-75 no A4.7 = A4.8, lines 29-30 = 28-29; Cowley 1923: 108-22, nos 30 = 31 [duplicates], lines 29 = 28; H.L. Ginsberg in Pritchard 1955: 491-92; H.H. Rowley in Winton Thomas (ed.), 1958: 260-65, pl. 16 (photograph of obverse); Grelot 1972: 406-15 no 102; Gressmann in Gressmann (ed.) 1926: 450-52 no 1; see also on this transaction, Porten 1968: 289-93; Kraeling 1953: 104-10.

293. CAD: P: 360-67 (*pīḫatu*, §1 'post, responsible position'; §2 'responsibility, duty'; § 3 'province, district'), specifically 365-67 §4 ('governor'); 367-69 (*bēl pīḫati*, 'governor'); Brinkman 1968: 303-304 and 296 n. 1940; Dušek 2007: 514-16.

294. Porten and Yardeni 1986: 1: 76-77 no A4.9; Cowley 1923: 122-24 no 32; Segert 1975: 499 no 24 (text in square script); Grelot 1972: 406-15 no 102; Ginsberg in Pritchard 1955: 492; Gressmann (ed.) 1926: 452 no 2.

is known already in the fourteenth century BC in a Canaanite gloss (explanation) of a Babylonian word in an Amarna letter, and also in Phoenician, as well as in earlier and later Aramaic dialects.[295]

Among the points which have been long discussed in the field of Biblical archaeology are the dates at which Ezra and Nehemiah came from Babylonia to Jerusalem. There are good arguments for dating the arrival of Ezra in Jerusalem in 458 BC, specifically in the seventh year of Artaxerxes II (Ezra 7:8),[296] and for placing the first mission of Nehemiah in the years 445-433 BC,[297] followed, after a return to Babylon, by a second mission in around 430 BC. This is said to have been 'at the end of days' (*lĕqēṣ yāmîm*; Nehemiah 13:6), a phrase which would usually refer to an indefinite period of time but taken by some here to indicate a year.[298]

I will conclude with a return to the Achaemenian homeland and the book of Esther. Cotton is thought of as a fairly modern textile but it is likely that it is referred to in Esther (1:6), in a passage describing the garden enclosure of Xerxes (*'ahašweroš*) at Susa. The text is rather obscure, but can be translated 'the garden had hangings of white and blue cotton', where the word rendered 'cotton', *karpas*, was very probably an Indo-Iranian loanword, as indicated by Sanskrit *karpāsa*, 'cotton',[299] suggesting that it had come into Persian from the east. That this is likely is shown by evidence of the use of cotton already in the third millennium BC at Mohenjo-Daro in the Indus Valley.[300]

Appendix I
The Earliest Old Persian Text
The Question of the Priority of the Bisitun Inscription

The Old Persian language is known only from a relatively limited corpus of inscriptions in a specially devised cuneiform script, and the suggestion that the great Bisitun inscription of Darius might have been the first Old Persian monumental text set up has been much discussed.

---

295. Hoftijzer and Jongeling 1995: 1: 321-29.
296. Williamson 1987: 55-69. Dušek argues, however, for 398BC as the date of Ezra's coming to Jerusalem (2007: 591-98 and 554).
297. Dušek 2007: 553-54.
298. See S. Talmon, 'qēṣ' in Botterweck, Ringgren and Fabry, 1974-2006: XIII: 78-86, specifically 82, where he suggests that it is possible that this passage 'describes a one-year absence of Nehemiah from Jerusalem', a suggestion adopted also by Dušek (2007: 573).
299. Mayrhofer 1953-76: I: 174-75; probably a loanword in Sanskrit from Austro-Asiatic, and in turn borrowed in Greek (*karpasos*), Burrow 1973: 379.
300. Marshall 1931: I: 33, 194; II: 585-86; and Gopal 1961: 61 n. 1; and on early cotton and its diffusion Watson 1983: 31-33.

Its priority is possibly implied by a statement in column IV, lines 88-92 (§70) of the inscription which reads (in the translation of R. Schmitt),

> Proclaims Darius the king: By the favour of Ahura Mazdā this (is) the form of writing (*dipičiçam* [*d-i-p-i-č-i-ç-m*]), which I have made, besides, in Aryan (*ariyā* [*a-r-i-y-a*]). Both on clay tablets (*pavastāyā* [*p-v-s-t-a-y-[a]*]) and on parchment (*čarmā* [*č-r-m-a*]) it has been placed. Besides, I also made the signature; besides, I made the lineage. And it was written down and was read aloud before me. Afterwards I have sent this form of writing (*dipičiçam*) everywhere into the countries (*dahyāva* [*d-h-y-a-[v]*]).[301]

In this text 'Aryan' evidently refers to the language of the inscription, Old Persian, though whether this applies also to the text written 'on clay tablets (*pavastāyā*) and on parchment (*čarmā*)' is perhaps open to debate. This passage is not included in the Babylonian version, nor in the surviving fragments of the Aramaic version, but it does appear in Elamite in ten lines in a separate additional 'box' above the figure of Darius in the sculptured area of the monument.[302] In this passage the Elamite

---

301. Schmitt 1991: 45, 73-74 (transliteration and translation [here the normalised form is followed in square brackets by the individual characters separated by hyphens]); for earlier publications, see Budge, King and Thompson 1907: 77-78 (copy, transliteration and translation, showing a very incomplete, damaged text); Weissbach 1911: 70-71 §70 (transliteration and translation of Old Persian); Kent 1953: 130 (transliteration), 132 (translation); and, more recently, Brandenstein and Mayrhofer 1964: 87-88 (transliteration); Borger and Hinz 1984: I.4: 448 (translation of Old Persian and Elamite); Lecoq 1997: 212-213 §70 (translation with notes); see also comment of Cameron in Dentan 1955: 88.

302. Budge, King and Thompson 1907: 157, Text L (text, transliteration and translation); Weissbach 1911: 70 §70 (= Bīs. l) (transliteration); Hinz 1952: 29 and 32-33 (transliteration and translation set out in nine sense units); and the text is given (under 'DB 70') in transliteration and translation, phrase by phrase with some overlapping, in Hinz and Koch 1987: I: 636 (under *har-ri-ya-ma*); II: 1123 (under *šá-iš-šá*); I: 594 (under *ha-la-at*); I: 392 (under *e-ip-pi*) = I: 662 (under *hi-iš*); I: 274 (under *tal-li-ik*); I: 259 (under v.*da-a-ya-u-iš*); I: 648 (under *ha-ti-ma*); I: 333 (under *tin-gi-ya*); and II: 1064 (under *sa-pi-iš*); the location of this Elamite passage is shown in Lecoq 1997: fig. 8, labelled '§70 (Élam.)', with combined translation, 212-13. Hinz also gives a transliteration of the text with a translation in 1952: 28-38; an article to which Levy 1954: 169-208 is largely a response. Diakonoff, in an interesting paper (1970: 98-124) concludes that *tuppi.me* in the Elamite version referred to a 'new kind of text' rather than a 'new system of writing', and on that basis concludes that §70 of the Elamite version at

equivalent of Old Persian *dipičiçam* is *tuppi-me*, where Akkadian *ṭuppu* (Sumerian DUB), 'tablet', appears as a loanword in both Old Persian *dipi* and Elamite *tuppi*.[303] In some contexts Elamite *tuppi* clearly referred to a clay tablet,[304] but in one administrative tablet from Persepolis there is reference to a *tup-pi*KUŠ, where KUŠ is the Sumerian ideogram marking a leather object, therefore *tup-pi*KUŠ or *tup-pi*[KUŠ] would signify 'tablet[leather]', leading in that case to Schmitt's translation 'document (written) on parchment'.[305] Moreover, concerning the terminations of *dipi-čiçam* and

Bisitun is irrelevant to the discussion. This distinction is not covincing, however, because reference in that passage to a 'new kind of text' could well have applied to a first use of Old Persian, whatever the script. Diakonoff accepts the arguments of C. Nylander that the inscriptions in the name of Cyrus at Pasargadae were set up by Cyrus the Great and were not later additions by Darius, but he rejects Nylander's further conclusion that only those in Babylonian and Elamite were made by Cyrus while those in Old Persian were later additions by Darius. Further, from an analysis of the writing conventions found in the Old Persian inscriptions he concludes that the Phoenician-Aramaic system was the main typological prototype for the alphabetic element of the Old Persian script, and that Late Babylonian, not Assyrian or Elamite, was the main influence for the cuneiform element. Moreover, he sees parallels in literary formulae with the Urartian cuneiform inscriptions (122) and, since the Urartian kingdom ended soon after 600 BC, he postulates a link by way of the Medes, the successors in the Urartian territory (modern Armenia), and he even speculates that what is known as Old Persian, and is described in the Bisitun Inscription as *ariyā*, might be defined more properly as 'a literary language common to Iranians' with a considerable element of Median in it (122). He suggests an analogy with the literary character of the Neo-Assyrian royal inscriptions, which show a 'spectrum of dialectal peculiarities', suggesting that the language of the Old Persian inscriptions might be characterised (adapting his suggestion) as '. . . literary Median with numerous "slips" into Persian . . ., the vocabulary is mostly Median but many of the technical terms are Persian'. These are interesting speculations, and Diakonoff acknowledges that this latter analysis of the language must be left to the judgement of Iranian scholars, but these points are not conclusive in the question of the origin of the Old Persian writing system. Concerning the Median language, no inscriptions have been found, and it is known only from words in Old Persian inscriptions and in personal names. A number of these words and names can be seen by turning the pages of Hinz 1975 marked 'medisch'; see also Mayrhofer 1968 (n. 153 above) 1-22.

303. *tup-pi-me* is preceded in the Elamite text by a horizontal wedge, normally the determinative for place names but sometimes used instead of a vertical wedge, as a determinative before nouns etc. (Paper 1955: 6-7 §2.4).

304. In some cases, it refers to the actual tablet on which it is written (*tup-pi hi*, 'this tablet'), e.g. Hallock 1969: 523 no PF 1940, line 29, see also other references 763-64; also, Hinz and Koch 1987: I: 365.

305. See also Hallock 1969: 588, no PF 1986, line 31, cited also in Hinz and Koch 1987: I: 365, under *h.tup-pi* (Pergament-Urkunde).

tuppi-me, Old Persian *-çiça* is reasonably interpreted as 'form; shape; appearance' on the basis of Middle Persian *čihr*,[306] and the Elamite suffix *-me* marks an abstract noun;[307] both therefore suggest some such sense in the context as 'document', without regard to the medium on which it was written.[308] The identity of the language of the inscription, *ariyā*, is given in Elamite as *har-ri-ia-ma*, and this is followed by the statement 'which had not been done before' (*ap-pa šá-iš-šá in-ni šá-ri*),[309] perhaps further supporting the view that this was the first time an Old Persian inscription was set up.

The statement which follows in the Old Persian text, 'on clay tablets (*pavastāyā*) and on parchment (*čarmā*)', is matched in the Elamite version in much the same sense, namely on 'clay (*ha-la-at*) and parchment (KUŠ)'. It is clear from its usage elsewhere that the meaning of Elamite *ha-la-at* was 'clay',[310] but Old Persian *pavastāyā* is less clearly defined. The Middle Persian form, *pōst*, 'skin, hide; bark, shell', and Sanskrit *pavásta-*, 'covering, cover',[311] give some indication, and Schmitt's rendering 'clay tablets' is based on the assumption that it referred to 'the thin clay envelope used to protect clay tablets'.[312] Concerning this suggestion, it should be noted that, while clay envelopes, not necessarily of 'thin' clay, were widely used on Babylonian and Assyrian tablets, none of those so far published were found among the Treasury or Fortification tablets at Persepolis, though some of these texts were in letter form.[313] *Čarmā* (*č-r-m-a*) occurs also in the Younger *Avesta* (*čarə̌man*) as well as Sanskrit (*cárman*), in each case with meanings in the range 'skin, hide, leather'.[314] A suggested derivation

306. Schmitt 1991: 73, comment, in which he supports the reading -**čiça** in preference to *-maiy* of Kent 1953: 130, 191, and Brandenstein and Mayrhofer 1964: 87, 116.
307. Paper 1955: 84-85 §6.10.1; Cameron 1948: 52-53.
308. Hinz and Koch 1987: I: 365, under *h.tup.pi.me* (near the foot of the page), give the definition '*Schrift*'.
309. Hinz and Koch 1987: II: 1123 ('*was es vordem nicht gab*').
310. Hinz and Koch 1987: I: 594.
311. Brandenstein and Mayrhofer 1964: 140, with bibliography; MacKenzie 1971: 69, *pōst*; Mayrhofer 1953-76: II: 238, *pavástam*.
312. Schmitt 1991: 73 n.; see also Kent 1953: 196 ('clay envelope of tablet') and 219; Borger and Hinz 1984: I.4: 448, '*Tontafeln*' (Old Persian), '*Ton*' (Elamite); Lecoq 1997: 212, '*tablette*'.
313. Hallock 1969: 26, 50-53.
314. Brandenstein and Mayrhofer 1964: 112; Bartholomae 1904: cols 582-83; Monier-Williams 1899: 390, citing many compound nouns with *carma-*, all with the sense 'skin, leather'; Mayrhofer 1953-76: I: 378 and III: 703; and 1992-2001: I: 537, citing cognate forms; also Turner 1966: 255 §4701, all senses in the range 'leather, skin, hide'.

of čarĕman and its cognates from Indo-European *(s)kér-men, 'cut off'
or the like,[315] would not support any subsidiary meaning for čarmā such
as 'papyrus'.[316]

The indication in the Old Persian version that this text was sent to all
the countries (dahyāva) is repeated in Elamite as da-a-ia-ú-iš, that is to
say, borrowing the Iranian word,[317] suggesting that the Elamite scribes
knew of no equivalent in their own language suitable to refer to the parts
of a large empire.

Appendix II
Parchment

The Bisitun inscription states that the text was disseminated on
parchment (čarmā), and this is indeed plausible. Parchment consists
of animal skin with the hairs removed and lightly cured with a surface
bulking of chalk and then stretched while drying. It can also be
produced by working with pastes of flour, chalk and fats such as egg
yolk. The date at which this process was first carried out is not precisely
known, but Egyptian tomb paintings of the New Kingdom (second
millennium BC) show stretching of skins, and calcium in some actual
leather samples of uncertain date may suggest that it was already in
use by that time,[318] and therefore quite possibly by the Achaemenian
period. Diodorus Siculus (first century BC) quotes Ctesias of Knidos,
who served as a physician under Artaxerxes II (early fourth century
BC), as referring to the Persian 'royal leathers' (basilikōn diphtherōn),[319]
in which diphtherā, 'leather', evidently had some such meaning as
'record'.

A possible hint that leather might have been used for the recording
of important documents in early Iran is found in a much later reference
in the Pahlavi composition, the Ardāy Wīrāz Nāmag (or Artāy Vīrāz
Nāmak) of the ninth century AD,[320] which claims that the Avesta ('pst'k)

---

315. Mayrhofer 1992-2001: I: 537.
316. W. Hinz argues strongly for leather rather than papyrus, particularly concerning
     the usage of the word in line 90 of the Old Persian version of the Bisitun text
     (1952: 34-35).
317. See Bartholomae 1904: cols 706-710, under dahyav-, with reference to Old
     Persian in cols 707-708.
318. C. van Driel-Murray in Nicholson and Shaw 2000: 303.
319. Persica, 2:32:4 (C.H. Oldfather, Diodorus Siculus, I, Loeb Classical Library
     [Cambridge, MA: Harvard University Press; and London: W. Heinemann,
     1933] 458-59); also, Jacoby 1958: 450 no 688, F5.
320. See Gignoux 1984; and, on this composition, see Boyce 1968: 48; Duchesne-

had been recorded on 'ox hides' (TWRA *pwstyh*, normalised as *gāw pōstīhā*)[321] before the time of Alexander the Great (i.e. in the fourth century BC). While this could not be true of manuscripts of the *Avesta*, which was not committed to writing until much later, it might preserve a correct record of the use of leather as a writing material at that date. In Graeco-Roman times parchment was leather, mainly the skins of sheep and goats, treated in a special way probably not much different from the process known in recent times which involved washing, liming, scraping, stretching and rubbing with chalk.[322] Pliny the Elder quotes the Roman author Marcus Varro (116-27 BC) as saying (in relation to the second century BC) that:

> When, owing to the rivalry between Ptolemy of Egypt and Eumenes of Pergamon about their libraries, Ptolemy suppressed the export of papyrus (*khartas*), parchment (*membranas*) was invented at Pergamum.[323]

Guillemin 1962: 41, 61; and, earlier, Browne 1902: 106, 118.

321. Gignoux 1984: 36-37 (transliteration and normalisation) 145 (translation), where TWRA, the conventional transcription of Aramaic *twr*, 'the ox', is an Aramaeogram, i.e. a word written in Aramaic but spoken *gāw* in Iranian; and *-ihā* in *pōstīhā* is a plural termination (Nyberg 1974: 278 §1.7)), perhaps introduced from modern Persian (Gignoux 1984: 37 n. 2); see also Bailey 1943: 151-52, line seven (also quoting a statement of the Tansar-nāma of the sixth century AD that Alexander [the Great] burnt nearly 12,000 ox-hide [*pūst i gāv*] of the 'book of the faith', i.e. the *Avesta* [1984: 156-57]. Iranian *gāw*, though etymologically cognate with English *cow* [both probably deriving from a hypothetical Indo-European forerunner *$g^w\bar{o}us$* or the like], had the wider range of meaning 'ox, bull, cow' [Bartholomae 1904: cols 505-509]; narrowing of the range of meaning of some words over the passage of time being a recognised linguistic phenomenon [see e.g. Robins 1971: 314]).

322. See e.g. Maunde Thompson 1912: 28-29, he refers also to rubbing with pumice but this was probably more the practice in the Roman world. He makes a general distinction between parchment made from sheep and goat skins, and vellum made from calf or kid or even newly-born or still-born calf or lamb skins. For a practical account of the process of producing parchment as practised in mediaeval Europe, see de Hamel 1992: 8-15. See also Reynolds and Wilson 1991: 3; Lewis 1974: 9 n. 8; Parkinson and Quirke 1995: 70-71; also, briefly, on parchment in the Roman world, Paoli 1963: 177.

323. *Natural History* 13:70, quoting the translation of H. Rackham, *Pliny, Natural History* IV (Loeb Classical Library) (Cambridge, MA: Harvard University Press; and London: W. Heinemann, 1971) 140-41. The full Latin designation of the material was *mebrana pergamena*.

This was the standard ancient view but, as already mentioned, parchment was probably in use well before that time.[324] A possible fifth-century BC reference to such use, on either papyrus or parchment, is found in the account by Thucydides of an episode in the Peloponnesian War when a Persian on his way to Sparta was captured and taken to Athens, 'and the Athenians had the dispatches (*epistolas*) which he was carrying and which were written in the Assyrian character (*tōn 'assuriōn grammatōn*) translated (*metagrap^{s}amenoi*) and read (*anegnōsan*)' (Peloponnesian War 4:50). In this the standard meaning of *metagrap^{h}ō* is 'write differently > translate' and that of *anagignōskō* is 'know again > read'. However, of particular significance in the present context, it is most likely that 'Assyrian character' or 'Assyrian writing' (*'assuriōn grammatōn*) referred to a text in the Aramaic script and language on parchment or papyrus, where the word *'assuriōn* had the meaning current in later Hebrew and Aramaic (*'aššûrî*) 'Hebrew square script',[325] in the fifth century BC the Imperial Aramaic forerunner of the formal Square Script, and not the sense sometimes assumed in the nineteenth century, 'cuneiform (on clay)'.[326] The fact that the Greeks were able to read the text supports this view,[327] and a similar instance is found in Herodotus' account of Darius setting up two pillars on the Bosporus, engraved, one in Assyrian (*'assuria*), i.e. Aramaic, and one in Greek (*'ellēnika*), characters (*grammata*) (*The Histories* 4:87), a combination comparable to that of the Lycian, Aramaic and Greek versions at Xanthos. This Aramaic script, which was adopted by the Jews during the Babylonian exile, was disseminated throughout the Achaemenid Empire. It is referred to in Talmudic sources as *ktb 'sryt*, 'Assyrian writing', and is known also as the Square Script. It is clearly seen from the second century BC onwards in the Dead Sea Scrolls from Qumran and a similar form is found in Palmyrene inscriptions, an early example of which, dated to 32 BC, was found at Dura Europos on the Euphrates.[328]

---

324. See, e.g., Easterling in Easterling and Knox (eds) 1985: 18-19; and Rostovtzeff 1941: I: 425, 541 and 564, with III: 1423 n. 221, 1447 n. 315 and 1451 n. 331, respectively; also, briefly, Casson 2001: 52.
325. E.g. Jastrow 1926: 127.
326. E.g. Jowett 1881: II: 250-51.
327. See comments on this passage by Levy 1954: 186-88.
328. The change of script in writing Hebrew and Aramaic is clear in the Qumran manuscripts, of which the majority are in the borrowed Aramaic form and only a small number in the archaic Hebrew form. On the latter, see Skehan, Ulrich and Sanderson 1992; see also Birnbaum 1971: col. 126, with 1954-57: 81ff.; and C.C. Torrey in Rostovtzeff, Brown and Welles 1939: 318-20, pl. LV.1 = Hillers and Cussini 1996: 169 no 1067m Doura 1 (32BC).

In the Biblical context it is worth noting that, when the Apostle Paul asked for his 'books (*biblion*) and parchments (*membrana*)' to be sent to him (2 Timothy 4:13), the Greek word *membrana* (< Latin *membrana* [= Greek *diphtherā*]) probably did refer to parchment proper,[329] while the 'books' were probably of papyrus (*khartēs*), a material referred to elsewhere in the New Testament as suitable for letters (2 John 12).

Appendix III
The Avesta

An important element in Zoroastrianism was the sacred book, or collection of texts, known as the *Avesta*.[330] The earliest known

---

329. See useful discussion in Marshall 1999: 819-21.
330. See Henning 1942: 46-47 = 1977: 157-58. ['Disintegration' in this paper refers to Henning's judgement that at the beginning of the twentieth century, with the publication by K.F. Geldner of his standard edition of the *Avesta*, 1886, 1889, 1895 and by C. Bartholomae of his *Wörterbuch*, 1904, the materials were available for major advances in the understanding of the text, but that, instead of such advances, 'a hypercritical attitude towards the text of the *Avesta*' prevailed, in spite of the fact that discoveries of previously unknown Middle Iranian languages had 'tended to show that the text as it stands is perfectly correct and not in need of any reconstruction' (41). There are interesting echoes of this judgement in the remarks of G.R. Driver in relation to the Old Testament in his Presidential Address in 1956 to the International Organization for the Study of the Old Testament, when, referring to the view that the text 'of the Hebrew Old Testament, being far remote from any archetype, must be desperately corrupt and called for extensive rewriting' and that, as a result, 'A flood of emendations descended on the unhappy pages of the Hebrew Bible.' He continues, 'Since the second war the pendulum has swung the other way and the substantial accuracy of the text is now a commonplace, even though it may be exaggerated. The careful study of it in the light of an increasing knowledge of the cognate languages has shown many words and phrases once thought incredible have in fact been correctly transmitted.' (Driver 1957: 4-5). This view has something of a forerunner in remarks of this father S.R. Driver concerning emendation to the text of the prophetic books, when he wrote, half a century earlier, '. . . the extensive alterations of text, and rejection of passages as later insertions, assumed by some modern scholars, partly on the ground of imperfect agreement with the context, partly on account of the supposed exigencies of metre, appear to me to rest upon an insufficient basis. It seems to me far from clear that the Hebrew prophets, most of whom were also poets, and evidently men swayed often by emotion, are to be regarded as necessarily developing their thought with exact logical precision; so that, – to say nothing of the possibility that their discourses may have come down to us in a condensed form, with connecting links omitted, – imperfect agreement with the context appears to me, except in extreme cases, to be a questionable ground for suspecting the originality of a passage.' (Driver,

manuscript dates from AD 1323,[331] but the text was probably put
into writing many centuries before that time, in the Sasanian period,
and conceivably as early as the Parthian period, though there is no
material evidence for that. Apart from references to the Avestan text
on ox hide in later Iranian sources,[332] the religious leader Mani (third
century AD)[333] is quoted in a Coptic Manichaean text (the *Kephalaia*),
found in 1930 at Medinet Madi in Egypt and probably dating from
about AD 400, as saying that 'Zoroaster (*zaradēs*) came to king
Hystaspes (*hustaspēs*) and preached in Persia' and that 'his disciples
after his death remembered (his words) and wrote the books which
they read to-day'.[334] On the basis of this Coptic reference W.B. Henning
had concluded, 'There is, therefore, no doubt that the Arsacid text of
the *Avesta* existed',[335] that is to say, a text of the *Avesta* in the Pahlavi

1906: x).] On the *Avesta* itself, see Kellens 1989: 35-44; and convenient summary
of the contents in J. Duchesne-Guillemin 1962: 31-40.

331. Bailey 1943: 168-69; Kellens 1989: 35.
332. See Appendix II above.
333. Mani was born in AD 216 under the Parthians. He began to preach in AD 240,
in the reign of the first Sasanian king Ardashir I (before AD 224-242), he was
permitted to preach freely throughout the Sasanian Empire under Shapur I
(AD 242-270), and this freedom continued under Hormizd I (AD 270-271).
Under Wahram I (AD 271-277), however, by the influence of the fanatical
Zoroastrian high priest Kartīr, he was imprisoned and died in captivity.
(Account of Mani's life, Widengren 1965: 23-42; and, more briefly in Yarshater
(ed.) 1983: 965-72; also, Rudolph 1977: 329-31; P.A. Mirecki in Freedman (ed.)
1992: 4: 503; and anonymous in F.L. Cross (ed.) 1997: 1027-28. Chronologies
differ among these treatments, as also with that in Yarshater (ed.) 1983: 178
(R.N. Frye).
334. Schmidt 1935: 6-7 (text and German translation on facing pages) lines 27-33; cited
by Henning 1942: 47 = 1977: 158; and by Duchesne-Guillemin 1962: 41; see also
Gardner 1995: 13 (translation of 7:27-33) with 10 (comment), and 18 (translation
of 12:10-20, mention of Buddha, Zarathustra and Jesus as earlier 'apostles'); also,
on this text in general, see Mirecki 1992: 505-506; and for a typical page from this
manuscript (not the pages in question) see Rudolph 1977: pl. 31.
335. Henning 1942: 47 = 1977: 158. In a similar way Diakonov and Livshits are
said to see possible evidence of a written *Avesta* as early as the first century BC
in the occurrence of the form *gwyrh* in the Parthian documents of that date
from Nisa in Turkmenistan, which they suggest may be interpreted as Gōš, the
name of the fourteenth day of the Zoroastrian month (Diakonov and Livshits
1966: 155 [I have been unable to consult this work]), a suggestion accepted
by Duchesne-Guillemin 1983: 868); and, as a possibility, 'gwyrh (= Gōš ?)' by
Gignoux (1972: 51). The use of a Zoroastrian day name at this date would not
necessarily, however, imply the existence of a written *Avesta*. Concerning the
day name Gōš, Boyce appears to give two different possible explanations of its
origin: (a) < Pahlavi *gwyrh* < Old Iranian **gav-ayar*, 'cow-day'? (1983: 815, with

script. This is rather thin evidence, however,[336] and M. Boyce points to the possibility that these 'books' were merely pseudepigraphic works known in the west in Zoroaster's name.[337]

Another ninth century AD reference to the recording of the *Avesta*[338] is found in the Pahlavi (Middle Persian) book, the *Dēnkard*,[339] where it is stated that 'Shapur king of kings son of Ardashir' (*šāpuhr šāhān šāh ī artaḥšahrān*), presumably referring to Shapur I (AD 240-272), collected various writings, including the *Avesta* (*apastāk*), and commanded that a copy (*paččēn*) be deposited in the Satrapal(?) Treasury (*ganj ī špyk'n*, literally 'Treasury which Satrapal[?]').[340] This would place the recording of the *Avesta* in the third century AD, but the historical value of such a statement should be judged in the light of a preceding passage in this text which runs:

> Darius son of Darius (*dārāy ī dārāyān*) commanded that two written copies (*napištak 2 paččēn*) of all *Avesta* and Zand (*hamāk apastāk ud zand*) as Zoroaster had received them

---

ns 4-5); or (b) < Avestan *Geush Urvan*, 'ox-soul' (1984: 19).

336. For a recent dismissal of the possibility of an 'Arsacid *Avesta*', see P.O. Sjærvø, in Kaye 2007: 2: 856-57.

337. M. Boyce in Gershevitch et al. 1968: 33 n. 2 (quoting H.H. Schaeder). The Greek writer Porphyry of Tyre (233-c.305AD), for instance, reports in his *Life of Plotinus* (16:6, 14) that Plotinus (c. AD 205-270) prepared refutations of a 'Book of Zoroaster' (Layton 1987: 182-84 [explanatory remarks and translation of chapter 16]); and there is a quotation from a 'Book of Zoroaster' in another Coptic document, the Apocryphon of John (15:29-19:9), discovered in 1945 at Nag Hammadi in Egypt (Layton 1987: 40-43, translation, and see 26; also by F. Wisse in Robinson (ed.) 1977: 107-109, translation), neither of these having any direct connection with the *Avesta*.

338. On the ninth century text, the Ardāy Wīrāz Nāmag, see Appendix II above.

339. On which, see M. Boyce in I. Gershevitch et al. 1968: 1: 43-45; J.P. de Menasce in Yarshater (ed.) 1983: 1170-76; and, earlier, E.W. West in Geiger and Kuhn (eds) 1896-1904: 91-98.

340. Bailey 1943: 219 (text in normalised transcription without translation, and the form possibly to be transliterated šasapīkān [a reading discussed by him on 230-31] given in Pahlavi script), cited as DkM, 412, lines 17-22, with comment on 156 (DkM referring to Madan 1911); also Shaki 1981: 114-25 (dating the text to the sixth century AD), specifically 116 (text, with slightly different normalisation, and šāhīgān for Bailey's possible šasapīkān with discussion 115 n. 2, citing the attested alternative writing *šspyk'nî*, for which MacKenzie has the normalisation *šasab*[satrap]-*īgān*, 'satrapal' [1971: 79]), 119 (translation), a reading not accepted by Shaki. Account of the manuscripts and editions of the *Dēnkard* (including full title of Madan's edition) in Nyberg 1964: xiv-xvii, both Shaki and Bailey quoting from Madan 1911 (cited as DkM), 412, lines 17 and 21-22. An earlier translation was given by West 1892: 414.

from Ohrmazd (*zartuhšt hač ōhrmazd patgraft*), one be kept
in the Satrapal[?] Treasury (*ganǰ ī špyk'n*), one in the Fortress
of Writing (*diz ī nipišt*).[341]

In this, *dārāy ī dārāyān* was Darius III (336-331 BC), the last
Achaemenid king, defeated by Alexander,[342] in other words assuming
that this took place in the fourth century BC.[343] Such statements suggest
that the *Dēnkard* is of doubtful value as a historical source.

In view of this, it can be no more than speculation that the *Avesta*
was committed to writing before the Sasanian period.[344] If there was
an earlier written *Avesta*, it would have been in the Pahlavi script, a
later form of the Aramaic alphabet of the Achaemenian period, which
consisted of only 22 characters with no specific vowel signs (only ', *w* and
y used as partial indicators),[345] and would have represented the original
text only very imperfectly. Because of the limitations of this alphabet, in
due course a special Avestan script was devised. This was based on the
Pahlavi alphabet, but it was enlarged to consist of 46 characters, made up
of consonants appropriate for an Iranian (Indo-European), as distinct
from a Semitic language, and fourteen vowels.[346] Henning argued that
the text recorded in this way would not have been copied from an already

---

341. Bailey 1943: 218, cited as DkM, 412, lines three to five, with 156; Shaki 1981: 115
(text), 118 (translation); early translation (as Dinkard 4:23) by West 1892: 413.

342. As indicated for instance in the ninth century Pahlavi book, the Bundahishn,
in which he is referred to as the predecessor of Alexander (34:8), on which, see
Boyce 1968: 40-41; translation of this passage in West 1880: 151.

343. This chronological relationship between Darius and Alexander is reflected also in
the romance known as the Eskandar-nāma (on which, see Hanaway 1998: 609-
12.), a composition, probably derived from Greek sources and known in a number
of versions, notably as an element in the eleventh-century Iranian national epic,
the Shāh-nāma of Ferdowsi, (English translation [with abridgements] in Levy
1967: 231-50, XVIII-XX, specifically 231-32; summarised in Brown 1902: 110-23,
specifically 118-19). This represents Eskandar/Sekandar (Alexander the Great), a
figure around whom stories gathered, not only as the successor, but also the half-
brother, of Dārā son of Dārāb, and as having travelled to such unlikely places as
Andalusia, the land of Rus, and the Land of Darkness in search of the Water of Life.

344. See Boyce 1968: 33 n. 2.

345. The script is set out, e.g., in Mackenzie 1971: xi; also in Back 1978: 10. The
following consonants were used to indicate long vowels in Pahlavi: ' (ā), *y* (ē, ī)
and *w* (ō, ū), in a way comparable to the use in Biblical Hebrew and Aramaic
(on which see Appendix VII above).

346. The script is set out, e.g., by Hoffmann 1989: 48, with explanation 47-51;
Bartholomae 1895-1901: 161 (forms), 152-53 (phonetic values); Jackson 1892:
xxxviii and 1; see also Henning 1942: 43-44 = 1977: 154-55; and, in a wider
context, Jensen 1970: 435 fig. 428.

existing hypothetical 'Arsacid text' but would have been taken down at dictation from 'carefully selected priests'.[347] The date of this development is debated, with views ranging between the fourth and sixth centuries AD.[348]

A possible, somewhat later, motive for putting the text of the *Avesta* in writing could have been that, following the Islamic conquest of Iran in the seventh century AD (Battle of Nihawand in AD 642 and murder of Yazdgird III, last Sasanian king, in AD 651), it would have become evident that 'Peoples of the Book', mainly Jews and Christians, were accorded better treatment than those without a book of their faith.[349]

The *Avesta* incorporates elements which probably go back to the second millennium BC[350] and, before it was recorded in writing, Zarathushtra's original, unelaborated, composition had been transmitted orally for many centuries.[351] Though Zarathushtra must have lived not later than the time of the Achaemenids, his actual dates are also much debated. W.B. Henning and R.C. Zaehner, place him in the seventh-sixth century BC,[352] H.W. Bailey dates him 'at least to 600 BC and probably to an earlier time',[353] while, on the basis of comparison of the archaic language of the Gāthās (the oldest part of the *Avesta*, hymns presumed to be compositions of Zarathushtra himself) with that of the Rigveda, M. Boyce argues for tentative dates in the second millennium, proposing variously and successively c.1400-1000 BC,[354] c.1700-1500 BC,[355] 1500-1300 BC[356] or 1400-1200 BC.[357]

---

347. Henning 1942: 48 = 1977: 159.
348. Henning 1942: 44 = 1977: 155 ('possibly in the fourth century'); Frye 1983: 162 (the special script was probably developed already in the time of Shapur II (309-379AD); Duchesne-Guillemin 1962: 45 (fourth century); Boyce and Grenet 1991: 16 (fifth or sixth century); see Bailey 1943: 172, 176 (mid-sixth century); Hintze 1998: 156-57 (probably not as early as the fourth century). See also Christensen 1944: 141-42, 515-17.
349. See e.g. Spuler 1995: 27-29.
350. See e.g. by Skjærervø 2007: 105-42, with proposed chronological chart 138.
351. Bailey 1943: 158-66.
352. Henning 1951: 43; Zaehner 1961: 33, 73.
353. Bailey 1943: 172.
354. Boyce 1975: 190-91. Such early dating of the *Avesta* is not new, see e.g. Moulton 1911: 48-49.
355. Boyce 1979: 18.
356. Boyce 1984a: I: 280.
357. Boyce 1984b: 22; Duchesne-Guillemin (1962: 135-38) questions the validity of dating one language by comparison with a neighbouring one, since languages, e.g. Danish and German, evolve at different speeds, and he cautiously favours a date near to the sixth century BC.

The name of the founder of Zoroastrianism appears as *Zaraθuštra* in the *Avesta*,[358] and as *Zōroastēr* in Greek texts. The name does not occur in the Old Persian inscriptions, but Gershevitch has suggested a hypothetical Old Persian *zara-uštra* going back to an original meaning 'camel-driver'.[359]

Appendix IV
Notes on the Word Apadāna

The word a*padāna* has been translated in various ways: 'temple (or edifice)' (Norris); '*salle d'apparat, salle du trône*' (Dieulafoy);[360] '*Säulenhalle*' (Weissbach); '*Schloss, Palast*' (Bartholomae);[361] 'palace' (Kent); 'royal audience hall', applied to the columned hall at Persepolis (Herzfeld);[362] and '*Palast, Säulenhalle, Audienzsaal*' (Brandenstein and Mayrhofer).[363]

An important clue to the meaning of this word is found in a trilingual inscription of Artaxerxes II (A²Sa) discovered in 1852 by W.K. Loftus in a columned building at Susa.[364] This inscription, repeated in varying states of preservation on four column bases, begins with the name of Artaxerxes (II) followed by his titles and ancestry – son (Old Persian *puça*) of Darius (II), son of Artaxerxes (I), son of Xerxes (I), son of Darius (I, the Great), son of Hystaspes, son of Achaemenes[365] – and goes on to say that 'Darius my great-great-grandfather (Old Persian *apaniyāka*) built (*akunaš*) this (*imam*) Apadana (*apadāna*)', that it was later burned and that he, Artaxerxes, had (re-)built (*akunām*) it.[366] In this, *akunaš* and

---

358. Bartholomae 1904: cols 1670-76; on the name, see also Mayrhofer 1977b: 105-106 no 416.
359. Gershevitch 1964: 38.
360. Dieulafoy 1884: II: 22.
361. Bartholomae 1904: col. 74.
362. E.g. Herzfeld 1935: 94: 'OP. *apadāna*, "royal audience hall"'.
363. Brandenstein and Mayrhofer 1964: 104.
364. Loftus 1857: 364-80, plan of the building on 366 (the four inscriptions marked 1-4) the inscriptions described, 370-72.
365. It may be noted that since Hystaspes was the son of Arsames, the son of Ariaramnes, the son of Teispes, the son of Achaemenes, in this context *puça*, 'son', had the meaning, great-great-grandson, or in other words 'descendant'. Similarly, Hebrew *bēn*, 'son', sometimes had the meaning 'grandson' (e.g. H. Haag, 'bēn' in Botterweck, Ringgren and Fabry, 1974-2006: II: 145-59, specifically 150 §2).
366. Text (A²Sa) in Kent 1953: 113, 154 (Old Persian transliteration, English translation); Weissbach 1911: 122-25 (Old Persian, Elamite and Babylonian transliteration, German translation); Mayrhofer 1978: 30-31 §7.1 (new

akunām are forms of the verb *kar-*, 'to do, make, build', which occurs also in Avestan *kar-*, 'to make',[367] so the sense 'rebuilt' is a reasonable rendering in the second occurrence. The core of the building referred to consisted of 36 columns in six rows of six, the inscriptions being located on the bases of four columns, two in the centre of each of the two northern rows, that is to say, forming a square at the north side. The details of the building were clarified in further excavations 30 years later (1884-86) by M. Dieulafoy who concluded that the 36 columns were probably placed within three walls on the west, north and east, outside which there were three double rows of six columns, and, on the basis of later analogies, he argued that the columned area was open to the south. He interpreted the four inscribed bases as marking the location of a throne, and he therefore described the building as a Throne Room.[368] It is now clear, however, that the south of the columned area was not open but that, as in the palace of Xerxes at Persepolis, it had a southern wall with a double entrance in the centre which led to a corridor connecting with the main palace of Darius.[369] The inscriptions clearly indicate that this building, or part of it, was known as an *apadāna*, written *a-p-d-a-n* in Old Persian, transcribed in the Elamite verson as *ha-ba-da-na* and Babylonian as *ap-pa-da-an*. This columned building forms a northern extension (rebuilt by Artaxerxes II after the fire described in his inscription A²Sa) of the

---

fragments found in 1958 and 1963, giving improved readings); Kuhrt 2007: 364-65 §9.22 (English translation); Lecoq 1997: 272-73 (French translation); early translation by E. Norris in Loftus 1857: 372. On Old Persian *ima-* 'this', see Kent 1953: 68-69 §199, and 174; Brandenstein and Mayrhofer 1964: 67, 127. Early discussion of the word 'apadana' in Dieulafoy 1884: 22-23 n. 1; Perrot and Chipiez 1890: 663-64 (quoting Darmesteter, 1883: II: 133).

367. Kent 1953: 179; Bartholomae 1904: cols 444-48.

368. Dieulafoy 1892: 323-58, with 342 fig. 221 (restored plan of the building, marking the inscribed column bases, with the Old Persian version facing the south), pl. XIV (elevation from the south, showing a suggested throne installation at the northern end), with *ibid.*, II (1890), pl. II (folding plan of the main tell); brief report on excavations in 1968-69 by Perrot 1970: 193-94, with pl. XIIb (view to south along western wall), c (view to east across northern and eastern wall); 1969-70 season in Perrot 1972: 181 with pl. IX; 1971 season in Perrot 1972: 183, with plan of the palace of Darius including Apadana (182 fig. 1); see also R. Boucharlat in Curtis (ed.) 1997: 57-60 with figs 22 (plan of the whole site), 23 (plan of the palace of Darius with Apadana), 24 (isometric view of the same); and Harper, Aruz and Tallon 1992, for a serviceable plan of the main tell at Susa (xvii fig.3), and useful description of the buildings by O.W. Muscarella, 216-19.

369. As, e.g., in Lecoq 1997: pl. 18; Harper et al. (eds) 1992: xvii fig.3; E. Porada in Gershevitch (ed.) 1985a: 807 fig. 6.

larger palace of Darius I at Susa, which itself occupies the northern part of the tell, and in which there was a small chamber with twelve columns but no large columned hall.

The word *apadāna* occurs in only one other Achaemenian inscription, also of Artaxerxes II (A²Ha), again trilingual, which was acquired by the British Museum in 1893. This consists of parts of two different rounded column bases of dark grey limestone from Hamadan, ancient Ecbatana the Median capital which remained an important city in Achaemenian times. One of these (BM.90854) has the end of a six-line Elamite version and a substantial part of a five-line Babylonian version (with the end missing), and the other (BM.90855) has the end of a five-line Babylonian version and a substantial part of a seven-line Old Persian version (with the end missing).[370] The distribution of the text of the Babylonian version shows that these fragments are from two different columns, demonstrating the, perhaps rather trivial, point that they were from a building with at least two columns. There have been archaeological investigations of different kinds at Tappeh-i Hekmataneh (or Tell Hagmatana), the ancient mound of Ecbatana, which lies in the built-up area of modern Hamadan, most recently by an Iranian team which found mudbrick buildings but uncovered no ground plan of a columned building.[371] So, though these inscriptions demonstrate that there was a building there containing at least two columns identifying it as part of an *apadāna*, there is no indication of what form it took or where it was situated.

---

370. Text A²Ha: first known from a photograph (noted by Pinches 1885: 132-33; the photograph, showing the inscriptions upside down, was subsequently published in Dieulefoy 1890-93: 389 fig. 236); the text then published while in private hands (Evetts 1890: 410-17); and subsequently Weissbach 1911: xxviii, 126-27 (who points out [126, note b] that the distribution of signs in the Babylonian text on the two fragments shows that they are from two different columns; a point already recognised by him in Geiger and Kuhn 1896-1904: 61 §20); Kent 1953: 114, 155; Lecoq 1997: 269; and see Knapton, Saraf and Curtis 2001: 99-117, specifically 102-104; Curtis and Tallis 2005: 61 nos 10 and 11 (with colour photographs); Kuhrt 2007: 2: 554-55 no 37, translation, with fig. 11.13 (499) (treating the two fragments as part of a single column). Hinz proposes the restoration of the word *apadāna* also in two imperfectly preserved inscriptions of Darius II from Susa (D²Sa and D²Sc; 1941: 249-51 and 253-55), and Kent accepts this restoration in D²Sa (1953: 154) but not in Hinz's D²Sc (= Scheil 1929: 40-41 no 5), which he assigns to Darius I as DSg (1953: 110, 144), and the restoration of *apadāna* in both is rightly questioned by Lecoq (1997: 114 and 115), and may be dismissed from the present consideration.

371. Summary of discoveries by Brown 1998: 80-81; and Knapton, Saraf and Curtis 2001: 106-109, 113-14 with plans at figs 6 (107) and, in more detail, 4 (105); also, Kleiss 1975: 76-77, fig. 3 (schematic plan of the site).

Possible light on the meaning of the word might be found in the occurrence of the form *'pdn* in a number of Parthian ostraca of the first century BC from Nisā (ancient Mithradātkert), the original Parthian capital, situated near the modern village of Bagir in the north-eastern foothills of the Kopet Dagh, about eight miles from Ashkabad in southern Turkmenistan. This site consists of two parts, both occupied in the Parthian period: New Nisā, the main city which has been excavated by Russian expeditions;[372] and Old Nisā, probably a royal residence with palaces, temples and tombs, excavated more recently by an Italian expedition.[373] Both sites, particularly Old Nisā, had columned buildings, demonstrating the use of this kind of architecture in the area. The ostraca, mostly from New Nisā, are receipts for tax in kind (*'wzbry*)[374] in the form of wine (*ḥmr*) from estates and vineyards, probably royal foundations let out to private persons.[375] Among these taxes are some from a vineyard (*krm'*) on an estate (*bn'*) referred to as *'pdn*.[376] In this context *'pdn* is assumed by the editors of the texts to have had the meaning 'palace',[377] and it might indicate that the rural residence of the estate was a substantial

---

372. Pugačenkova 1958.

373. Invernizzi 2007: 163-77; also, summary by Schlumberger 1983: 1037-41, with fig. 5; and earlier in Schlumberger 1970: 34-39.

374. On this, see Lukonin 1983: 744.

375. See Lukonin 1983: 659-60.

376. Transliterations and translations in Diakonoff and Livshits 1976: nos 1-34. These texts are in Middle Persian written in a script derived from the Aramaic alphabet of the Achaemenian period, but the words *ḥmr, krm'* and *bn'* are Aramaic logograms, that is to say they are written in Aramaic but would have been read in Persian as *mad* (*maδ*), *raz*, and *dastkird* respectively (Gignoux 1972: 52, 55 and 49), in the same way as *viz.* (abbreviation of Latin *videlicet*) would be read by an educated English speaker as 'that is to say'. These are examples of a Middle Persian writing practice known as *huzwāreš, uzwārišn* or *zavarishn*, under which, by the Sasanian period, Persian words were written with Aramaeograms (Aramaic logograms), that is to say with their Aramaic equivalents but read as Persian (*ḥmr* to be read as *mad* etc.). There is clear evidence (absence of Aramaic loanwords in New Persian etc.) which shows that by this date the scribes had no knowledge of the Aramaic language, and that for them the forms were simply graphic representations of the Persian words (therefore reasonably described as heterograms). On the evidence for this conclusion, and the writing convention in general, see Durkin-Meisterernst 2004: 585-88; and, for an older discussion, with the same conclusion, on the basis of the more limited evidence available a century ago, see Browne 1902: 66-67, 72-77.

377. Diakonoff and Livshits 1976: I: 10; also Gignoux 1972: 46. On later forms of the word, see Henning 1942: 40-56, specifically 110 n. 1 = 1977: 151-67, specifically 195 n. 1.

columned building. This can be no more than speculation, but it would allow the possibility that the word referred to a columned building, less formal than those at Susa and Ecbatana.

One point to consider in this matter is the fact that, while the column base A²Sa identifies the building of which it was part as an *apadāna*, a different, inscribed column base from Susa (A²Sd) is identified in the Old Persian text as part of 'this hadish' (*imām hadiš*), where *hadiš* had the meaning 'seat, abode, palace' or the like.[378] The precise find spot of this column is not recorded, so the type of building involved cannot be defined. The noun *hadiš* is found also in a trilingual inscription of Xerxes on the portico and the terrace of the palace of Darius at Persepolis (XPc), which refers to 'this palace' (*ima hadiš*) built by Darius,[379] and where the Babylonian equivalent of *hadiš* is *bītu* (*bi-it a-ga-a*, literally 'house this'), a very general term. This palace of Darius is a building with columns but quite different in plan from that with columns labelled *apadāna* at Susa. The noun *hadiš* is found also in the Foundation Charter of Darius at Susa (DSf),[380] referring to the palace described in that text, but fragments were found scattered all over the site[381] so it cannot be associated with

---

378. Kent 1953: 213; Bartholomae 1904: col. 1759, '*Wohnsitz, Palast*'; and col. 1753 (from ¹*had-*, '*sich setzen*' – 'to sit'); Brandenstein and Mayrhofer 1964: 122, '*Palast, Residenz, Pfalz*' (imperial palace) etc.; Hinz 1973: 135, '*Palast*', literally '*Sitz*' (seat), from *had-*, '*sich setzen*'. This inscription is known also in one of the clay tablet fragments mentioned above, see n. 51. Of interest from the Biblical point of view is the fact that this inscription goes on to say that the building would be for Artaxerxes a *paradayadām* (*p-r-d-y-d-a-m*), a word found in Avestan as *pairidaēza-*, perhaps '(walled) enclosure' (Bartholomae 1904 col. 865; Kent 1953: 195, 'pleasant retreat'; Hinz 1975: 179, under *pardaiδa-*, favouring the sense 'domain' (*Domäne*); Brandenstein and Mayrhofer 1964: 137 (under *paridaida-*, '*Lustgarten, Wildpark*'). Lecoq questions the reading *p-r-d-y-d-a-m* and proposes **p-r-i-d-i-d-a-m*, **pari-daidām*, with some such meaning as 'I have consecrated' (1990: 209-11; and 1997: 116), but in Scheil's hand-copy of the text the reading is clearly *p-r-d-y-d-a-m* (1929: 91). Gershevitch 1964: 34 suggests that the form (**paridaidā-*) is best explained as a 'transposition into cuneiform characters' of an Aramaic **prdyd*. The word *pairidaēza* was borrowed in the Old Testament as *pardēs* (Nehemiah 2:8, and also perhaps by way of later scribal revision in Song of Solomon 4:13 and Ecclesiastes 2:5), and as *paradeisos* in Greek texts already in the early fourth century BC (Xenophon), in the Septuagint (Genesis 2:15; 3:23; 13:10; Isaiah 51:3 etc.), and in the New Testament at Luke 23:43; 2 Corinthians 12:4; Revelation 2:7 (see Danker 2010: 761; J. Jeremias in Kittel (ed), 1964-76: V: 765-73).

379. Weissbach 1911: xxiv, 110-13; Kent 1953: 112, 149; Lecoq 1997: 253.

380. On which (inscription DSf) see n. 415 below.

381. Scheil 1921: 4.

any one building. There the Babylonian equivalent is *e-kal a-ga-a*, 'this *ēkallu*,'[382] where *ēkallu* (from Sumerian *é.gal*, 'big house') usually had the meaning 'palace'. This evidence of usage suggests that *hadiš* was a general term which could be applied to any kind of large building, including, but not specifically, an *apadāna*.[383]

The etymology of *apadāna* has been a matter of debate.[384] The Old Persian writing system consists mainly of consonantal signs followed by inherent vowels[385] but it includes separate signs for the three vowels *a*, *i* and *u*, which are taken within a word to indicate vowel length. In the form *a-p-d-a-n* (traditionally transliterated *a-pᵃ-dᵃ-a-nᵃ*) the element *-d-a-* (or *-dᵃ-a-*) is normalised as *-dā-*, but the Old Persian script had no way of distinguishing between *a-* and *ā-* at the beginning of a word,[386] so this spelling might have represented either *apadāna* or *āpadāna*. In the specially devised Avestan script (which was an augmented version of the Pahlavi alphabet, itself derived from the Aramaic script of the Achaemenian period) there are separate characters for *a* and *ā*, and one possibility proposed for the interpretation of the word is that the first element *ap-* might have represented *āp-*, 'water', common in Avestan and later Iranian languages.[387] Concerning the element *-dāna*, possible suggested interpretations include: (a) 'receptacle', from the base *dhā-*,[388] which might lead to some such meaning as 'reservoir'; or (b) 'building, house, structure', from the base *dam-*, 'to build',[389] which might lead to a meaning like 'water shrine'.[390]

---

382. Convenient synoptic transliteration, in Herzfeld 1938: 13, lines 22 and 16, respectively.
383. This was already the conclusion of Dieulafoy 1884: 2: 23 in n. 1. A third word found in reference to buildings in Old Persian inscriptions, *tačara*, is usually taken to mean 'palace': Kent, 'palace' (1953: 186); Hinz, '*Palast*' (1975: 231); Brandenstein and Mayrhofer, '*etwa Wohnpalast, Privatpalast*' (perhaps dwelling-palace, private palace) with further references (1964: 144); Lecoq suggests possibly a corridor or entrance portico (1997: 101, with discussion of both *hadiš* and *tačara*).
384. See, e.g., Lecoq 1997: 115.
385. See n. 9 above.
386. Kent 1953: 13 §21.
387. Bartholomae 1904: cols 325-29 (because the word *auten* does not occur in the *Avesta*, and Bartholomae could only cite Old Persian references, it is entered in his *Wörterbuch* with a short initial vowel *a-* [col.74]); see also Brandenstein and Mayrhofer 1964: 103 (*ap-*, '*Wasser*'); and Boyce, '*āb*' in 1985: 27.
388. Zaehner 1961: 159, 331; Brandenstein and Mayrhofer 1964: 114, **dhā-na-* (under *daivadāna-*).
389. Gershevitch 1964: 35, Appendix VIII.
390. I owe this suggestion to Dr Sharokh Razmjou.

Possible support for this idea might be found in the statement in both A²Sa and A²Ha that the apadāna was built by the favour of Ahura Mazda, Anahita and Mithra. Anahita and Mithra both predated the introduction of Zoroastrianism but were brought in due course into the official pantheon. Anahita was particularly associated with water[391] and Mithra had an early association with water, though his main attributes – contract, war etc. – were different.[392] However, Ahura Mazda (the supreme god)[393] had no special association with water and the building at Susa which is most clearly associated with the word *apadāna* is on the ancient tell and not immediately at a natural water source – though water could, of course, have been brought to it on donkey back from the River Shaur which runs not far from the tell.[394] It is perhaps relevant to note that, while in the Susa Apadana column base inscriptions (A²Sa) all three of these god's names are written with a preceding divine determinative (DINGIR = *ilu*), in the Hamadan column base text (A²Ha) it is written only with Ahura Mazda and Mithra but not with Anahita (*an-na-i-tu*),[395] suggesting a not very high view of Anahita at the site. These points do not give strong support to such an interpretation. More recent French excavations (1973, 1975 and 1976) have exposed another palace at Susa, in the plain to the west of the main tell on the further side of the River Shaur. Seven fragments of inscribed column bases found in the remains show that this was built, at least in part, by Artaxerxes II. These inscriptions are in Old Persian, Elamite and Babylonian and all but one

391. Boyce 1985: 1003-1006; and, briefly, Schwartz in Gershevitch (ed.) 1985a: 2: 670-71; Anāhitā is mentioned particularly in the Avestan Yasht 5 which came to be called the Ābān Yašt, the 'Hymn to the Waters', literally 'waters hymn'. In it she is referred to as Arĕdvī Sūrā Anāhitā, Anāhitā having been merged by the time of the Achaemenian period with the goddess Arĕdvī Sūrā, literally 'humid mighty' or the like (Boyce 1982: I: 71-75); see also Malandra 1983: 117-30, introduction and translation of Yasht 5; and the earlier translation with introduction by Darmesteter 1884: 52-84.

392. See, e.g., Gershevitch 1959: 26-44; Boyce 1982: I: 25-31; also, briefly, on Mithra, Schwartz in Gershevitch 1985a: 2: 670; also Malandra 1983: 55-75, introduction and translation of Yasht 10 (the Mihr Yašt, 'Hymn to Mithra'); and the earlier translation with introduction by Darmesteter in 1884: 119-158 (Mihir Yast).

393. On Ahura Mazda see, conveniently, Schwartz in Gershevitch 1985a: 667-68.

394. The Shaur is a small river that rises close to, and is probably fed from, the Karkhah, a little over three miles (five kilometres) north of Susa, and runs close to the west of the mound and into the Ab-i-Diz, a tributary of the River Karun (on this, see le Rider 1965: 262-63, with map 256; and Ghirshman 1950: 218-19, with map 207).

395. This is the case on both fragments (Weissbach 1911: 127 (BM.90854) and 126 n.b (BM.90854).

bears the text already known as A²Sd, the name Artaxerxes being found complete in an Old Persian fragment (*a-r-t-ḫ-š-ç-a*) and mostly complete in an Elamite fragment (*ir-tak-ik-šá-áš-*).³⁹⁶ The word *apadāna* does not occur in them, and in any case none of them is associated with any specific part of the structure. Though these were not found *in situ*, it is probable that they appertain to the principal building uncovered, which had 64 columns in eight rows of eight.³⁹⁷

A similar situation might possibly have obtained at Ecbatana. The Greek historian Polybius, writing in the second century BC, refers to a temple or shrine (*naos*) of Anahita (*ainēs*) there (*The Histories* 10:27:12)³⁹⁸, and he says in reference to the top or citadel (*akran*) of the city that 'under this there was a palace' (*hupo de tautēn 'esti basileia*) (10:27:6-7).³⁹⁹ He refers to columns (*kionas*) in the porticoes (*stoais*) and collonades (*perustulois*) in the building complex (*The Histories* 10:27:10, also 12), so it would be quite plausible for a *naos*, whether a temple or just a shrine,⁴⁰⁰ to have stood within such a complex. It has been suggested that this passage might have referred to a building beside the Nazar Beyk watercourse which flows round the east side of Tappeh-i Hekmataneh, the main mound.⁴⁰¹ Polybius describes this palace as a complex of buildings occupying an area about seven stades in circumference, something amounting to not much short of four-fifths of a mile around.⁴⁰² The Tappeh-i Hekmataneh mound is only a little over

---

396. Vallat, 1979: 145-54, specifically 146 (= fig. 43) nos 7 and 5, respectively.
397. Boucharlot and Labrousse 1979: 19-136, with folding plan fig. 37; also, briefly, Boucharlat in Curtis (ed.) 1997: 61-62. Lecoq cites a suggestion of M.-J. Steve that the Old Persian form *p-r-d-y-d-a-m* (on which see n. 379 above) which occurs in the text of Artaxerxes II (A²Sd) might be analysed as 'outside' (*para-*) 'wall' (*didām*), i.e. 'extra-mural', and to have referred to this newly excavated palace, but he, Lecoq, objects, probably rightly, that this word occurs in a context that requires a noun and not an adjective ('extra-mural') or adverb ('extra-murally').
398. On Anaitis, Anaia and Ainēs as Hellenised forms of Anahita, see Walbank 1967: 235.
399. The text, conveniently, in Paton 1925: 166-67, where 'under' (*hupo*), 'this' (*auten*), referring back to 'top, height, citadel' or the like (*akra* in the accusative), has the sense 'under', even 'towards under'; on *basileia*, see Mauersberger 1956: cols 316-317, under *basileios*, B (2; neuter), *basileia* being neuter plural.
400. For the usage of *naos* in Greek texts, see a convenient summary by O. Michel in Kittel (ed.) 1964-76: IV: 880-81.
401. Knapton, Sarraf and Curtis, 2001: 114 and 100, with a translation of the whole passage, and citation of Hellenistic and Parthian references to a temple of Anaitis at the site.
402. Taking the *stadion* as about 606.75 feet (185 metres), 7 x 606.75 = 4,247.25 feet (1,295 metres), about 80 per cent of a mile.

half a mile long and, taking the width from the bank of the watercourse, a little over a quarter of a mile wide,[403] making the circumference of the whole mound only about a mile and a half, so the palace complex would have had to be very much smaller for the possibility of a shrine of Anahita by the water to make sense. This text relates of course to the Hellenistic period, so, assuming the dimensions to be accurate, a palace complex could well have been enlarged since Achaemenid times. This might support the connection of Anahita with a columnned building near water but it remains highly speculative.

Appendix V
An Aspect of the Geography of the Achaemenid Empire
The Place Names hst, srk *and* prkn *on Green Chert Objects from Persepolis*

This point does not have a direct relation to the Old Testament, but it does illustrate the extent of the Empire of which Judah was a part. The Achaemenid Empire extended over a very large area and, apart from knowledge of the 'Royal Road' which ran from Susa to Sardis and which, according to Herodotus, took about three months to traverse,[404] and a probable route from Ecbatana to Bactria, there is little contemporary information about the details of other travel within it. Some indication of what was possible in the late fourth century BC is found in lives of Alexander the Great which record routes he and contingents of his forces followed in Asia, though what was feasible for military expeditions may not always have been suitable for regular trade connections. It is perhaps more realistic, therefore, to take the evidence of Arab geographers of the Abbasid period as indicative of the main earlier travel routes. From this evidence it can be seen, for instance, that travel from Kandahar to Persepolis was fairly straightforward, by way of Zaranj, the Great Desert (Dasht-i Lût), Kirman, Sirjan and Shiraz,[405] a journey which, however, would probably have taken over a month.[406]

It is possible to argue that *hst*, *srk* and *prkn* are the names of places from which the green chert mortars, pestles and dishes were passed first to Arachosia and then to Persepolis, so it is appropriate to consider possible locations at which this mineral might have been found. The

---

403. About 930 yards (850 metres) long by about 490 yards (450 metres) wide as measured on the plan.

404. Herodotus, *The Histories*, 5:52-53; also 8.98 (on couriers), and Xenophon, *Cyropaedia*, 8:6:17-18. See Cook 1983: 107-109, with (rather crude) map, fig. 13 (181); Burn 1962: 111-12; also, on this and subsequent communication systems in the Hellenistic and Roman periods, Klauck 2006: 61-63.

405. See le Strange 1905: 10-11, with map I (opp. 1).

406. Bernard 1972: 165-76, specifically 168 n. 6.

stone is described in the excavation report as 'hard green stone which has been identified as impure chert' where the 'green colour is caused by impurities such as clay and probably glauconite'.[407] One standard reference work defines chert as 'layers or irregular concretions of chalcedonic silica occurring, usually, in limestone formations'[408] and other sources indicate that chert is to be found as nodules in sedimentary rocks.[409] P. Bernard quotes Sayyid Hachem Mirzad, former Director of Mines in Afghanistan, as stating that this kind of stone (green chert) is found in modern Kandahar, Helmand and Farah Provinces,[410] each of which includes, in the north, the outliers of the Hindu Kush.

The Hindu Kush is part of a young fold mountain system, running through the Alps, Greece, Turkey, Persia and the Himalayas, which was formed by the thrusting of the African geological plate against the Eurasian plate causing the folding of stratified rocks, many of them limestone (the Alpine Orogeny of the Tertiary Era).[411] It is a reasonable speculation that outcrops of green chert are to be found in different locations throughout this fold mountain system. If this analysis is correct, the sources of the material used for the Persepolis objects could well have been in this same geological formation. It is reported, for instance, that in modern times in the Farghana Valley north of the Hindu Kush there have been discoveries of 'quantities of valuable non-ferrous and other mineral resources'.[412]

The question is somewhat complicated by the fact that the Aramaic inscriptions use two different words to qualify the word *gll*, 'stone', which refers to the material on which they are written.[413] These words, *kptwk* (once on a mortar) and *'hšynpyn* (on three mortars and one pestle), are Old Persian loanwords, from *kapautaka* and *ahšaina*, respectively, probably indicating colour. The Old Persian forms are both otherwise known from a trilingual inscription describing the building of the palace of Darius

---

407. Schmidt 1957: 53, this identification having been provided by Mrs Hans Ramberg.
408. Wyatt 1986: 51.
409. See, e.g., B. Aston, J. Harrell and I. Shaw, in Nicholson and Shaw 2000: 28-29 and Table 2.5 (21); Kirkaldy 1971: 195-96; and Smith 1962: 427-30; 1972: 430-35.
410. Bernard 1972: 165-76, specifically 173-74 with ns 8 and 1.
411. See, e.g., map in Kirkaldy 1971: fig. XV.7 (234), the area stippled; the geological plates can be further analysed as the African pushing, in turn, against an Arabian, an Iranian and then the Eurasian plate.
412. Caroe 1967: 21.
413. *Gll* is cognate with Biblical Aramaic *gĕlāl*, 'stone block', found in Ezra 5:8; 6:4, and with Hebrew *gal*, 'pile', as used in the place-name *haggilgāl*, 'the pile of stones', being the place where the Hebrews first crossed the Jordan (Joshua 4:19-24), (Koehler and Baumgartner 2001: II: 1845, and I: 190-91, respectively), rendered 'Gilgal' in English Versions.

at Susa (DSf), sometimes referred to as the Susa Foundation Charter,[414] where each term defines a semi-precious stone (*kāsaka*).[415] In the Babylonian version the equivalent of *kāsaka hya kapautaka*[416] ('kapatauka stone') is [aban]*uqnu*, usually taken as 'lapis lazuli', but in some contexts possibly 'turquoise',[417] a material which can range in colour through green, greenish-blue and blue to grey. Such a meaning for *gll kptwk* may find support from Middle Persian *kapōt* and New Persian *kabūd*, both of which have the meaning 'blue', and Sanskrit *kapóta*, 'pigeon, dove',[418] pointing, perhaps, to 'blue-grey' or 'grey'. The inscription (DSf) gives the source of this material as Sogdia (Sugda),[419] an area in the western outliers of the

---

414. Inscription D(arius)S(usa)f (known from various fragments) [the words in question occur: *kapautaka* in line 37, *aḫšaina* in line 39]: Scheil 1929: 3-34 ('*Charte de fondation du palais*'; transliteration, translation and commentary of the three versions); Herzfeld 1931: 29-81 (copies of the three versions, pls V-VII; interlinear transliterations, translations and commentary) [II, '*Die Gatha des Dareios*', speculates on the literary form of the inscription]; Herzfeld 1938: 13-17, the relevant passage on 15 (revised presentation, with copy of Old Persian version only); Kent 1953: 110, 142-44; Brandenstein and Mayrhofer 1964: 86-87 (transliteration); H.W. Bailey in Arberry 1953: 179-80 (transliteration, translation and mention of occurrences of some words in later Iranian languages); Brown 1969: 199-201 no 127 (introduction and translation); Steve 1974: 135-61 (new fragments of the text with resulting transliteration of Old Persian [145-47] and Babylonian [155-57], with translation of the Babylonian text [158-59], passages relevant to *kapautaka* and *aḫšaina* on 146, 157, 159); Lecoq 1997: 234-37 (French translation set out in fourteen sense sections without line numbers, the relevant passage in §10; see also 111-12); Wiesehöfer 1996: 26-27 (English translation); M.W. Stolper in Harper, Aruz and Tallon (eds) 1992: 271-72 no 190 (with photograph of the best preserved Old Persian copy: Louvre Sb.2789); Curtis and Tallis 2005: 56 no 1 (with colour photograph of Louvre Sb.2789 and English translation)
415. Brandenstein and Mayrhofer 1964: 130.
416. Scheil 1929: 8-9 (Babylonian lines 26-27) 18-19 (Old Persian, lines 37-38); Herzfeld 1938: 15 (transliteration of all three versions interlinearly); the Elamite version has *ka₄-si-ka₄ ap-pa ka₄-ba-u-da-ka₄*, simply repeating the Old Persian (*ap-pa = hya*, 'this').
417. See von Soden 1959-81: III: 1426 ('*Lapislazuli, Lasurstein, Türkis*', ('*grün-blau*'); Black, George and Postgate 1999: 424-25; Campbell Thompson 1936: 129-32; Lecoq proposes '*la turquoise bleue* (?)' (1997: 236); CAD: U and W: 195-202 (lapis lazuli).
418. Kent 1953: 178; Hinz 1975: 147; Brandenstein and Mayrhofer 1964: 129, and the text, DSf, line 37 (87); Mayrhofer 1953-76: I: 157-58; 1992-2001: I: 303, *kapóta-*.
419. At this point in the text another stone is mentioned, also originating in Sogdia, Old Persian *s-i-k-b-r-u-š* (*sinkabruš*) (Kent 1953: 209, 'carnelian'; Brandenstein and Mayrhofer 1964: 142, '*eine Edelsteinart*', with other references; Elamite

Hindu Kush, mainly on the middle course of the Oxus (Amu Darya) River, which includes Badakshan, known today as a rich source of lapis lazuli,[420] a stone which is found, sometimes as nodules, in association with limestone deposits which have been impregnated with intrusive igneous rock.[421] In the same way the inscription gives the Babylonian equivalent of *kāsaka hya aḫšaina*[422] ('*aḫšaina* stone') as [aban]*šadānu*, commonly taken to have been 'haematite',[423] though it did not always have precisely this meaning, as is shown by an inscribed 'magnetite' duck-weight which describes itself as made of *šadānu*.[424] It is not appropriate to expect strict consistency in ancient identifications and in this case both types of stone are mainly black in colour. Comparison of the Old Persian form with Avestan *aḫšaēna*, 'dark colour'[425] and cognate forms in Middle Iranian languages (Khotanese, Tocharian) which have the meaning 'pigeon, dove'[426] have led to the suggestion that *gll 'ḫšynpyn* was 'turquoise'.[427] The inscription gives the source of *aḫšaina* stone as Chorasmia (Huvarazmi). The core area of Chorasmia lay in the delta of the Oxus on the south of the Aral Sea and on the lower course of the river, an alluvial area unlikely to have been the

ši-in-qa-ab-ru-iš (Hinz and Koch 1987: II: 1138, '*Karneol*'), Babylonian [aban]*šingabrû* (CAD: Ṣ: 200 '(a precious stone, carnelian?)'; Black, George and Postgate 1999: 338, 'a red stone'.

420. Herrmann 1968: 21-57, with useful discussion of the sources of the stone, 22-29.

421. Bauer 1968: II: 438-45; McClintock 1983: 66-67; Börner 1962: 225-26; Smith 1962: 436-38; 1972: 444-47.

422. Scheil 1929: 8-9 (Babylonian, lines 27-28) 18-19 (Old Persian, line 39); Herzfeld 1938: 15. The Elamite version has ka_4-*si*-ka_4 *ap-pa ak-še-na*, again simply repeating the Old Persian.

423. CAD: Š: I: 36-38; Campbell Thompson 1936: 85-88. It may be noted that, like chert, haematite is found in limestone formations (Kirkaldy 1971: 194-95).

424. George 1979: 134 mo. 47.

425. Bartholomae 1904: col. 51.

426. Brandenstein and Mayrhofer 1964: 101. Another possible indication arises from the likelihood that this word was borrowed in Greek in the designation of the Black Sea as *pontos axeinos*, 'dark(-coloured) sea', a place name misunderstood by subsequent Greek-speakers as 'sea' (*pontos*) 'without' (*a-*) 'foreigner' (*xeinos*) = 'inhospitable sea', and consequently modified to *pontos euxeinos*, 'hospitable sea' (*eu-* ['good'] *xeinos* ['foreigner']). This may be concluded from the statement, for instance, of the Latin author Ovid, *dictus ab antiquis Axenus ille fuit*, 'from antiquity this was called Axenus' (*Tristia* 4:4:55-56; trans A.L. Wheeler, [Loeb Classical Library] [Cambridge, MA: Harvard University Press; and London: W. Heinemann, 1924] 181-82), pointing in that case to a dark blue(-green) sense.

427. Kent 1953: 165; Hinz 1975: 25; Brandenstein and Mayrhofer 1964: 101, and the text, DSf, line 39 (87).

source of any kind of stone, but at times it included some parts towards the east between the Oxus and Jaxartes, and also parts on the west in the Ustyurt plateau between the Aral and Caspian Seas.[428] It has also been noted that formerly the Oxus River had another arm which flowed into the Caspian Sea south of Krasnovodsk,[429] pointing to the possibility that at that time Chorasmia might have extended considerably further to the southwest.[430] If such an extension had included the geological formation of the Nebit Dagh near to Krasnovodsk on the east side of the Caspian, and the more substantial Kopet Dagh to the south-east, all part of the fold mountain system,[431] this could be a possibility. The likelihood of this as a source of minerals such as green chert could only be determined, however, by geological investigation.[432]

The use of these two Old Persian words in the inscription of Darius, the only instance of their occurrence in the known Old Persian texts, shows that in that context they referred to different materials, whereas in referring in Aramaic to the material of the green chert objects they can have referred only to variations in colour or some distinction of that kind. Moreover, the perception of colour is subjective, and it could be that the use of these terms in Aramaic merely reflects the impressions of different scribes. This illustrates the well known fact that there is often uncertainty in the definition of words for minerals, plants, animals and colours. Consistency is not to be expected on the part of scribes, not least because they may not have been well informed themselves about what they were describing.[433]

---

428. Knobloch 1972: 73 and map 4.
429. Marked in le Strange 1905: map I; and Gershevitch (ed.) 1985a: maps 11 and 16; Herzfeld mentions this branch of the river in a characteristically interesting discussion of Chorasmia (1968: 325).
430. Hinz 1941: 222-57, specifically 235-36.
431. On this range, Talish-Elburz-Northern Khorasan-Paropamisus-Hindu Kush, see Brice 1966: 177-83, area 3c, and maps figs 33 and 34.
432. As already indicated by Naveh and Shaked 1973: 457.
433. In the context of colour perception, it has been suggested that there was no specific word for 'blue' in Akkadian, Aramaic, Hebrew or Greek (Brenner 1982: 12 and 222 n. 37). The word 'blue' is used in many English Versions of the Bible particularly in accounts of the tabernacle (Exodus 25-28, 35-39), but this renders tĕkēlet which properly means 'purple' (Brenner 1982: 145-46). This suggestion needs some modification as far as Akkadian is concerned, however, since Akkadian uqniātum, uqnītum and uqnû might each have had the meaning 'blue' in some contexts (Black, George, Postgate 1999: 424-25). Though 'blue' may not have been represented in some word stocks, 'green' was well covered in each of these languages (Akkadian (w)arqu; Old Aramaic yrq; Hebrew yereq, yārôq [see Brenner 1982: 100-102; D. Kellerman, in Botterweck

These considerations of colour vocabulary do not affect the conclusion that, if the three names *hst*, *srk* and *prkn* refer to locations from which green chert objects were sent to Arachosia (Kandahar), they are likely to have been in the general Hindu Kush and related fold mountain system. With this in mind, it is reasonable to seek possible identifications with geographical names found in later written sources.[434] *Hst* could be identified with Khǎšt on the western border of Farghânah, partly in modern Uzbekistan, Tajikistan and Kyrgyzstan, ancient Sogdia, on the western extension of the Hindu Kush.[435] *Srk* could perhaps be identified with Sirōk (Sarakēnē, later Sarakhs) on the Tajand (later Herat) River, south-west of Merv (Marv) in ancient Margiana (in modern Turkmenistan) in the Nebit Dagh-Kopet Dagh area already mentioned and both therefore plausible mineral-producing areas.[436] For *prkn*, more than one possibility has been proposed: (a) the area of later Farghânah (more strictly Farġânah) again in the north-east,[437] postulating the sound changes |p>f|r|k>ġ|n|, where a p>f change is not improbable, and, while /k/, an unvoiced stop, and /ġ/ (*ġayn*), a voiced continuant, both of which can be classified as velars (articulated between the back of the tongue and the back part of the palate) is conceivable,[438] so a sound change k>ġ is not impossible; (b) the area of Bāriz Kūh south-east of Kirman, finding a correspondence between Parikanioi and Bāriz,[439] presumably assuming the sound changes |p>b|r|k>z|n>Ø|, where, while a change p>b and loss

and Ringgren (eds) 1974-2006: VI: 362-68]; and Greek *k^hlōros*) and might have served in contexts where in the west 'blue' would be a more appropriate rendering, so it is not reasonable to press colour terms too rigidly.

434. Conveniently discussed by Naveh and Shaked 1973: 446-48, who take up some suggestions considered but rejected by Bowman 1970: 20-22.

435. See le Strange 1905: 483, map IX (433); and Naveh and Shaked 1973: 447-48 on Khǎšt.

436. See le Strange 1905: 395-96, map VIII (335); for other possibilities of names see Naveh and Shaked 1973: 447 n. 9. On Margiana, Old Persian *Margu*, see briefly Lecoq 1997: 144; and Kent 1953: 202.

437. Frye 1962: 46, with 263 n. 63, citing Diakonov and Herzfeld 1968: 329-30 (placing the Parikanioi of Herodotus < Hecataeus in Farghānah; on the Parikanioi, see also proposal [c] below); and Naveh and Shaked (1973: 447 n. 16) cite a spelling of the name as *plk'n* in the *Greater Bundahišn* in the edition of Anklesaria and Anklesaria 1908: 87; presumably also to be seen in Anklesaria 1956, neither of these volumes was available in London. On the Bundahishn, see also D.N. MacKenzie, 'Bundahišn', in Yarshater (ed.) 1990: 547-51.

438. Beeston 1970: 18; see also a traditional description of the pronunciation, Wright 1896: 6 (ġ (ﻍ), a gutteral *g*), 7 (*k*, just like our *k*); and Bateson 1967: 4 (making a distinction between ġ as a velar, *k* as a palatal); the very small difference in point of articulation of the tongue with the back of the palate (palatal) or the velum (velar) can be seen, e.g., in Gleason 1961: 242 figure and 244 chart.

439. Bivar 1985: 25-42, specifically 30-35.

of a final /n/ is not improbable, the sound change k>z is improbable; or (c) the territory occupied by the Parikanioi mentioned by Herodotus (*The Histories* 3:92; 7:68, 86) who were perhaps located in the area of later Gedrosia, modern Makran,[440] situated to the south west of Arachosia.[441] Of these possible locations, *hst* and *srk* would have been connected with Arachosia (Kandahar) by plausible routes as known in Abbasid times: Khāšt via Samarkand, Bukhara and Merv to Herat; and Sirōk via Herat; and from there in both cases to Farah, then to Karnin, Khwash, Haruri, Bost[442] and eastwards to Kandahar.[443] The detour to the west, to the south then back to the east involved in this route would be required by the need to skirt round the western outliers of the Hindu Kush, and indeed between Merv and Herat the Ardewan Pass rises to about 4,800 feet (c.1526 metres).[444] Concerning the three proposed identifications for *prkn*: (a) Farghanah would be in the same general area as *hst* and *srk*; (b) Bāriz Kūh, in the vicinity of Kirman, would be near the route from Kandahar to Persepolis, entailing a journey to Kandahar and back again; and (c) there is no obviously direct route from Makran to Kandahar.[445] These considerations may suggest that, if *hst*, *srk* and *prkn* were outposts in the eastern empire, it is more probable that *prkn* is to be identified with Farghana – proposal (a) – in the same mountainous area as Khāšt (Ḥāšt)[446] and not far from Sirōk, rather than with the vicinity of Kirman (b) or Makran (c).

An alternative possibility concerning these three terms, *hst*, *srk* and *prkn*, is that they were not geographical locations in the Empire but referred simply to parts of the palace at Persepolis. This was proposed by I. Gershevitch, who argues that *hst* can be connected with *hasta-*, known in the Avestan compound form *pasuš.hasta*, 'sheep-fold' (where *pasuka-* = 'domesticated quadruped'[447]), and that this is etymologically related

440. As argued by Bernard 1972: 171-72; see also Hinz 1975: 179-80, who cites a possible connection with the New Persian place name Pargān in the area of Kerman/Makran mentioned in *Farhang-i juġrāfiā-yi Īrān*, a survey compiled by the Geographical Bureau of the Iranian Army (on which see Gershevitch et al. 1968: 187).

441. See, e.g., Lecoq 1997: 145, 152, and map, 14-15; map in Frye 1962: 257; references on the name, Schmitt 1967: 137 with n. 156; on Makran, le Strange 1905: 329-33, map VII (323).

442. On Bost, see Davary 1974: 201-208 (map of environs, 202); also, Fischer 1990: 383-85; and on modern Bost = Lashkargāh, le Strange 1905: 237.

443. See map in Brice 1966: 33 fig. 7.

444. Brice 1966: 28, 179-80; located at 34 43 N, 62 10 E.

445. On this area, Gedrosia, see Cary 1949: 194-96.

446. On this north-eastern area, see Cary 1949: 198-200 and map, 195; for travel routes in the Abbasid period, see le Strange 1905: map I (facing 1).

447. Bartholomae 1904: col. 880.

to Old Persian *hadiš*, 'palace', *hasta* therefore being a building on the terrace. He further argues that *prkn* can be read as Avestan *frakana*, 'dug-out', and hence 'basement room' somewhere in the Palace; and that *srk*, sometimes written *srwk*, can be connected with *sāruka*, interpreted as 'castle' on the basis of later Persian *sārūq*, and Old Persian **sāru*- and its Sanskrit cognate *śālā*, 'hall', referring therefore to the Treasury building at Persepolis.[448] On this basis he speculates that, when the commandant (*sgn*) held an audience in the

> Hasta, the Frakana, or the Treasury itself, a sub-treasurer installs himself on a rug just inside the entrance, a scribe beside him. As each caller, usually military men [*sic*], presents himself, he hands his gift for the Commandant to the sub-treasurer, obsequiously identifying himself by name. The sub-treasurer inspects the gift, hands it to the scribe, and dictates the text, which is stereotyped except for the caller's name and the description of the object.[449]

In other words, he proposes that the inscriptions would have been added after the arrival of these items of tribute at Persepolis, and that they served to indicate their place of storage. The fact that the inscriptions are in ink and therefore possibly fugitive might support this latter interpretation, there is, however, no indication that handling in modern times has caused the ink to rub off, so this is probably not a very significant factor. While Gershevitch sees these procedures as taking place in different locations at Persepolis, his reconstruction could presumably just as well apply in Arachosia, and his etymological speculations could also be relevant for the names of locations out in the Empire. Indeed, the association of the word *byrt'*, 'city, fortified town',[450] with each of the three names does not appear appropriate to

---

448. Gershevitch 1974: 45-75, specifically 53-54; accepted etymologically by Hinz 1975: 371-85, specifically 373; but not as locations at Persepolis (see 1975: 118 [**hasta*-], 179-80 [**parikāna*-], 222 [**sāruka*-]); see also Hoftijzer and Jongeling 1995: 1: 291 (*hst*); 2: 803 (*srk₂*), 938-39 (*prkn₂*), considering them as probable place-names, but citing the alternative suggestions, 'basement room' (*hst*), 'shrine, cell' (*srk₂*), 'cella(?)' (*prkn₂*); see also Williamson 2004: 214 n. 9; and Boyce 1982: 148-49, both also favouring the view that they were geographical names and not locations in the palace.

449. Gershevitch 1974: 71.

450. That *byrt'* is likely to have referred to a city or town and not merely to part of the Palace at Persepolis is suggested by the comparable use of the word in the Aramaic text at Xanthos where it occurs in the introductory passage *byrḥ sywn*

parts of the palace at Persepolis, so their interpretation as geographical names, not necessarily precisely those discussed above, is probably to be preferred.

Appendix VI
Suene/Syene

While dealing with the place-name Suene, it is worth mentioning another probable occurrence in a passage in Isaiah (49:8-26) which prophesies the restoration of Israel at the coming of the Messiah. In this, the Authorised Version has the rendering 'they will come from afar – some from the north, some from the west, and some from the region of Sinim' (Isaiah 49:12). The Greek writer Claudius Ptolemy who was active in the second century AD refers in his *Outline of Geography* to what is clearly China by the name *sinai* (7:3),[451] and this and other such references have led to a long-held view that it was plausible to take Biblical Sinim as a reference to China.[452] In the traditional Rabbinic (Masoretic) spelling of this passage in the Hebrew text this name is written with the consonants *synym* which could suggest the pronunciation 'sînîm' appearing to support this, but in the great Isaiah Scroll (1QIs^a) from Qumran this name is spelled *swnyym*,[453] making it highly probable that this is another reference to *swn*, Syene.[454] The form can be analysed as *swn-yym*, where the ending *-yym*, probably to be vocalised as *-iyîm*, is the equivalent of English '-ites' or '-ians', and refers therefore to 'Syenites' or 'Syenians', that is 'inhabitants of Syene'. This means that this passage in Isaiah refers to the north, the west, and the southern limit of Egypt, something recognised by the Revised Standard Version of the Bible, which was published in 1952 and was able to take account of the Isaiah manuscript discovered at Qumran in 1947.

šnt ḥd 'rtḥšš mlk' b'wrn byrt', 'In the month Siwan year one of Artaxerxes the king in 'Orna (Greek Xanthos) the city' (see above).

451. For an earlier discussion of Ptolemy's place names, see Gerini 1897: 551-77, specifically 575-77 in support of the conclusion Sinai = China.

452. Wilhelm Gesenius devotes three pages to a discussion of *sînîm* in 1835-1853: II (1840): 948-50, with the cautious conclusion that the name referred to a remote land in the east or south.

453. Burrows 1950: pl. XLI, transcribed by Burrows as *synyym*, but clearly *swnyym* in the photograph of the manuscript; and it is given correctly as *swnyym* in *Biblia Hebraica Stuttgartensia*, rev. ed. 1977: 753, footnote apparatus.

454. This is, of course, on the assumption that the Qumran manuscript has a text superior to that of the Masoretic text.

Bibliography

Aharoni, Y. 1979. *The Land of the Bible: A Historical Geography*, 2nd rev. ed., London: The Westminster Press

Altheim, F., and R. Stiehl. 1963. *Die Aramäische Sprache unter den Ach*ämeniden, Frankfurt am Main: Klostermann

Amiran, R. 1967. 'Persian-Achaemenid Impact on Palestine', in A.U. Pope (ed.), *A Survey of Persian Art from Prehistoric Times to the Present*, XIV, Proceedings of the IVth International Congress of Iranian Art and Archaeology, Oxford: Oxford University Press, 3017-23

Amiran, R. 1972. 'Achaemenian Bronze Objects from a Tomb at Kh. Ibsan in Lower Galilee', *Levant* 4: 135-38

Anderson, J.K. 1974. *Xenophon*, London: Duckworth & Co.

Andrews, A. 1967. *The Greeks*, London. New ed. 1971 reissued as *Greek Society*, Harmondsworth: Penguin

Anklesaria, T.D. 1908. *Bûndahishn*, Bombay: British India Press

Anklesaria, T.D. 1956. *Zand-Ākāsīh: Iranian or Greater Bundahišn. Transliteration and Translation in English*, Bombay

Arberry, A.J. (ed.). 1953. *The Legacy of Persia*, Oxford: The Clarendon Press

Armayor, O.K. 1978. 'Herodotus' Catalogues and the Persian Empire in the Light of the Monuments and the Greek Literary Tradition', *Transactions of the American Philological Association* 108: 1-9

Back, M. 1978. *Die Sassanidischen Staatsinschriften*, Acta Iranica 18, Leiden: Brill

Bailey, H.W. 1943. *Zoroastrian Problems in the 9th Century Books*, Oxford. Repr. 1971 with new Introduction, Oxford: The Clarendon Press

Balkan, K. 1959. 'Inscribed Bullae from Daskyleion-Ergili', *Anadolu*, Ankara, 4: 123-28

Bar-Kochva, B. 1976. *The Seleucid Army: Organization & Tactics in the Great Campaigns*, Cambridge: Cambridge University Press

Bartholomae, C. 1895-1901. 'Awestasprache und Altpersisch', in W. Geiger and E. Kuhn (eds), *Grundriss der Iranischen Philologie*, Vol. I, Strassburg: 152-248.

Bartholomae, C. 1904. *Altiranisches Wörterbuch*, Strassburg. Repr. 1961, Berlin: Walter de Gruyter

Bateson, M.C. 1967. *Arabic Language Handbook*, Washington, DC: Georgetown University Press

Bauer, M. 1904. *Precious Stones*, London. Repr. 1968 with addenda, New York: Warner Books

Beaulieu, P.A. 1989. *The Reign of Nabonidus, King of Babylon 556-539 B.C.*, Yale Near Eastern Researches 10, New Haven, CT, and London: Yale University Press

Beckerath, J., von. 1984. *Handbuch der Ägyptischen Königsnamen*, Mainz: Philipp von Zabern

Beeston, A.F.L. 1970. *The Arabic Language Today*, London: Hutchinson University Library

Benveniste, E. 1966. *Titres et noms propres en iranien ancien*, Paris: C. Klinckseick

Berger, P.-R. 1974-75. 'Die Kyros-Zylinder mit dem Zusatzfragment BIN II Nr.32 und die Akkadischen Personennamen im Danielbuch', *Zeitschrift für Assyriologie* 64:192-234

Bernard, P. 1972. 'Les mortiers et pilons inscrits de Persépolis', *Studia Iranica* 1: 165-76

Betts, A.V.G., and V.N. Yagodin. 2007. 'The Fire Temple at Tash-k'irman Tepe, Chorasmia', in J. Cribb and G. Herrmann (eds), *After Alexander. Central Asia before Islam*, Proceedings of the British Academy 133, Oxford: Oxford University Press, 435-53

Beyerlin, W. (ed.). 1978. *Near Eastern Texts Relating to the Old Testament*, London: SCM Press

Bezold, C. 1911. 'Recensionen', *Zeitschrift für Assyriologie* 25: 393-94

Birnbaum, S.A. 1954-57. *The Hebrew Scripts* II: *The Plates*, London: Palaeographia

Birnbaum, S.A. 1971. *The Hebrew Scripts* I: *The Text*, Leiden: Brill

Bivar, A.D.H. 1971. 'A Hoard of Ingot-Currency of the Median Period from Nūsh-i Jān, near Malayir', *Iran* 9: 97-111

Bivar, A.D.H. 1985. 'A Persian Fairyland', *Acta Iranica* 24, Mary Boyce Festschrift 1, Leiden: Brill, 25-42

Black, J., A. George and N. Postgate. 1999. *A Concise Dictionary of Akkadian*, Wiesbaden: Harrassowitz Verlag

Blass, F., and A. Debrunner. 1961. *A Greek Grammar of the New Testament and Other Early Christian Literature*, trans. and rev. by R.W. Funk, Cambridge: Cambridge University Press, and Chicago, IL: Chicago University Press

Blomqvist, J. 1982. 'Translation Greek in the Trilingual Inscription of Xanthus', *Opuscula Atheniensia I*, Stockholm, 14: 11-20

Bockisch, G. 1969. 'Die Karer und ihre Dynasten', *Klio* 51: 117-75

Borger, R. 2003. *Mesopotamisches Zeichenlexikon*, Alter Orient und Altes Testament, 305, Münster: Ugarit-Verlag

Borger, R., and W. Hinz. 1984. 'Die Behistun-Inschrift Darius' des Großen', in O. Kaiser (ed.) *Texte aus der Umwelt des Alten Testaments* I.4, *Historische-chronologische Texte*, Gütersloh: Gütersloher Verlagshaus Gerd Mohn, 419-50

Börner, R. 1962. *Minerals, Rocks and Gemstones*, Edinburgh: Oliver & Boyd

Börner, R. 1962. *Minerals, Rocks and Gemstones*, Edinburg: Oliver & Boyd

Botterweck, G.J., H. Ringgren and H.-J. Fabry (eds). 1974-2006. *Theological Dictionary of the Old Testament*, 1-15, Grand Rapids, MI: Eerdmans

Boucharlat, R., and A. Labrousse. 1979. 'Le palais d'Artaxerxès II', *Cahiers de la Délégation Archéologique Française en Iran* 10: 19-136

Bouzek, J. 1997. 'Cimmerians', in E.M. Meyers et al. (eds), *The Oxford Encyclopedia of Archaeology in the Near East* 2, New York and Oxford: Oxford University Press, 11-12

Bowman, R.A. 1970. *Aramaic Ritual Texts from Persepolis*, Oriental Institute Publications XCI, Chicago: University of Chicago Press

Bowra, C.M. 1933. *Ancient Greek Literature*, Oxford: Oxford University Press

Boyce, M. 1968. *Middle Persian Literature* (Handbuch der Orientalistik), Leiden: Brill, 32-66

Boyce, M. 1975. *A History of Zoroastrianism*, Vol. I (Handbuch der Orientalistik), Leiden: Brill

Boyce, M. 1979. *Zoroastrians. Their Religious Beliefs and Practices*, London: Routledge & Kegan Paul

Boyce, M. 1982. *A History of Zoroastrianism*, Vol. II (Handbuch der Orientalistik), Leiden: Brill

Boyce, M. 1983. 'Iranian Festivals', in E. Yarshater (ed.), *The Cambridge History of Iran, Vol. 3: The Seleucid, Parthian and Sasanian Periods, Part 2*, Cambridge: Cambridge University Press, 792-815

Boyce, M. 1984a. 'Persian Religion in the Achaemenid Age', in W.D. Davies and L. Finkelstein (eds), *The Cambridge History of Judaism*, Vol. I: 279-307

Boyce, M. 1984b. *Textual Sources for the Study of Zoroastrianism*, Manchester: Manchester University Press

Boyce, M. 1985. 'Anāhīd', in E. Yarshater (ed.), *Encyclopaedia Iranica*, Vol. 1: 1003-1006

Boyce, M. 2003. 'Haoma', in E. Yarshater (ed.), *Encyclopaedia Iranica*, Vol. 11: 659-67

Boyce, M., and F. Grenet. 1991. *A History of Zoroastrianism*, Vol. III (Handbuch der Orientalistik), Leiden: Brill

Brandenstein, W., and M. Mayrhofer. 1964. *Handbuch des Altpersischen*, Wiesbaden: Harrassowitz Verlag

Brenner, A. 1982. *Colour Terms in the Old Testament*, Journal for the Study of the Old Testament, Supplement Series 21, Sheffield: Sheffield University Press

Bresciani, E. 1987. 'Aršāma', in E. Yarshater, ed., *Encyclopaedia Iranica*, Vol. 2: 546

Briant, P. 2002. *From Cyrus to Alexander: A History of the Persian Empire*, Winona Lake, IN: Eisenbrauns

Brice, W.C. 1966. *South-West Asia*, London: University of London Press

Brinkman, J.A. 1968. *A Political History of Post-Kassite Babylonia 1158-722 BC*, Analecta Orientalia 43, Rome: Pontifical Bible Institute

Brinkman, J.A. 1969. Review of W. von Soden and W. Rollig, *Das Akkadische Syllabar* in *Wiener Zeitschrift für die Kunde des Morgenlandes* 62: 295-98

Brinkman, J.A. 1989. 'The Akkadian Words for "Ionia" and "Ionian"', in R.F. Sutton (ed.), *Daidalikon: Studies in Memory of Raymond V. Schoder S.J.*, Wauconda, IL: Bolchazy-Carducci, 53-71

Brown, J.P. 1969. *The Lebanon and Phoenicia: Ancient Texts Illustrating their Physical Geography and Native Industries. 1. The Physical Setting and the Forest*, Beirut: American University

Brown, S.C. 1998. 'Ecbatana', in E. Yarshater (ed.), *Encyclopaedia Iranica*, Vol. 8: 80-84

Browne, E.G. 1902. *A Literary History of Persia*, Vol. I, London: T.F. Unwin. Repr. 1956, Cambridge: Cambridge University Press

Browning, R. 1969. *Medieval and Modern Greek*, London: Hutchinson

Bruce, F.F. 1971. *New Testament History*, rev. ed., London: Oliphants

Budge, E.A.W., L.W. King and R.C. Thompson. 1907. *Sculptures and Inscriptions of Darius the Great on the Rock of Behistûn in Persia*, London: British Museum

Bulman, J.M. 1973. 'The Identity of Darius the Mede', *Westminster Theological Journal* 35: 247-67

Burkert, W. 1985. *Greek Religion*, Oxford: Blackwell

Burn, A.R. 1962. *Persia and the Greeks*, London: Edward Arnold

Burney, C., and D.M. Lang. 1971. *The Peoples of the Hills: Ancient Ararat and Caucasus* London: Weidenfeld & Nicolson

Burrow, T. 1973. *The Sanskrit Language*, new ed., London: Faber & Faber

Burrows, M. 1950. *The Dead Sea Scrolls of St. Mark's Monastery, Vol. I: The Isaiah Manuscript and the Habakkuk Commentary*, New Haven, CT: American Schools of Oriental Research (ASOR)

Butler, E.M. 1948. *The Myth of the Magus*, Cambridge: Cambridge University Press

CAD (The Chicago Assyrian Dictionary): A-Z. 1961-2010. A.L. Oppenheim et al. (eds), *The Assyrian Dictionary*, Chicago: The Oriental Institute

Cameron, G.G. 1932. 'New Light on Ancient Persia', *Journal of the American Oriental Society* 52: 304

Cameron, G.G. 1948. *Persepolis Treasury Tablets*, Oriental Institute Publications LXV, Chicago: University of Chicago

Campbell Thompson, R. 1936. *Dictionary of Assyrian Chemistry and Geology*, Oxford: Oxford University Press

Cardascia, G. 1951. *Les Archives des Murašû: Une famille d'hommes d'affaires babyloniens a l'Époque Perse (455-403 av. J.-C.)*, Paris: Imprimerie Nationale

Caroe, O. 1967. *Soviet Empire: The Turks of Central Asia and Stalinism*, 2nd ed., London: Macmillan

Cary, M. 1949. *The Geographic Background of Greek and Roman History*, Oxford: The Clarendon Press

Casson, L. 2001. *Libraries in the Ancient World*, New Haven, CT: Yale University Press

Chaudhuri, N.C. 1979. *Hinduism*, Oxford: Oxford University Press

Chavalas, M.W. 2006. *The Ancient Near East*, Historical Sources in Translation, Oxford: Blackwell

Christensen, A. 1944. *L'Iran sous les Sassanides*, 2nd ed.; Copenhagen: E. Munksgaard

Christides, A.F. (ed.). 2007. *A History of Ancient Greek*, Cambridge: Cambridge University Press

Clay, A.T. 1919. *Neo-Babylonian Letters from Erech*, Yale Oriental Series 3, New Haven, CT: Yale University Press

Cogan, M. 2000. In W.W. Hallo and K.L. Younger (eds), *The Context of Scripture, Vol. 2: Monumental Inscriptions from the Biblical World*, Leiden: Brill

Colless, B.E. 1992. 'Cyrus the Persian as Darius the Mede in the Book of Daniel', *Journal for the Study of the Old Testament* 56: 113-26

Coogan, M.D. 1976. *West Semitic Personal Names in the Murašû Documents*, Harvard Semitic Monographs 7, Missoula, MT: Scholars Press

Cook, J.M. 1983. *The Persian Empire*, London: Dent

Cooke, G.A. 1903. *A Text-Book of North-Semitic Inscriptions*, Oxford: The Clarendon Press

Cowley, A.E. 1923. *Aramaic Papyri of the Fifth Century B.C.*, Oxford: The Clarendon Press

Cross, F.L., and E.A. Livingstone (eds). 1997. *The Oxford Dictionary of the Christian Church*, 3rd rev. ed., Oxford: Oxford University Press

Cross, F.M. 1963. 'The Discovery of the Samaria Papyri', *Biblical Archaeologist* 26: 110-21

Cross, F.M. 1969. 'Papyri of the Fourth Century B.C. from Dâliyeh', in D.N. Freedman and J.C. Greenfield (eds), *New Directions in Biblical Archaeology*, Garden City, NY: Doubleday, 41-62

Cross, F.M. 1974. 'The Papyri and Their Historical Implications', in P.W. and N.L. Lapp (eds), *Discoveries in the Wâdī ed-Dâliyeh*, Annual of the American Schools of Oriental Research 41, Cambridge, MA: ASOR, 17-29

Cross, F.M. 1975. 'A Reconstruction of the Judean Restoration', *Journal of Biblical Literature*, 94: 4-18; and 1998. *From Epic to Canon: History and Literature in Ancient Israel*, rev. and expanded, Baltimore and London: Johns Hopkins University Press, 151-72

Cross, F.M. 1985. 'Samaria Papyrus 1: An Aramaic Slave Conveyance of 335 B.C.E. Found in the Wâdī ed-Dâliye', *Eretz-Israel* 18: 7*-17*

Cross, F.M. 1998. *From Epic to Canon: History and Literature in Ancient Israel*, Baltimore and London: Johns Hopkins University Press

Cross, F.M. 2003. *Leaves from an Epigrapher's Notebook*, Harvard Semitic Studies 51, Winona Lake, IN: Eisenbrauns

Cross F.M., and P.W. Lapp. 1974. 'An Account of the Discovery', in P.W. and N.L. Lapp (eds), *Discoveries in the Wâdī ed-Dâliyeh*, Annual of the American Schools of Oriental Research 41, Cambridge, MA: ASOR

Curtis, J. 1993. 'William Kennett Loftus and his Excavations at Susa', *Iranica Antiqua* 28: 1-55.

Curtis, J.E. (ed.). 1997. *Mesopotamia and Iran in the Persian Period*, London: British Museum

Curtis, J., and N. Tallis (eds). 2005. *Forgotten Empire: The World of Ancient Persia*, London: British Museum

Curtis, V.S., and S. Stewart (eds). 2005. *Birth of the Persian Empire (The Idea of Iran Vol.1)* London: I.B. Tauris

Dandamaev, M. 1993. 'The Cyrus Cylinder', in E. Yarshater (ed.), *Encyclopaedia Iranica* 6: 521-22

Danker, F.W. (rev. and ed.). 2010. W. Bauer's *A Greek-English Lexicon of the New Testament and other Early Christian Literature*, trans. by W.F. Arndt and F.W. Gingrich, 3rd rev. ed., Chicago and London: University of Chicago Press

Darmesteter, J. 1884. *The Zend-Avesta, Vol. II: The Sīrōzahs, Yasts and Nyāyis*, Sacred Books of the East 23, Oxford: Oxford University Press

Darmesteter, J. 1883. *Études iraniennes, Vol. I: Grammaire historique du persan, Vol. II: Mélanges d'histoire et de litérature iranienne*, Paris: F. Vieweg

Davary, D. 1974. 'Die Ruinenstadt Bost am Helmand', in *Monumentum H.S. Nyberg, Vol. I, Acta Iranica*, Series 2, Leuven: Peeters, 201-8

Davies, J.K. 1993. *Democracy and Classical Greece*, 2nd ed. (1st ed., 1978), Cambridge, MA: Harvard University Press

Davies, W.D., and L. Finkelstein (eds). 1984. *The Cambridge History of Judaism, Vol. I: Introduction; The Persian Period*, Cambridge: Cambridge University Press

Delling, G. 1967. '*Magos*', in G. Kittel and G. Friedrich (eds), 1964-1976. *Theological Dictionary of the New Testament*, Grand Rapids, MI: Eerdmans, 4: 356-59

Delaunay, J. A. 1974. 'A propos des "Aramaic Ritual Texts from Persepolis" de R.A. Bowman', *Acta Iranica*, 2, Leiden: Brill, 193-217

Dentan, R.C. 1955. *The Idea of History in the Ancient Near East*, New Haven, CT: Yale University Press

Diakonoff, I.M. 1970. 'The Origin of the "Old Persian" Writing System and the Ancient Oriental Epigraphic and Annalistic Traditions', in M. Boyce and I. Gershevich (eds), *W.B. Henning Memorial Volume*, London: Lund Humphries, 98-124

Diakonoff, I.M. 1981. 'The Cimmerians', in *Monumentum G. Morgenstierne, I, Acta Iranica*, Leiden: Brill, 103-40

Diakonov, I.M., and V.A. Livshits. 1966. 'Novye nakhodki dokumentov v staroi Nise', *Peredneaziatskii Sbornik*, II, Moscow

Diakonoff, I.M., and V.A. Livshits. 1976. *Part II, Inscriptions of the Seleucid and Parthian Periods and of Eastern Iran and Central Asia: Vol. II: Parthian, Parthian Economic Documents from Nisa*, Texts I, London: Lund Humphries on behalf of Corpus Inscriptiorum Iranicarum

Dietrich, M., et al. 2001. *Texte aus der Umwelt des Alten Testaments: Erganzungslieferung*, Gütersloh: Gütersloher Verlagshaus Gerd Mohn, 194-99

Dietrich, M., O. Loretz and J. Sanmartín. 1995. *The Cuneiform Alphabetic Texts from Ugarit, Ras Ibn Hani and other Places*, 2nd enlarged ed., Münster: Ugarit-Verlag

Dieulafoy, M. 1884. *L'art antique de la Perse: Achéménides, Parthes, Sassanides, II: Monuments de Persépolis*, Paris: Librarie centrale d'architecture

Dieulafoy, M. 1890-93. *L'acropole de Suse*, Paris: Librarie Hachette

Dieulafoy, M. 1892. *L'acropole de Suse d'après les fouilles exécutées en 1884, 1885, 1886 sous les auspices du Musée du Louvre, IV: L'Apadana et l'Ayadana*, Paris: Librairie Hachette

Dillard, R.D., and T. Longman. 1994. *An Introduction to the Old Testament*, Grand Rapids, MI: Eerdmans

Dillon, M., and L. Garland. 1994. *Ancient Greece: Social and Historical Documents from Archaic Times to the Death of Socrates (c.800-399 B.C.)*, London: Routledge

Donner, H., and W. Röllig. 1964. *Kanaanäische und Aramäische Inschriften*, Wiesbaden: Harrassowitz Verlag

Dougherty, R.P. 1923. *Archives from Erech: Time of Nebuchadrezzar and Nabonidus*, Goucher College Cuneiform Inscriptions 1, New Haven, CT: Yale University Press

Dougherty, R.P. 1928. 'Writing upon Parchment and Papyrus among the Babylonians and the Assyrians', *Journal of the American Oriental Society* 48: 109-35

Driel, G., van 1989. 'The Murašûs in Context', *Journal of Economic and Social History of the Orient* 32: 203-26

Driel-Murray C., van. 2000. 'Leatherwork and Skin Products', in P.T. Nicholson and I. Shaw (eds), *Ancient Egyptian Materials and Technology*, Cambridge: Cambridge University Press, 299-319

Driver, G.R. 1954. *Aramaic Documents of the Fifth Century BC*, Oxford: The Clarendon Press, and rev. ed., abridged, without the plates, 1957

Driver, G.R. 1957. 'Presidential Address', *Volume du Congrès, Strasbourg, 1956, Vetus Testamentum*, Supplement 4, Leiden: Brill, 4-5

Driver, G.R. 1976. *Semitic Writing from Pictograph to Alphabet*, Schweich Lectures 1944, 3rd ed., London: Oxford University Press

Driver, G.R., and J.C. Miles. 1952. *The Babylonian Laws*, Vol. I, Oxford: The Clarendon Press

Driver, G.R., and J.C. Miles. 1955. *The Babylonian Laws*, Vol. II, Oxford: The Clarendon Press

Driver, S.R. 1906. *The Minor Prophets: Nahum, Habakkuk, Zephaniah, Haggai, Zechariah, Malachi*, The Century Bible, Edinburgh: T.C. & E.C. Jack

Duchesne-Guillemin, J. 1953. 'Les noms des eunuques d'assuérus', *Le Muséon*, Louvain, 66: 105-108

Duchesne-Guillemin, J. 1962. «Mana», *La religion de l'Iran ancien*, Vol. I: III, Paris: Presses Universitaires de France

Duchesne-Guillemin, J. 1983. 'Zoroastrian Religion', in E. Yarshater (ed.), *The Cambridge History of Iran*, 3:2: 866-908

Dumézil, D. 1970. *Archaic Roman Religion*, I-II, Chicago: University of Chicago Press

Durkin-Meisterernst, D. 2004. 'Huzwāreš', in E. Yarshater (ed.), *Encyclopaedia Iranica*, 12: 585-88

Dušek, J. 2007. *Les manuscrits araméens du Wadi Daliyeh et la Samarie vers 450-332 av.J.-C.*, Leiden–Boston: Brill

Easterling, P.E., and B.M.W. Knox (eds). 1985. *The Cambridge History of Classical Literature, I: Greek Literature*, Cambridge: Cambridge University Press

Ebeling, E. 1934. *Neubabylonische Briefe aus Uruk*, Berlin: Verlag des Herausgebers

Ebeling, E. 1952. 'Die Rüstung eines babylonischen Panzerreiters nach einem Vertrage aus der Zeit Darius II', *Zeitschrift für Assyriologie* 50: 203-13

Eilers, W. 1964. 'Kyros: Eine namenkundliche Studie', *Beiträge zur Namenforschung* 15: 180-236

Eliade, M. 1979. *A History of Religious Ideas*, 1, London: Collins

Erman, A., and H. Grapow. 1925-1931. *Wörterbuch der Aegyptischen Sprache*, I-V, 3rd ed. (1961), Berlin: Akademie-Verlag

Evetts, B.T.A. 1890. 'A Trilingual Inscription of Artaxerxes Mnemon', *Zeitschrift für Assyriologie* 5: 410-17

Faulkner, R.O. 1962. *A Concise Dictionary of Middle Egyptian*, Oxford: Oxford University Press for the Griffith Institute

Finkel, I.L. (ed.). 2013. *The Cyrus Cylinder*, London and New York: I.B. Tauris

Finkel, I.L., and M.J. Seymour. 2008. *Babylon: Myth and Reality*, London: British Museum

Fischer, K. 1990. 'Bost, 1, The Archaeological Site', in E. Yarshater (ed.), *Encyclopaedia Iranica*, 4: 383-85

Flinders Petrie, W.M. 1930. *Beth-Pelet*, I, British School of Archaeology in Egypt, Vol. XLVIII, London

Fohrer, G. 1970. *Introduction to the Old Testament*, London: SPCK

Folmer, M.L. 1995. *The Aramaic Language in the Achaemenid Period: A Study in Linguistic Variation*, Orientalia Lovaniensia Analecta 68, Louvain: Peeters

Fowler, J.D. 1988. *Theophoric Personal Names in Ancient Hebrew*, Sheffield: Sheffield Academic Press

Fredericks, D.C. 1988. *Qohelet's Language: Re-evaluating its Nature and Date*, Lewiston, NY: Edwin Mellon

Freedman, D.N. (ed.). 1992. *The Anchor Bible Dictionary* 1-6, Garden City, NY: Doubleday

Friedrich, J. 1932. *Kleinasiatische Sprachdenkmäler*, Berlin: Walter de Gruyter

Frye, R.N. 1968. *The Persian Empire*, Wiesbaden: Harrassowitz Verlag

Frye, R.N. 1982. 'The "Aramaic" Inscription on the Tomb of Darius', *Iranica Antiqua* 17: 85-90

Frye, R.N. 1983. 'The Political History of Iran under the Sasanians', in E. Yarshater (ed.), *The Cambridge History of Iran*, 3: 1: 116-80

Galling, K. (ed.). 1968. *Textbuch zur Geschichte Israels*, 2nd ed., Tübingen: Mohr Siebeck

Gardiner, A.H. 1961. *Egypt of the Pharaohs*, Oxford: Oxford University Press

Gardner, I. 1995. *The Kephalaia of the Teacher: The Edited Coptic Manichaean Texts in Translation with Commentary*, Leiden: Brill

Garrison, M.B., and M. Cool Root. 2001. *Seals on the Persepolis Fortification Tablets, Vol. I: Images of Heroic Encounter*, Part 1, Text (OIP 117), Chicago: The Oriental Institute

Garstang, J. 1929. *The Hittite Empire*, London: Constable

Geiger, W., and E. Kuhn (eds). 1895-1901. *Grundriss der Iranischen Philologie*, Vol. I, Strassburg: K.J. Trübner

Geiger, W., and E. Kuhn (eds). 1896-1904. *Grundriss der Iranischen Philologie*, Vol. II, Strassburg: K.J. Trübner

Geldner, K.F. 1886. *Avesta, die heiligen Bücher des Parsen, Vol. I: Yasn*, Stuttgart: W. Kohlhammer

Geldner, K.F. 1889. *Avesta, die heiligen Bücher des Parsen, Vol. II: Vispered und Khorde Avesta*, Stuttgart: W. Kohlhammer

Geldner, K.F. 1895. *Avesta, die heiligen Bücher des Parsen, Vol. III: Vendidad*, Stuttgart: W. Kohlhammer

Geldner, K.F. 1951. *Der Rig-Veda*, Harvard Oriental Series 33-35, Cambridge, MA: Harvard University Press

Geller, M., J.C. Greenfield and M.P. Weitzman (eds). 1995. *Studia Aramaica. New Sources and New Approaches*, Journal of Semitic Studies, Supplement 4, Oxford: Oxford University Press

George, A. 1979. 'Cuneiform Texts in the Birmingham City Museum', *Iraq* 41: 121-40

Gerini, G.E. 1897. 'Notes on the Early Geography of Indo-China, I', *Journal of the Royal Asiatic Society*: 551-77

Gershevitch, I. 1959. *The Avestan Hymn to Mithra*, Cambridge: Cambridge University Press

Gershevitch, I. 1964. 'Zoroaster's Own Contribution', *Journal of Near Eastern Studies* 23: 12-38

Gershevitch, I., et al. 1968. *Iranistik, Vol. 2: Literatur, Part 1*, (Handbuch der Orientalistik), Leiden: Brill

Gershevitch, I. 1983. Editor's Preface to preliminary monograph publication of R.T. Hallock, 'The Evidence of the Persepolis Tablets', 1971, published subsequently, without the Preface, in I. Gershevitch (ed.), *The Cambridge History of Iran, Vol. 2: The Median and Achaemenid Periods*, Cambridge: Cambridge University Press, 588-609

Gershevitch, I. 1974. 'An Iranist's View of the Soma Controversy', in P. Gignoux and
    A. Tafazzoli (eds), *Mémorial Jean de Menasce*, Louvain: Peeters
Gershevitch, I. (ed.). 1985a. *The Cambridge History of Iran*, 2, Cambridge:
    Cambridge University Press
Gershevitch, I. 1985b. 'The Evidence of the Persepolis Tablets', in I. Gershevitch
    (ed.), 1985a: 588-609
Gesenius, G. (W.). 1835-1853. *Thesaurus Philologicus Criticus Linguae Hebraeae et
    Chaldaeae Veteris Testamenti*, Vols I-III, Leipzig: Vogel
Gesenius, W. 1987-2010. Ed. by D.R. Meyer, H. Donner and U. Rüterswörden,
    Hebräisches und Aramäisches Handwörterbuch über das Alte Testament, 1-6,
    18th ed., Berlin: Springer Verlag
Gesenius, G. 1837. *Scripturae Linguaeque Phoeniciae Monumenta quotquot
    Supersunt*, Leipzig: Vogel
Ghirshman, R. 1950. 'Masjid-i-Solaiman. Résidence des Premiers Achéménides',
    Syria 27: 205-20
Gibson, J.C.L. 1971. *Textbook of Syrian Semitic Inscriptions, Vol. 1: Hebrew and
    Moabite Inscriptions*, Oxford: Oxford University Press
Gibson, J.C.L. 1975. *Textbook of Syrian Semitic Inscriptions, Vol. 2: Aramaic
    Inscriptions.* Oxford: Oxford University Press
Gignoux, Ph. 1972. *Glossaire des Inscriptions Pehlevies et Parthes*, Corpus
    Inscriptionum Iranicarum, II, Supp. 1, London: Lund Humphries
Gignoux, Ph. 1984. *Le livre d'Arda Viraz: translittération, transcription et traduction
    du texte pehlevi*, Institut Français d'Iranologie de Téhéran, Bibliothèque
    iranienne 30, Paris
Gleason, H.A. 1961. *An Introduction to Descriptive Linguistics*, rev. ed., New York:
    Holt, Rinehart and Winston
Godley, A.D. (trans.). 1971. *Herodotus*, III, Loeb Classical Library, London: W.
    Heinemann; and Cambridge, MA: Harvard University Press
Gopal, L. 1961. 'Textiles in Ancient India', *Journal of the Economic and Social
    History of the Orient* 4: 53-69
Görg, M. 1991. *Aegyptiaca-Biblic:. Notizen und Beiträge zu den Beziehungen
    zwischen Ägypten und Israel*, Ägypten und Alte Testament 11, Wiesbaden:
    Harrassowitz Verlag
Grant, M. 1970. *The Ancient Historians*, London: Weidenfeld & Nicolson
Grayson, A.K., and D.B. Redford (eds). 1973. *Papyrus and Tablet*, Englewood
    Cliffs, NJ: Prentice-Hall
Grayson, A.K. 1975. *Assyrian and Babylonian Chronicles* (Texts from Cuneiform
    Sources) 5, Locust Valley, NY: J.J. Augustin
Green, P. 1991. *Alexander of Macedon, 356-323 BC: A Historical Biography*, rev. ed.,
    Berkeley, Los Angeles and Oxford: University of California Press
Green, P. 1996. *The Greco-Persian Wars*, Berkeley, Los Angeles and London:
    University of California Press
Greenfield, J.C. 1981. 'Aramaic Studies and the Bible', in J.A. Emerton (ed.), *Congress
    Volume Vienna 1980*, Supplements to *Vetus Testamentum* 32, Leiden: Brill, 110-30
Greenfield, J.C., and B. Porten. 1982. *The Bisitun Inscription of Darius the Great:
    Aramaic Version*, Corpus Inscriptionum Iranicarum I.V, London: Lund
    Humphries

Grenier, J.-C. 1993. *Museo Gregoriano Egizio*, Guide Cataloghi Musei Vaticani 2, Rome: L'Erma di Bretschneider

Grelot, P. 1972. *Documents araméens d'Égypte*, Littératures anciennes du Proche-Orient 5, Paris: Les Editions du Cerf

Gressmann, H. (ed.). 1926. *Altorientalische Texte zum Alten Testament*, Berlin and Leipzig: Walter de Gruyter

Gropp, D.M. 1992. 'Samaria (Papyri)', in D.N. Freedman et al. (eds), *The Anchor Bible Dictionary*, New York, NY: Doubleday, Vol. 5: 931-32

Gropp, D.M. 2001. *Wadi Daliyeh, II: The Samaria Papyri from Wadi Daliyeh*, Discoveries in the Judaean Desert XXVIII, Oxford: The Clarendon Press

Haerinck, E. 1973. 'Le Palais Achéménide de Babylone', *Iranica Antiqua* 10: 108-32

Hallo, W.W., and K.L. Younger (eds). 1997. *The Context of Scripture, Vol. I: Canonical Compositions*, Leiden: Brill

Hallo, W.W., and K.L. Younger (eds). 2000. *The Context of Scripture, Vol. II: Monumental Inscriptions*, Leiden: Brill

Hallo, W.W., and K.L. Younger (eds) 2002. *The Context of Scripture, Vol. III: Archival Documents*, Leiden: Brill

Hallock, R.T. 1969. *Persepolis Fortification Tablets*, Oriental Institute Publications XCII, Chicago

Hallock, R.T. 1985. 'The Evidence of the Persepolis Tablets', in I. Gershevitch (ed.), 1985: 588-609

Hamel, C., de.1992. *Medieval Craftsmen: Scribes and Illuminators*, London: British Museum

Hanaway, W.L. 1998. 'Eskandar-nāma', in E. Yarshater (ed.), *Encyclopedia Iranica* 8: 609-12

Hannig, R. 1995. *Großes Handwörterbuch Ägyptisch-Deutsch (2800-950 v.Chr.)*, Mainz: Phillip von Zabern

Haran, M. 1978. *Temples and Temple Service in Ancient Israel*, Oxford: The Clarendon Press

Harper, P.O., J. Aruz and F. Tallon. 1992. *The Royal City of Susa: Ancient Near Eastern Treasures in the Louvre*, New York: Metropolitan Museum of Art

Harris, Z.S. 1939. *Development of the Canaanite Dialects*, American Oriental Series 16, New Haven, CT: American Oriental Society

Harris, Z.S. 1941. 'Linguistic Structure of Hebrew', *Journal of the American Oriental Society* 61: 143-67

Henning, W.B. 1942. 'The Disintegration of the Avestic Studies', *Transactions of the Philological Society*: 40-56; see *Acta Iranica* 1977: 15: 151-67

Henning, W.B. 1951. *Zoroaster, Politician or Witch-doctor?* Oxford: The Clarendon Press

Henning, W.B. 1958. 'Mitteliranisch', in *Iranistik, Linguistik* (Handbuch der Orientalistik), 1.4.1, Leiden: Brill, 21-130

Herrmann, G. 1968. 'Lapis Lazuli: The Early Phases of its Trade', *Iraq* 30: 21-57

Herzfeld, E. 1926. 'Reisebericht', *Zeitschrift der Deutschen Morgenländischen Gesellschaft*, 80: 225-84

Herzfeld, E. 1931. 'Die Magna Charta von Susa', I, 'Text und Commentar', *Archäologische Mitteilungen aus Iran* 3: 29-81; II, 'Die Gatha des Dareios', *Archäologische Mitteilungen aus Iran* 3: 83-124

Herzfeld, E. 1935. *Archaeological History of Iran*, Schweich Lectures 1934, London: H. Milford

Herzfeld, E. 1937. 'Die Silberschüsseln Artaxerxes' des I. und die goldene Fundamenturkunde des Ariaramnes', *Archälogische Mitteilungen aus Iran* 8: 5-51

Herzfeld, E. 1938. *Altpersische Inscriften, Archäologische Mitteilungen aus Iran*, Ergänzungsband 1, Berlin: Reimer

Herzfeld, E. 1968. *The Persian Empire: Studies in Geography and Ethnography of the Ancient near East, Edited from the Posthumous Papers by G. Walser*, Wiesbaden: Harrassowitz Verlag

Hill, G.F. 1922. *Catalogue of the Greek Coins of Arabia Mesopotamia and Persia: Catalogue of the Greek Coins in the British Museum*, London: British Museum

Hillers, D.R., and E. Cussini. 1996. *Palmyrene Aramaic Texts*, Baltimore and London: Johns Hopkins University Press

Hintze, A. 1998. 'The *Avesta* in the Parthian Period', in J. Wiesehöfer (ed.), *Das Partherreich und seine Zeugnisse*, Historia Einzelschriften 122:147-61, Stuttgart: Franz Steiner Verlag

Hinz, W. 1941. 'Zu den altpersischen Inschriften von Susa', *Zeitschrift der Deutschen Morgenländischen Gesellschaft* 95: 222-57

Hinz, W. 1952. 'Die Einführung der altpersischen Schrift: Zum Absatz 70 der Behistun-Inschrift', *Zeitschrift der Deutschen Morgenländischen Gesellschaft* 102: 28-38

Hinz, W. 1972. *The Lost World of Elam*, London: Sidgwick and Jackson

Hinz, W. 1973. *Neue Weg im Altpersischen*, Göttinger Orientforschungen, III.1, Wiesbaden: Harrassowitz Verlag

Hinz, W. 1975. *Altiranisches Sprachgut der Nebenüberlieferungen*, Wiesbaden: Harrassowitz Verlag

Hinz, W. 1975. 'Zu den Mörsern und Stösseln aus Persepolis', in *Monumentum H.S. Nyberg, Vol. 1, Acta Iranica*, Series 2, I, Leiden: Brill, 371-85

Hinz, W., and R. Borger. 1984. 'Die Behistun-Inschrift Darius' des Großen', in O. Kaiser (ed.), *Texte aus der Umwelt des Alten Testaments* I.4, *Historische-chronologische Texte*, Gütersloh: Gütersloher Verlagshaus Gerd Mohn, 419-50; 448

Hinz, W., and H. Koch. 1987. *Elamisches Wörterbuch, Archäologisches Mitteilungen aus Iran*, Erganzungsband 17, I-II, Berlin: Reimer

Hoffmann, K. 1989. 'Avestan Language', in E. Yarshater (ed.), *Encyclopaedia Iranica*, 3: 47-51

Hoftijzer, J., and K. Jongeling. 1987. *Dictionary of North-West Semitic Inscriptions*, 1-2, Leiden: Brill

Hornblower, S., and A. Spawforth (eds). 2003. *The Oxford Classical Dictionary*, 3rd ed. rev., Oxford: Oxford University Press

Howatson, M.C. (ed.). 1989. *The Oxford Companion to Classical Literature*, 2nd ed., Oxford: Oxford University Press

Hoyland, R.G. 2001. *Arabia and the Arabs*, London and New York: Routledge

Humbach, H. 1974. 'Aramaeo-Iranian and Pahlavi', *Acta Iranica*, Series 2, Leiden: Brill, 237-43

Iliffe, J.H. 1935. 'A Tell Fār'a Tomb Group Reconsidered: Silver Vessels of the Persian Period', *Quarterly of the Department of Antiquities of Palestine* 4: 182-86

Invernizzi, A. 2007. 'The Culture of Parthian Nisa between Steppe and Empire', in J. Cribb and G. Herrmann (eds), *After Alexander: Central Asia before Islam*, Proceedings of the British Academy 133:163-77, London

Jackson, A.V.W. 1892. *An Avesta Grammar in Comparison with Sanskrit*, Stuttgart: W. Kohlhammer; repr. 1968, Darmstadt: Wissenschaftliche Buchgesellschaft

Jacob, E. 1958. *Theology of the Old Testament*, London: Hodder & Stoughton

Jacoby, F. 1958. *Die Fragmente der Griechischen Historiker, Part III, Geschichte von Staedten und Voelkern: Horographie und Ethnographie, C: Autoren ueber eizelne Laender*, Leiden: Brill

Jastrow, M. 1926. *A Dictionary of the Targumim, the Talmud Babli and Yerushalmi and the Midrashic Literature*, 2nd ed., New York: Choreb

Jeffery, L.H. 1961. *The Local Scripts of Archaic Greece*, Oxford: Oxford University Press

Jenkins, I. 2006. *Greek Architecture and its Sculpture*, London: British Museum

Jensen, H. 1970. *Sign, Symbol and Script*, 3rd ed., London: Allen & Unwin

Joüon, P., and T. Muraoka. 1991. *A Grammar of Biblical Hebrew*, I-II, Rome: Pontifical Bible Institute

Jowett, B. 1881. *Thucydides Translated into English with Introduction, Marginal Analysis, Notes and Indices*, Oxford: The Clarendon Press

Kaiser, O. (ed.). 1984. *Texte aus der Umwelt des Alten Testaments*, I.4, Historisch-chronologische Text, Gütersloh: Gütersoher Verlagshaus Gerd Mohn

Kalinka, E. 1901. *Tituli Lyciae lingua Lycia conscripti*, Tituli Asiae Minores, 1, Vienna

Kaltner, J., and S.L. McKenzie (eds). 2002. *Beyond Babel: A Handbook of Biblical Hebrew and Related Languages*, Resources for Biblical Study 42, Atlanta: Society of Biblical Literature

Kaufman, S.A. 1974. *The Akkadian Influences on Aramaic*, Chicago: University of Chicago Press

Kaye, A.S. 2007. *Morphologies of Asia and Africa*, Winona Lake, IN: Eisenbrauns

Kellens, J. 1989. 'Avesta', in E. Yarshater (ed.), *Encyclopaedia Iranica*, 3: 35-44

Kent, R.G. 1953. *Old Persian: Grammar, Texts, Lexicon*, American Oriental Series 33, 2nd ed., New Haven, CT: American Oriental Society

Kenyon, K.M. 1974. *Digging Up Jerusalem*, London: Thames & Hudson

King, L.W., and R.C. Thompson. 1907. *The Sculptures and Inscription of Darius the Great on the Rock of Behistûn in Persia*, London: British Museum

Kirkaldy, J.F. 1971. *General Principles of Geology*, 5th ed. London: Hutchinson

Kitchen, K.A. 2003. *On the Reliability of the Old Testament*, Grand Rapids, MI, and Cambridge: Eerdmans

Kitchen, K.A., and P.J.N. Lawrence. 2012. *Treaty, Law and Covenant*, I-II, Wiesbaden: Harrassowitz Verlag

Kittel, G., and G. Friedrich (eds). 1964-1976. *Theological Dictionary of the New Testament*, Grand Rapids, MI: Eerdmans, 1-10

Klauck, H.-J. 2006. *Ancient Letters and the New Testament*, Waco, TX: Baylor University Press

Kleiss, W. 1975. 'Fundnotizen zu einigen Säulenbasen aus West-Iran', *Archäologische Mitteilungen aus Iran* 8: 75-79

Knapton, P., M.R. Saraf and J. Curtis. 2001. 'Inscribed Column Bases from Hamadan', *Iran* 39: 99-117

Knobloch, E. 1972. *Beyond the Oxus: Archaeology, Art and Architecture of Central Asia*, London: Benn

Koehler, L., and W. Baumgartner et al. 2001. *The Hebrew and Aramaic Lexicon of the Old Testament: Study Edition*, I-II, trans. and ed. by M.E.J. Richardson, Leiden and Boston: Brill; Stuttgart: W. Kohlhammer

Koldewey, R. 1914. *The Excavations at Babylon*, London: Macmillan & Co.

Koldewey, R., ed. by F. Wetzel. 1931. *Die Königsburgen von Babylon, I: Die Südburg*, Wissenschaftliche Veröffentlichung der Deutschen Orientgesellschaft 54, Leipzig: J.C. Hinrichs

Koldewey, R., ed. by F. Wetzel. 1932. *Die Königsburgen von Babylon, II: Die Hauptburg und der Sommerpalast Nebukadnezzars im Hügel Babylon*, Wissenschaftliche Veröffentlichung der Deutschen Orientgesellschaft 55, Leipzig: J.C. Hinrichs

Koldewey, R. 1990. *Das wieder erstehende Babylon*, 5th ed. ed. by B. Hrouda, Munich: Beck

Kraeling, E.G. 1953. *The Brooklyn Museum Aramaic Papyri*, New Haven, CT: Yale University Press

Kuhrt, A. 2007. *The Persian Empire: A Corpus of Sources from the Achaemenid Period*, I-II, London: Routledge

Kutscher, E.Y. 1982. *A History of the Hebrew Language*, Jerusalem: Magnes; and Leiden: Brill

Landsberger, B., and T. Bauer. 1926-27. 'Zu neuveröffentlichten Geschichtsquellen der Zeit von Asarhaddon bis Nabonid', *Zeitschrift für Assyriologie* 37: 61-98

Langdon, S. 1912. *Die Neubabylonishen Königsinschriften*, Vorderasiatische Bibliothek 4, Leipzig: J.C. Hinrichs

Layton, B. 1987. *The Gnostic Scriptures: A New Translation with Annotations and Introductions*, New York: Doubleday

Le Strange, G. 1905. *The Lands of the Eastern Caliphate*, Cambridge: University Press

Lecoq, P. 1990. 'Paradis en vieux Perse?', in F. Vallat (ed.), *Contribution à l'histoire de l'Iran: mélanges offerts à Jean Perrot*, Paris: Editions Recherche sur les Civilisations, 209-11

Lecoq, P. 1997. *Les inscriptions de la Perse achéménide*, Paris: Gallimard

Lehman, W.P. 1992. *Historical Linguistics*, 3rd ed., London and New York: Routledge

Leith, M.J.W. 1997. *Wadi Daliyeh, I: The Wadi Daliyeh Seal Impressions*, Discoveries in the Judaean Desert XXXIV, Oxford: The Clarendon Press

Lemaire, A., and H. Lozachmeur. 1987. 'Bīrāh/byrt' en araméen', *Syria* 64: 261-66

Lemaire, A. 1995. 'The Xanthos Trilingual Revisited', in Z. Zevit, S. Gitin and M. Sokoloff (eds), *Solving Riddles and Untying Knots: Biblical, Epigraphic and Semitic Studies in Honor of Jonas C. Greenfield*, Winona Lake, IN: Eisenbrauns, 423-32

Leuze, O. 1935. *Die Satrapieneinteilung in Syrien und im Zweistromlande von 520-320*, Schriften der Königberger Gelehrten Gesellschaft, 11.4, Halle (Saale): Niemeyer

Levy, J. 1954. 'The Problems Inherent in Section 70 of the Behistun Inscription',
    Hebrew Union College Annual 25: 169-208
Levy, R. 1967. *The Epic of the Kings*, London and Boston: Routledge & Kegan Paul
Lewis, D.M., et al. (eds). 1994. *Cambridge Ancient History, Vol. VI: The Fourth
    Century BC*, Cambridge: Cambridge University Press
Lewis, N. 1974. *Papyrus in Classical Antiquity*, Oxford: The Clarendon Press
Liddell, H.G.D., and R. Scott, rev. by H.S. Jones. 1940. *A Greek-English Lexicon*, 9th
    ed., Oxford: The Clarendon Press
Lidzbarski, M. 1898. *Handbuch der Nordsemitischen Epigraphik*, I-II, Weimar: E. Felber
Loftus, W.K. 1857. *Travels and Researches in Chaldaea and Susiana*, London: J.
    Nisbet & Co.
Long, V.P., D.W. Baker and G.J. Wenham (eds). 2002. *Windows into Old Testament
    History*, Grand Rapids, IN, and Cambridge: Eerdmans
Lukonin, V.G. 1983. 'Political, Social and Administrative Institutions: Taxes and
    Trade', in E. Yarshater (ed.), *The Cambridge History of Iran*, 3: 2: 681-746
Madan, D.M. 1911. *The Complete Text of the Pahlavi Dinkard*, I-II, Bombay
Macalister, R.A.S. 1912. *The Excavation of Gezer, 1902-1905 and 1907-1909*, I,
    London: J. Murray
Macdonell, A.A. 1917. *A Vedic Reader for Students*, Oxford: The Clarendon Press
MacKenzie, D.N. 1971. *A Concise Pahlavi Dictionary*, London: Oxford University
    Press
MacKenzie, D.N. 1990. 'Bundahišn', in E. Yarshater (ed.), *Encyclopaedia Iranica*, 4:
    547-51
Malandra, W.W. 1983. *An Introduction to Ancient Iranian Religion: Readings from
    the Avesta and the Achaemenid Inscriptions*, Minneapolis, MN: University of
    Minnesota Press
Mallory J.P., and D.Q. Adams. 2006. *The Oxford Introduction to Proto-Indo-
    European and the Proto-Indo-European World*, Oxford: Oxford University
    Press
Marshall, I.H. 1999. *The Pastoral Epistles*, International Critical Commentary,
    London: T. & T. Clark
Marshall, J. (ed.). 1931. *Mohenjo-Daro and the Indus Civilization*, Vols I-III,
    London: Arthur Probsthain
Mauersberger, A. 1956. *Polybius-Lexikon*, I, Berlin: Akademie-Verlag
Maunde Thompson, E. 1912. *An Introduction to Greek and Latin Palaeography*,
    Oxford: The Clarendon Press
Mayrhofer, M. 1953-76. *Kurzgefaßtes etymologisches Wörterbuch des Altindischen
    – A Concise Etymological Sanskrit Dictionary*, 1-3, Heidelberg: Carl Winter
    Universitätsverlag
Mayrhofer, M. 1968. 'Die Rekonstruktion des Medischen', *Anzeiger der Phil.-Hist.
    Klasse der Österreichischen Akademie der Wissenschaften* 105: 1-22
Mayrhofer, M. 1977a. *Zum Namengut des Avesta*, Sitzungsberichte der
    Österreichischen Akademie der Wissenschaften, Phil.-Hist. Klasse 308: 5,
    Vienna
Mayrhofer, M. 1977b. *Iranisches Personennamenbuch, Vol. I: Die Altiranischen
    Namen, Part 1: Die Avestischen Namen*, Vienna: Österreichischen Akademie
    der Wissenschaften

Mayrhofer, M. 1978. *Supplement zur Sammlung der Altpersischen Inschriften,*
    Österreichischen Akademie der Wissenschaften, Phil.-Hist. Klasse 338: 7,
    Vienna

Mayrhofer, M. 1979. *Iranisches Personennamenbuch, Vol. I: Die Altiranischen*
    Namen, Part 2: Die Altpersischen Namen, Vienna: Österreichischen Akademie
    der Wissenschaften

Mayrhofer, M. 1992-2001. *Etymologisches Wörterbuch des Altindoarischen,* 1-3,
    Heidelberg: Carl Winter Universitätsverlag

Mazar, B. 1957. 'The Tobiads', *Israel Exploration Journal* 7: 137-45, 229-38

Mazzucchi, C.M. 1979. 'Sul sistema di accentazione dei testi greci in età romana e
    bizantina', *Aegyptus* 59: 145-67

McClintock, W.F.P. 1983. *Gemstones in the Geological Museum: A Guide to the*
    Collection, 4th ed. rev. by P.M. Statham, London: HMSO

Meissner, B. 1920-25. *Babylonien und Assyrien,* 1-2, Heidelberg: Carl Winter
    Universitätsverlag

Mellink, M. 1991. 'The Native Kingdoms of Anatolia', in D.M. Lewis et al. (eds),
    Cambridge Ancient History, III: 2: 619-65

Metzger, M., E. Laroche, A. Dupont-Sommer and M. Mayrhofer. 1979. *Le Stèle*
    Trilingue de Létôon, Fouilles de Xanthos, VI, Paris: Klincksieck

Millard, A.R. 2003. 'Words for Writing in Aramaic', in M.F.J Baasten and W.Th.
    van Peursen (eds), *Hamlet on a Hill: Semitic and Greek Studies Presented to*
    Professor T. Muraoka on the Occasion of this Sixty-Fifth Birthday, Orientalia
    Lovaniensia Analecta 118, Louvain: Peeters, 349-55

Miller, J. 1950. 'Pixodaros', in Pauly-Wissowa, *Realencyclopädie der classischen*
    Altertumswissenschaft, Neue Bearbeitung, Stuttgart: J.B. Metzler,
    Vol. XX_2 = XL: cols 1893-94

Mirecki, P.A. 1992. 'Manichaeans and Manichaeism', in D.N. Freedman (ed.), 1992,
    4: 502-11

Mitchell, T.C. 1991. 'The Babylonian Exile and the Restoration of the Jews in
    Palestine (586-c.500 BC)', in D.M. Lewis et al. (eds), *Cambridge Ancient*
    History, III: 2: 410-60

Mitchell, T.C. 1996. 'Furniture in West Semitic Texts', in G. Herrmann (ed.), *The Furniture*
    of Western Asia Ancient and Traditional, Mainz: Philipp von Zabern, 49-60

Mitchell, T.C. 1997. 'Achaemenid History and the Book of Daniel', in J.E. Curtis
    (ed.), *Mesopotamia and Iran in the Persian Period,* London: British Museum,
    68-78

Mitchell, T.C. 1988; enlarged ed., 2004. *The Bible in the British Museum,* London:
    British Museum

Monier-Williams, M. 1899. *A Sanskrit-English Dictionary,* Oxford: The Clarendon
    Press

Mordtmann, A.D. 1860. 'Aus Briefen des Hrn. Dr. Mordtmann an Prof. Brockhaus',
    Zeitschrift der Deutschen Morgenländischen Gesellschaft 14: 555-56

Morony, M.G. 1984. *Iraq after the Muslim Conquest,* Princeton, NJ: Princeton
    University Press

Moscati, S., et al. 1964. *An Introduction to the Comparative Grammar of the Semitic*
    Languages, Wiesbaden: Harrassowitz Verlag

Moulton, J.H. 1911. *Early Religious Poetry of Persia,* Cambridge: University Press

Naveh, J., and S. Shaked. 1973. 'Ritual Texts or Treasury Documents?', *Orientalia* 42: 445-57

Naveh, J. 1970. *The Development of the Aramaic Script*, Proceedings of the Israel Academy of Sciences and Humanities, V.1, Jerusalem

Neusner, J. 1994. *Introduction to Rabbinic Literature*, New York: Doubleday

Newman, J. 1932. *The Agricultural Life of the Jews in Babylonia*, Oxford: Oxford University Press

Newsome, J.D. 1975. 'Toward a New Understanding of the Chronicler and his Purposes', *Journal of Biblical Literature* 94: 201-17

Newton, C.T. 1862. *A History of Discoveries at Halicarnassus, Cnidus and Branchidae*, I, London: Day & Son

Nicholson, P.T., and I. Shaw (eds). 2000. *Ancient Egyptian Materials and Technology*, Cambridge: Cambridge University Press

Nyberg, H.S. 1974. *A Manual of Pahlavi, Part II: Glossary*, Wiesbaden: Harrassowitz

O'Flaherty, W.D. 1975. *Hindu Myths*, Harmondsworth: Penguin

Oates, J. 1979. *Babylon*, London: Thames & Hudson

Obermeyer, J. 1929. *Die Landschaft Babylonien im Zeitalter des Talmuds und des Gaonats*, Frankfurt am Main: Kauffmann

Olmo Lete, G. del. 2004. *Canaanite Religion According to the Liturgical Texts of Ugarit*, Bethesda, MD: CDL Press

Olmo Lete, G. del, and J. Sanmartín. 2004. *A Dictionary of the Ugaritic Language in the Alphabetic Tradition*, 2nd rev. ed., Leiden: Brill

Oppenheim, A.L. 1985. 'The Babylonian Evidence of Achaemenian Rule in Mesopotamia', in I. Gershevitch (ed.), *The Cambridge History of Iran*, 2: 529-87

Oppenheimer, A. 1983. *Babylonia Judaica in the Talmudic Period*, Tübinger Atlas des Vorderer Orients, B, 47, Wiesbaden: Dr Ludwig Reichert Verlag

Oren, E. 1973. 'Migdol: A New Fortress on the Edge of the Eastern Nile Delta', *Bulletin of the American Schools of Oriental Research* 256: 7-44

Palmer, L.R. 1980. *The Greek Language*, London: Faber & Faber

Paoli, U.E. 1963. *Rome: Its People, Life and Customs*, London: Longmans, Green & Co.

Paper, H.H. 1955. *The Phonology and Morphology of Royal Achaemenid Elamite*, Ann Arbor, MI: University of Michigan Press

Parkinson, R., and S. Quirke. 1995. *Papyrus*, Egyptian Bookshelf, London: British Museum

Parpola, S. 1987. *The Correspondence of Sargon II*, Part I, State Archives of Assyria I, Helsinki: Helsinki University Press

Paton, W.R. (trans.). 1925. *Polybius, The Histories*, IV, Loeb, London: W. Heinemann; and Cambridge, MA: Harvard University Press

Pauly, A., G. Wissowa and W. Kroll (eds). 1893-1972. *Realencyclopädie der classischen Altertumswissenschaft* (Pauly-Wissowa), I-XVII, Stuttgart: J.B. Metzler

Perrot, J. 1970. 'Suse et Susiane', *Iran* 8: 190-94

Perrot, J. 1971. 'Missione de Suse', *Iran* 9: 178-81

Perrot, J. 1972. 'Suse et Susiane', *Iran* 10: 181-83

Perrot, G., and C. Chipiez. 1890. *Histoire de l'art dans l'antiquité, V: Perse, Phrygie, Lydie et Carie, Lycie*, Paris: Hachette et Cie

Pezard, M., and E. Pottier. 1926. *Catalogue des antiquités de la Susiane (Mission J. de Morgan)*, Paris: E. Leroux

Pinches, T.G. 1882. 'On a Cuneiform Inscription Relating to the Capture of Babylon by Cyrus, and the Events which Preceded and Led to it', *Transactions of the Society of Biblical Archaeology* 7: 139-76

Pinches, T.G. 1885. Short communication in *Proceedings of the Society for Biblical Archaeology* 7: 132-33

Polzin, P. 1976. *Late Biblical Hebrew: Toward an Historical Typology of Biblical Hebrew Prose*, Harvard Semitic Monographs, 12, Missoula, MT: Scholars Press

Porten, B. 1968. *Archives from Elephantine: The Life of an Ancient Jewish Military Colony*, Berkeley and Los Angeles: University of California Press

Porten, B., and A. Yardeni, 1986. *Textbook of Aramaic Documents from Ancient Egypt, Vol. 1: Letters*, Jerusalem: The Hebrew University

Potts, D. 2005. 'Cyrus the Great and the Kingdom of Anshan', in Curtis and Stewart (eds) 2005, 7-28

Pritchard, J.B. (ed.). 1955. *Ancient Near Eastern Texts Relating to the Old Testament*, 2nd ed., Princeton, NJ: Princeton University Press

Pugačenkova, G.A. 1958. *Puti Razvitija Arḫitektury Yužnogo Turkmenistana pory rabovladenija i feodillizma*, Trudi Yužno-Turkmenistanskoyi Arḫeologičeskoyi Kimpleksnoyi Ekspedyicyii, VI, Moscow

Rabinowitz, I. 1956. 'Aramaic Inscriptions of the Fifth Century BC from a North-Arab Shrine in Egypt', *Journal of Near Eastern Studies* 15: 1-9

Rawlinson, H.C., and T.G. Pinches. 1884. *Cuneiform Inscriptions of Western Asia*, V, London

Reicke, B., and L. Rost. 1962-66. *Biblisch-Historisches Handwörterbuch* 1-3, Göttingen: Vandenhoeck & Ruprecht

Reiner, E. 1972. 'Tall-e Malyan – Inscribed Material', *Iran* 10: 177

Reiner, E. 1973. 'The Location of Anšan', *Revue d'assyriologie* 67: 57-62

Reynolds, L.D., and N.G. Wilson. 1991. *Scribes and Scholars: A Guide to the Transmission of Greek and Latin Literature*, 3rd ed., Oxford: Oxford University Press

Rider, G. le. 1965. *Suse sous les Séleucides et les Parthes*, Mémoires de la Mission Archéologique en Iran 38, Paris: Geuthner

Robins, R.H. 1971. *General Linguistics: An Introductory Survey*, 2nd ed., London: Longmans

Robinson, E.S.G. 1958. 'The Beginings of Achaemenid Coinage', *Numismatic Chronicle* 18: 187-93

Robinson, J.M. (ed.). 1977. *The Nag Hammadi Library*, Leiden: Brill

Rogers, R.W. 1912. *Cuneiform Parallels to the Old Testament*, Oxford: Oxford University Press

Rosenthal, F. 1939. *Die Aramaistische Forschung seit Th. Nöldeke's Veröffentlichungen*, Leiden: Brill

Rosenthal, F. 1961. *A Grammar of Biblical Aramaic*, Wiesbaden: Harrassowitz

Rostovtzeff, M. 1932. *Seleucid Babylonia: Bullae and Seals of Clay with Greek Inscriptions*, Yale Classical Studies 3, New Haven, CT: Yale University Press

Rostovtzeff, M.I., F.E. Brown and C.B. Welles. 1939. *The Excavations at Dura-Europos: Preliminary Report of the Seventh and Eighth Seasons of Work, 1933-1934 and 1934-1935*, New Haven, CT: Yale University Press

Rostovtzeff, M. 1941. *The Social and Economic History of the Hellenistic World*, I-III, Oxford: The Clarendon Press

Rudolph, K. 1977. *Gnosis*, Eng. trans. by R.M. Wilson, Edinburgh: T. & T. Clark

Sáenz-Badillos, A. 1993. *A History of the Hebrew Language*, Cambridge: Cambridge University Press

Schaudig, H. 2001. *Die Inschriften Nabonids von Babylon und Kyros' des Großen*, Alter Orient und Altes Testament 256, Münster: Ugarit-Verlag

Scheil, V. 1929. *Inscriptions des Achéménides à Suse*, Mémoires de la mission archéologique de Perse XXI, Paris: E. Leroux

Schiffman, L.H., and J.C. VanderKam, J.C. (eds). 2000. *Encyclopedia of the Dead Sea Scrolls*, I-II, Oxford and New York: Oxford University Press

Schlumberger, D. 1970. *L'Orient hellénisé: l'art Grec et ses héritiers dans l'Asie non méditerranéenne*, Paris: Editions Albin Michel

Schlumberger, D. 1983. 'Parthian Art', in E. Yarshater (ed.), *The Cambridge History of Iran*, 3: 2: 1027-54

Schmidt, C. 1935. *Kephalaia*, I, Manichäische Handschriften der Staatlichen Museen Berlin, Stuttgart: W. Kohlhammer

Schmidt, E.F. 1957. *Persepolis, II: Contents of the Treasury and Other Discoveries*, Oriental Institute Publications LXIX, Chicago: Chicago University Press

Schmidt, E.F. 1970. *Persepolis, III: The Royal Tombs and Other Monuments*, Oriental Institute Publications LXX, Chicago: Chicago University Press

Schmitt, R. 1967. 'Medisches und persisches Sprachgut bei Herodot', *Zeitschrift der Deutschen Morgenländischen Gesellschaft* 117: 119-45

Schmitt, R. 1987. 'Arachosia', in E. Yarshater (ed.), *Encyclopaedia Iranica*, 2: 246-47

Schmitt, R. 1989. 'Atossa', in E. Yarshater (ed.), *Encyclopaedia Iranica*, 3: 13-14

Schmitt, R. 1991. *The Bisitun Inscriptions of Darius the Great: Old Persian Text*, Corpus Inscriptionum Iranicarum I/I, Texts I, London: SOAS

Schmitt, R. 1993. 'Cyrus vi. Cyrus the Younger', in E. Yarshater (ed.), *Encyclopaedia Iranica*, 6: 524-26

Schürer, E. 1973-87. *The History of the Jewish People in the Age of Jesus Christ (175 BC- AD 135)*, I-III, New English Version; rev. and ed. by G. Vermes, F. Millar, M. Goodman and M. Black, Edinburgh: T. & T. Clark

Searight, A., J. Reade and I. Finkel. 2008. *Assyrian Stone Vessels and Related Material in the British Museum*, Oxford: Oxbow Books

Segal, M.H. 1927. *A Grammar of Mishnaic Hebrew*, Oxford: The Clarendon Press

Segal, M.H. 1936. *Dqdwq lšwn hmšnh*, Tel Aviv

Segert, S. 1975. *Altaramäische Grammatik*, Leipzig: VEB Verlag Enzyklopädie

Seidl, U. 1976. 'Ein Relief Dareios' I in Babylon', *Archäologische Mitteilungen aus Iran* NF 9: 125-30

Shaki, M. 1981. 'The *Dēnkard* Account of the History of the Zoroastrian Scriptures', *Archiv Orientalni*, 49

Skehan, P.W., E. Ulrich and J.E. Sanderson. 1992. *Qumran Cave 4, IV: Palaeo-Hebrew and Greek Biblical Manuscripts* (Discoveries in the Judaean Desert) (Vol. IX), Oxford: The Clarendon Press

Skjærervø, P.J. 2007. 'The Videvdad: Its Ritual-Mythical Significance', in V.S. Curtis and S. Stewart (eds), *The Age of the Parthians*, London: I.B. Tauris, 105-42

Smith, C.F.H. 1972. *Gemstones*, 13th ed., revised by F.C. Phillips, London

Smith, S. 1924. *Babylonian Historical Texts Relating to the Capture and Downfall of Babylon*, London: Methuen

Smyth, H.W. 1956. *Greek Grammar*, rev. ed. by G.M. Messing, Cambridge, MA: Harvard University Press

Soden, W. von 1959-1981. *Akkadisches Handwörterbuch*, I-III, Wiesbaden: Harrassowitz Verlag

Soden, W. von, and W. Röllig. 1967. *Das Akkadische Syllabar*, Analecta Orientalia 42, 2nd ed, Rome: Pontifical Bible Institute

Soggin, J.A. 2001. *Israel in the Biblical Period*, Edinburgh: T. & T. Clark

Speiser, E.A. 1954. 'The Terminative-Adverbial in Canaanite-Ugaritic and Akkadian', *Israel Exploration Journal* 4: 108-15 = J.J. Finkelstein and M. Greenberg (eds), *Oriental and Biblical Studies: Collected Writings of E.A. Speiser*, Philadelphia, PA: University of Philadelphia Press, 1967: 494-505

Speiser, E.A. 1963. 'Background and Function of the Biblical Nāśī', *Catholic Biblical Quarterly* 25: 111-17

Spuler, B. 1995. *The Age of the Caliphs: History of the Muslim World*, Princeton, NJ: Princeton University Press

Starr, I. 1990. *Queries to the Sun God: Divination and Politics in Sargonid Assyria*, State Archives of Assyria, IV, Helsinki: Helsinki University Press

Stern, E. 1982. *The Material Culture of the Land of the Bible in the Persian Period (538-332 BC)*, Warminster: Aris & Phillips

Stern, E. (ed.). 1993. *The New Encyclopedia of Archaeological Excavations in the Holy Land*, Vols 1-4, New York: Simon and Schuster

Stern, E. 2001. *Archaeology of the Land of the Bible, II: The Assyrian, Babylonian and Persian Periods (732-332 BC)*, New York and London: Doubleday

Steve, M.-J. 1974. 'Inscriptions des Achéménides à Suse (suite)', *Studia Iranica* 3: 135-61

Stolper, M.W. 1976. 'A Note on Yahwistic Personal Names in the Murašû Texts', *Bulletin of the American Schools of Oriental Research* 222: 22-25

Stolper, M.W. 1984. *Texts from Tall-i Malyan, I: Elamite Administrative Texts (1972-1974)*, Philadelphia, PA: Babylonian Fund

Stolper, M.W. 1985. *Entrepreneurs and Empire: the Murašu Archive, the Murašu Firm and Persian Rule in Babylonia*, Publications of the Netherlands Historical-Archaeological Institute, 54, Leiden: Brill

Stolper, M.W. 1994. 'Mesopotamia 482-330 BC', in D.M. Lewis et al. (eds), *Cambridge Ancient History*, VI: 234-60

Stolper, M.W. 1992. 'Murashu, Archive of', in D.N. Freedman et al. (eds), *The Anchor Bible Dictionary*, 4: 927-28

Strack, H.L., and G. Stemberger. 1991. *Introduction to the Talmud and Midrash*, Edinburgh: T. & T. Clark

Stronach, D. 1978. *Pasargadae*, Oxford: The Clarendon Press

Stronach, D. 1990. 'On the Genesis of the Old Persian Cuneiform Script', in F. Vallat (ed.) 1990, 195-203

Stuart Jones, H. 1895. *Ancient Writers on Greek Sculpture*, London: Macmillan & Co., repr. Chicago: Argonaut Inc., 1966

Sumner, W.M. 1972. 'Tall-e Malyan', *Iran* 10: 176

Tadmor, M. 1974. 'Fragments of an Achaemenid Throne from Samaria', *Israel Exploration Journal* 24: 37-43

Teixidor, J. 1978. 'The Aramaic Text in the Trilingual Stele from Xanthus', *Journal of Near Eastern Studies* 37: 181-85

Thomas, D. Winton (ed.). 1958. *Documents from Old Testament Times*, London: Thomas Nelson & Sons

Tufnell, O. 1953. *Lachish III (Tell ed-Duweir): The Iron Age* (Text and Plates), London, New York and Toronto: Oxford University Press

Turner, R.L. 1966. *A Comparative Dictionary of the Indo-Aryan Languages*, London: Oxford University Press

Unger, E. 1931. *Babylon, die Heilige Stadt nach der Beschreibung der Babylonier*, Berlin and Leipzig; 2nd ed. with preliminary notes by R. Borger, Berlin: Akademie-Verlag, 1970

Usher, S. 1969. *The Historians of Greece and Rome*, London: Hamish Hamilton

Vallat, F. 1970. 'Fragments de Suse (1969-1970)', *Revue d'assyriologie* 64: 171

Vallat, F. 1972. 'Epigraphie Achemenide', *Cahiers de la Délégation Archéologique Française en Iran* 2: 203-11

Vallat, F. 1979. 'Les inscriptions du palais d'Artaxerxès II', *Cahiers de la Délégation Archéologique Francaise en Iran* 10: 145-54

Vallat, F. (ed.). 1990. *Contribution à l'histoire de l'Iran: mélanges offerts à Jean Perrot*, Paris: Editions Recherche sur les Civilisations

Vaux, R. de. 1961. *Ancient Israel: Its Life and Institutions*, London: Darton, Longman & Todd

Vincent, L.H. 1923. 'La date des épigraphes d''Araq el Émir', *Journal of the Palestine Oriental Society* 3: 55-68

Voigtlander, E.N. von. 1978. *The Bisitun Inscription of Darius the Great: Babylonian Version*, CII.1.ii.1, London: Humphries

Wagner, M. 1966. *Die Lexikalischen und Grammatikalischen Aramaismen im alttestamentlichen Hebräisch*, Berlin: Töpelmann

Walbank, F.W. 1967. *A Historical Commentary on Polybius*, Vol. II, Oxford: The Clarendon Press

Walker, C.B.F. 1980. 'Elamite Inscriptions in the British Museum', *Iran* 18: 75-81

Waters, M.W. 2000. *A Survey of Elamite History*, State Archives of Assyria, Studies XII, Helsinki: Helsinki University Press

Watson, A.M. 1983. *Agricultural Innovation in the Early Islamic World*, Cambridge: Cambridge University Press

Weippert, H. 1988. *Palästina in vorhellenistischer Zeit*, Handbuch der Archäologie, Vorderasien, II.1, Munich: Beck

Weissbach, F.H. 1903. *Babylonische Miscellen*, Wissenschaftliche Veröffentlichungen der deutschen Orient-Gesellschaft 4, Leipzig: J.C. Hinrichs

Weissbach, F.H. 1911. *Die Keilinschriften der Achämeniden*, Vorderasiatische Bibliothek 3, Leipzig: J.C. Hinrichs

Weissbach, F.H. 1937. 'Achämenidisches', *Zeitschrift der Deutschen Morgenländischen Gesellschaft* 91: 81-87, 643-51

Welles, C.B. (trans.). 1963. *Diodorus Siculus; Library of History*, Vol. VII, Books XVI.66-XVII, Loeb Classical Library 422, London: W. Heinemann; and Cambridge, MA: Harvard University Press

Wenham, J.W. 1965. *The Elements of New Testament Greek*, Cambridge: Cambridge University Press

West, E.W. 1880. *Pahlavi Texts*, Vol. I (F.M. Müller [ed.], Sacred Books of the East, Vol. V), Oxford: Oxford University Press

West, E.W. 1892. *Pahlavi Texts*, Vol. IV (F.M. Müller [ed.], Sacred Books of the East, Vol. XXXVII), Oxford: Oxford University Press

Widengren, G. 1965. *Mani and Manichaeism*, London: Weidenfeld & Nicholson

Widengren, G. 1968. *Les Religions de l'Iran*, Paris: Payot

Wiesehöfer, J. 1996. *Ancient Persia from 550 BC to 650 AD*, London and New York: I.B. Tauris

Wiesehöfer, J. 1994. *Achaemenid History, Vol. VIII: Continuity and Change*, Leiden: Brill, 390

Wiesehöfer, J. (ed.). 1998. *Das Partherreich und seine Zeugnisse* (Historia Einzelschriften 122), Stuttgart: Franz Steiner Verlag

Williamson, H.G.M. 1977. 'Eschatology in Chronicles', *Tyndale Bulletin* 28: 115-54

Williamson, H.G.M. 1982. *1 and 2 Chronicles*, The New Century Bible Commentary, Grand Rapids, MI: Eerdmans; and London: Marshall, Morgan & Scott

Williamson, H.G.M. 1987. *Ezra and Nehemiah* (Old Testament Guides), Sheffield: Sheffield Academic Press

Williamson H.G.M. 2004. *Studies in Persian Period History and Historiography*, Forschungen zum Alten Testament 38, Tübingen: Mohr Siebeck

Winternitz, M. 1910. *A General Index to the Names and Subject Matter of the Sacred Books of the East*, Oxford: The Clarendon Press

Wiseman, D.J., et al. 1965. *Notes on Some Problems in the Book of Daniel*, London: The Tyndale Press

Wiseman, D.J. 1985. *Nebuchadrezzar and Babylon*, The 1983 Schweich Lectures on Biblical Archaeology, Oxford: Oxford University Press

Wiseman, D.J. 1991. 'Babylonia 605-539 BC', in D.M. Lewis et al. (eds), *Cambridge Ancient History*, III: 2: 229-51

Wright, W. 1896. *A Grammar of the Arabic Language*, Vol. I, 3rd ed., Cambridge: Cambridge University Press

Wyatt, A. 1986. *Challinor's Dictionary of Geology*, 6th ed., Cardiff: University of Wales Press

Yarshater, E. (ed.). 1983. *The Cambridge History of Iran, Vol. 3: The Seleucid, Parthian and Sasanian Periods, Part 2*, Cambridge: Cambridge University Press

Yarshater, E. (ed.). 1985-2011. *Encyclopaedia Iranica*, 1-15 and continuing, Costa Mesa, CA

Young, I., R. Rezetco and M. Ehrensvärd. 2008. *Linguistic dating of Biblical Texts*, London: T. & T. Clark

Zadok, R. 1976. 'The Connections between Iran and Babylonia in the Sixth Century BC', *Iran* 14: 61-78

Zadok, R. 1985. *Geographical Names According to New- and Late-Babylonian Texts* (Tübinger Atlas des Vorderer Orients, B, 7/8; Répertoire Géographiques des Textes Cunéiform 8/9), Wiesbaden: Reichert

Zadok, R. 1986. 'Notes on Esther', *Zeitschrift für Alttestamentlich Wissenschaft* 98: 105-109

Zadok, R. 2002. *The Earliest Diaspora: Israelites and Judeans in Pre-Hellenistic Mesopotamia*, Tel Aviv: Tel Aviv University

Zaehner, R.C. 1961. *The Dawn and Twilight of Zoroastrianism*, London: Weidenfeld & Nicolson

Zevit, Z., et al. (eds). 1995. *Solving Riddles and Untying Knots: Biblical, Epigraphic and Semitic Studies in Honor of Jonas C. Greenfield*, Winona Lake, IN: Eisenbrauns

6

The Textual Connections
between the Cyrus Cylinder and the Bible,
with Particular Reference to Isaiah

Shahrokh Razmjou

Introduction

Until the nineteenth century, historical understanding of the Near East was limited to two main sources: the Bible (mainly the Old Testament) and the classical sources (Greek and Roman). After the remarkable archaeological discoveries of the nineteenth century and the decipherment of cuneiform scripts, more textual evidence came to light, which unlike the Bible and classical sources contained first-hand evidence. The increasing number of new texts containing a huge amount of information quickly exceeded the number of previous sources. This sudden expansion of ancient historical knowledge led to a rewriting of the history of the Ancient Near East using the newly found sources.

The scholars who translated the texts were astonished to find parallels with the Old Testament stories in the tablets. This was particularly so after George Smith (1840-76) identified the story of the Flood amongst the newly found cuneiform documents. It confirmed the idea of such a connection and brought the sources to the attention of the scholarly world and to the general public. The so-called Epic of Creation tablet, with surprising similarities to some parts of Genesis, was another example that drew more attention to the Biblical link with these texts. The newly found sources were apparently much older than the Old Testament, which created even more excitement amongst the public and scholars about a possible connection.

In the beginning some theologians, overwhelmed by the new discoveries, declared that the newly found sources confirmed the accuracy of the Biblical accounts. However, with the development of studies, this approach changed over time, as there were also clear contradictions and different contextual insights. The cuneiform texts contained extensive detailed information regarding ancient Mesopotamian civilisations, including unknown rulers, peoples and events, which were not mentioned in the Bible. Consequently, the cuneiform texts turned into first-hand sources, older than existing ones.

The Cyrus Cylinder

The Cyrus Cylinder, discovered in 1879 in the ruins of Babylon by Hormuzd Rassam, was another important document with a close connection to the Old Testament that came to light. It contained the words of King Cyrus (559-530 BC), previously known through the Old Testament and the classical sources. The Cylinder was considered to be another example of an ancient text whose contents had similarities with Biblical accounts. Rassam discovered the Cylinder in the southern part of Amran, in the ruins of Babylon, probably inside the remains of the ancient Imgur-Enlil wall (Razmjou 2010: 23; Curtis 2013: 34-35). At the time of its discovery, Rassam had no idea about the contents of the Cylinder and its importance. Without knowing the name of the king, he packed the Cylinder together with other finds and tablets and sent them to London.[1]

After the arrival of the crates in London, in the same year (1879) Theophilus G. Pinches (1856-1934), a cuneiform specialist at the British Museum, was the first person to examine and study the broken Cylinder and noticed with excitement that the Cylinder belonged to King Cyrus and referred to his capture of Babylon. Some parts of the text were the direct triumphant words of Cyrus himself, which made the text a significant and valuable historical document. Pinches informed Henry C. Rawlinson (1810-95) about this find. Realising the importance of the text, Rawlinson, in a letter to Pinches, expressed his urgent desire to copy and study the Cylinder (Razmjou 2010: 27-28; Taylor 2012: 60). Rawlinson described the Cylinder to scholars in a talk on 17 November 1879 at the Royal Asiatic Society in London.[2] The news was published the next day in *The Times* newspaper and

1.   Later, Rassam confirmed this in a letter to Samuel Birch at the British Museum. See Razmjou 2010: 22-23.
2.   Rawlinson's translation was based on a full copy made by Pinches.

The Cyrus Cylinder, British Museum 90920

introduced the text for the first time to the public. The following year,
in 1880, Rawlinson published his translation of the Cylinder for the
first time in the *Journal of the Royal Asiatic Society,* which brought the
Cylinder to the centre of attention.[3]

The Cyrus Cylinder, written on a barrel-shaped cylinder of clay, is
inscribed in 45 lines in Babylonian cuneiform.[4] The first nineteen lines
are about Cyrus and, from line 20 onwards, Cyrus speaks in the first
person about his deeds in Babylon. The text is written in a traditional
Babylonian style, but it has been also suggested that its author took the
Ashurbanipal inscription as a literary model (Harmatta 1971; Curtis and

3.   After Rawlinson, the text was also translated by other scholars such as
     Weissbach (1911), Eilers (1971), Oppenheim (in Pritchard 1969: 315-16),
     Schaudig (2001: 550-56), Michalowski (in Arnold and Michalowski 2006: 418-
     20), Finkel (2012) and van der Spek (2014). The latest translation into Persian
     was made by the author directly from the Cylinder.
4.   The Cylinder is broken and damaged. Borger identified a fragment in the
     collection of Yale University, later joined to the Cylinder. Two fragments
     were also identified at the British Museum recently and belong to a flat tablet,
     containing parts of the text on the Cyrus Cylinder, see Razmjou 2010: 37-38;
     Finkel 2012: 18-19; Curtis 2013: 45.

Tallis 2005: 59; Finkel 2012: 26). Later, additional Babylonian texts such as the *Nabonidus Chronicle* and the *Verse Account* came to light, which together with a number of administrative, economic and prophecy texts, added more to the knowledge about Cyrus and the events in Babylon, before and after the fall of the city.

The Classical and Old Testament Sources

The classical sources: the classical texts, which had been considered as reliable and accurate over millennia, also appeared to have numerous contradictions with the Babylonian sources in the same way. All classical sources, for example, when referring to the fall of Babylon, contain a story about a battle to explain the capture of the city, mainly generated by Herodotus.[5] Even the book *Cyropaedia*, written about the life of Cyrus by Xenophon (c.430-354 BC), who seemed to be in close contact with a member of the Persian royal family, Prince Cyrus the Younger, is in fact a novel-like biography of Cyrus as a model ruler. Xenophon's story seems to have been influenced by Herodotus and features additional military clashes during the capture of Babylon, which are entirely fictional (Razmjou 2012: 115). We know that these stories were meant to be recited to the public rather than being kept inaccessible in a sealed archive with other manuscripts. Of course, in the minds of the ancient people, the fall of the legendary city of Babylon could not have happened without a fierce battle. Accounts of Cyrus battling to capture Babylon seem to be a genre of narrative style, containing additional fictional matter in order to dramatise the story and make it more attractive to the audience.

Other Babylonian textual evidence, including accounts of daily life, also contradict the Greek accounts. Some cuneiform tablets, written in Babylon or Sippar just a few days after the fall of the city, show a continuation of normal life with no trace of a chaotic or critical situation resulting from regime change.[6] Indeed, they prove that Babylon fell without a battle as daily life went on without interruption. This was probably due to prearranged treaties with the Babylonian elite and priesthood, and a disciplined army that avoided bloodshed and looting. All this can be understood from the Babylonian textual evidence. Apparently, the authors of the classical sources had some basic knowledge

---

5.   Herodotus (*The Histories* I.189-91) recounts that Cyrus captured the city by diverting the River Euphrates. For some insights, see Razmjou 2012: 115.

6.   British Museum numbers: 60744, 101100, 30418. See Strassmaier 1889: 3, *Cyrus*: 1, 2, 4, 5, 10; Razmjou 2010: 52-53.

about the fall of Babylon and mixed it with fictitious narratives. Such classical stories were written long after the events had taken place by writers who were not alive at the time and did not witness them.

The Old Testament: the case with regard to the Old Testament narratives seems to be slightly different from the classical texts. The latter, in fact, contain more general information including non-Greek/ Roman political history, whereas the Old Testament books speak only about events related to the Jewish people. Despite this narrow focus and comparatively limited information regarding the fall of Babylon, the Old Testament seems to be closer to the Babylonian sources. This may suggest a possible literary connection.

In the Old Testament Cyrus is mentioned in the books of Isaiah, Ezra, Daniel and 2 Chronicles. However, unlike classical sources, none of these books contains any reference to the series of events which led to the fall of Babylon. The only background to Cyrus' capture of Babylon mentioned in the Old Testament is exclusively related to the Jewish captivity and nothing more is stated. In fact, the only reason for the fall of Babylon according to the Old Testament was the desire of the Judean god, Yahweh to help the Judeans return from exile and rebuild the temple in Jerusalem. There is not a single reference to any internal Babylonian affairs or socio-political issues and absolutely nothing is mentioned about King Nabonidus.

Consequently, the focus of the Old Testament account is generally on two main subjects. The first depicts the character of Cyrus as the chosen one, as he is highly praised in the Old Testament for liberating the Jews from their captivity. The second subject relates to the freedom of the Jews to return to their homes. These two subjects form the background to Cyrus' capture of Babylon as far as the Old Testament is concerned. The whole matter is seen from a purely Jewish perspective.

Comparison between the Old Testament Sources and the Cyrus Cylinder

Although the Old Testament and the Cyrus Cylinder come from two different scribal traditions, a comparison of the texts demonstrates interesting closeness and similarity. By juxtaposing the texts, one can see a resemblance between some parts of the Cyrus Cylinder and chapters 40-55 in the Book of Isaiah. This part of the book is written by an anonymous prophet, known as the 'Deutero-Isaiah/Second Isaiah'. This second Isaiah was a great supporter of Cyrus. He highly praised Cyrus, even honouring him through the words of Yahweh, by calling him 'Messiah' (מָשִׁיחַ= *māšîaḥ*) (Isaiah 45:1).

The resemblance with the Cyrus Cylinder is evident wherever there is a reference to Cyrus in the Old Testament. The intimacy of terms and sentences in the Cyrus Cylinder cannot be found in any classical text. By comparing sentences, it becomes more evident that the Cyrus Cylinder and the Old Testament might have shared the same source, displaying similar content and perspective. The most evident similarities can be seen in some phrases and sentences, as presented below.[7]

Both texts (the Cyrus Cylinder and the Book of Isaiah) refer to the hand of God (Marduk/Yahweh) holding or protecting Cyrus when introducing him as a king. Although holding the hand of a king might have been an established tradition in the period, this seems to be more a Babylonian expression, representing a sign of legitimacy.

> Cyrus Cylinder (12): He took the hand of Cyrus, king of the city of Anshan (Finkel 2012: 5).
>
> Isaiah (45:1): . . . whose right hand I take hold of . . .

Both texts refer to Cyrus being accompanied by God, who was moving with him:

> Cyrus Cylinder (15): . . . like a friend and companion, he [Marduk] walked at his side . . . (Finkel 2012: 5).
>
> Isaiah (45:2): I [Yahweh] will go before you . . .

Both gods Marduk and Yahweh speak about how they call Cyrus by name and announce his title:

> Cyrus Cylinder (12): [Marduk] called him by his name, proclaiming him aloud for the kingship over all of everything (Finkel 2012: 5).
>
> Isaiah (45:3): . . . I [Yahweh] am the Lord, . . ., who summons you by name.
>
> Isaiah (45:4): . . . I [Yahweh] summon you by name and bestow on you a title of honour . . .

In the Cyrus Cylinder, the god (Marduk) speaks about the people from different geographical regions and distant lands, coming before

---

7. For the Cyrus Cylinder, the recent translation by Irving Finkel (2012: 4-7) is used in this paper; for the Old Testament, the New International Version is used.

Cyrus with their products and goods, bowing down and kissing his feet. In the Cylinder, Cyrus refers to the same occasion himself, in his own words:

> Cyrus Cylinder (18): All the people of Tintir, of all Sumer and Akkad, nobles and governors, bowed down before him and kissed his feet, rejoicing over his kingship . . . (Finkel 2012: 5).

> Cyrus Cylinder (28-30): . . . all kings who sit on thrones, from every quarter, from the Upper Sea to the Lower Sea, those who inhabit [remote distric]ts [and] the kings of the land of Amurru who live in tents, all of them, brought their weighty tribute into Shuanna, and kissed my feet (*ibid.* 6).

A similar formula is used in Isaiah, where Yahweh speaks about people from distant lands coming to Cyrus with their products and bowing before him:

> Isaiah (45:14): This is what the Lord says: 'The products of Egypt and the merchandise of Cush, and those tall Sabeans – they will come over to you and will be yours; they will trudge behind you, coming over to you in chains. They will bow down before you and plead with you . . .'

This comparison can be seen in other phrases too, where peoples and nations prostrate before Cyrus and subject themselves to him:

> Cyrus Cylinder (13): He [Cyrus] made the land of the Guti and all the Median troops prostrate themselves at his feet . . . (Finkel 2012: 5).

> Isaiah (45:1): . . . to subdue nations before him . . .

In another part in the Cyrus Cylinder, Marduk orders him directly to take the way to Babylon:

> Cyrus Cylinder (15): Marduk . . . ordered that he [Cyrus] should go to Babylon. He had him take the road to Tintir [Babylon] (Finkel 2012: 5).

In Isaiah, Yahweh is the one who calls Cyrus directly and takes him to Babylon:

> Isaiah (45: 15): I [Yahweh] have called him [Cyrus]. I will bring him [to Babylon] and will succeed in his mission.

Both texts have a clear reference to Cyrus' determination to enable the peoples in different lands to settle and live in peace:

> Cyrus Cylinder (36): I [Cyrus] have enabled all the lands to live in peace (Finkel 2012: 7).

> Isaiah (32:18): My people [Yahweh's] will live in peaceful dwelling-places, in secure homes, in undisturbed places of rest.

> Isaiah (32:17): The fruit of righteousness will be peace . . .

While referring to Cyrus, both the Cyrus Cylinder and the Old Testament mention their gods (Marduk or Yahweh) and their power over heaven and earth:

> Cyrus Cylinder (1): When . . . Marduk, King of the whole of heaven and earth . . . (Finkel 2012: 4).

> 2 Chronicles (36:23): This is what Cyrus king of Persia says: 'The Lord, the God of heaven, has given me all the kingdoms of the earth . . .'

In both texts there are references to the good heart of Cyrus in relation to Marduk and Yahweh. This is mentioned twice in the Bible:

> Cyrus Cylinder (14-15): Marduk . . . saw with pleasure his fine deeds and true heart and ordered that he should go to Babylon (Finkel 2012: 5).

> Ezra (1:1): . . . the Lord moved the heart of Cyrus king of Persia to make a proclamation throughout his realm . . .

> 2 Chronicles (36:22): . . . the Lord moved the heart of Cyrus king of Persia to make a proclamation

In the Cyrus Cylinder, Cyrus shepherded the people. Isaiah also refers to Cyrus as a shepherd:

Cyrus Cylinder (13): . . . while he [Cyrus] shepherded in justice and righteousness the black-headed people . . . (Finkel 2012: 5).

Isaiah (44:28): [The Lord] who says of Cyrus, 'He is my shepherd'.

Both the Cyrus Cylinder and the Old Testament refer to the deeds of Cyrus, which make their gods rejoice and be pleased:

Cyrus Cylinder (26): Marduk the great lord, rejoiced at [my good] deeds (Finkel 2012: 6).

Isaiah (44:28): . . . and will accomplish all that I please.

Cyrus is a liberator in both texts, freeing the people from bonds or exile:

Cyrus Cylinder (26): I freed them from their bonds (Finkel 2012: 6).

Isaiah (45:13): . . . he (Cyrus) will . . . set my exiles free.

In both texts, Cyrus appears as a builder, who reconstructs temples, shrines and holy places:

Cyrus Cylinder (31-32): . . . the sanctuaries across the river Tigris – whose shrines had earlier become dilapidated, the gods who lived therein, and made permanent sanctuaries for them (Finkel 2012: 6-7).

Isaiah (44:28): . . . he [Yahweh] will say of Jerusalem, 'Let it be rebuilt', and of the temple, 'Let its foundations be laid'.

Ezra (1.2): This is what Cyrus *king of Persia says*: 'The Lord, . . . he has appointed me to build a temple for him at Jerusalem in Judah'.

Ezra (6:3): In the first year of King Cyrus, the king issued a decree concerning the temple of God in Jerusalem: 'Let the temple be rebuilt as a place to present sacrifices, and let its foundations be laid'.

As can be seen, there are a number of similarities between the Cyrus Cylinder and the Old Testament, particularly in the book of Isaiah. Both sources speak about:

1. The hand of God protecting/holding Cyrus.
2. God accompanying Cyrus on his mission.
3. God calling Cyrus by name and announcing his title/ kingship.
4. People from distant lands coming with tributes/gifts and subjugating themselves to Cyrus.
5. God ordering Cyrus to move towards Babylon.
6. Restoring peace and making people settle in peace.
7. The god who protects Cyrus being ruler of heaven and earth.
8. God recognising the good heart of Cyrus and moving him to make a proclamation and take the road to Babylon.
9. Cyrus being referred to as a shepherd/shepherding the people.
10. God being happy and rejoicing about the deeds of Cyrus.
11. Cyrus freeing captives and deported people.
12. Cyrus being a builder/reconstructor of temples, shrines and holy places.

Although it is not always easy to interpret the connections and adaptations of ancient literary sources, the possibility of a textual link can be attested. The fact that ancient texts such as the Cyrus Cylinder and the Old Testament derive from two separate scribal traditions does not make such a connection impossible. Surprisingly, when the narrative is about Cyrus and the capture of Babylon, the narratives become closer to each other. This close link cannot be accidental, and it can only be explained by considering a possible literary connection between the texts. Most certainly, if one has been literally adapted from the other, it was the Judean texts, influenced by the strong Babylonian scribal tradition, rather than the other way round, that is, Babylonian scribes copying from the captives.

Most of the aforementioned subjects and terms were commonly in use in the Ancient Near East, also among the Judeans, but the expressions suggest a stronger link with Mesopotamia. The narratives in the Old Testament probably represent Mesopotamian terms and traditions that might have been adapted during the Babylonian exile. For example, holding the hand of god is a well-known Babylonian term and tradition. Since the Kassite Period (1595-1155 BC) every new king in Babylon had to 'take the hand of Marduk/Bēl' as a sign of legitimacy. This was also an important part of the Babylonian rites marking the spring and the beginning of the New Year, specifically during the *akītu* celebrations

(Black and Green 1992: 137; Roaf 2002: 201-202). In Babylonian terms, this was probably more than a literary expression. The rite actually took place in the sanctum of Esagila, before the statue of Marduk. The presence of the king had great importance and his absence could be the sign of a bad omen. In the Nabonidus Chronicle the bitter tone of the scribe illuminates the poor view taken of the king's absence:

> Nabonidus, the king, stayed in Teima. . . . The king did not come to Babylon for the ceremony . . . the god Nabû did not come to Babylon, the god Bēl did not go out of Esagila in procession; the festival of the New Year was omitted (Grayson 1975: 106).

The text refers to the continuous ten-year absence of the king. The absence of Nabonidus to perform the rite of 'taking the hand of Marduk' seems to be one of the causes of the anger against him in Babylon. Such a rite is not known or reported amongst the Jews. Although there are numerous references in the Old Testament to the 'hand of God' or the 'right hand of God' as a protecting hand (such as in Psalms, Exodus, Isaiah or Lamentations), these might have been written in the post-exilic period or added in the Persian, Hellenistic or even Roman Periods. It should also be noted that Biblical references to 'the hand of God' or 'the right hand of God' were more literary expressions than a physical act. In Babylon, the kings needed to hold the hand of the actual statue of Marduk but this was not the case for the Jews. Consequently, the literary use of such terms by Jewish scribes with reference to conferring political legitimacy might have been a loan terminology, adopted during the Judean exile in Babylon.

In the same way, the idea of a god accompanying a king and moving around with him can be found frequently in Mesopotamian texts, and a similar expression is also attested in the Old Testament.

Some other expressions may have been shared amongst the peoples of the Ancient Near East, such as the act of kissing feet and the bringing of goods and gifts to show submission to a ruler. This symbolic act of submission was very common and widely practised *vis-à-vis* rulers in the Ancient Near East. This rite was also practised in the region towards the elders of the family for millennia and even today is still alive in some traditional societies.[8]

8. A form of such practice can be seen nowadays in some parts of the Near East, Central Asia, India, Pakistan and Afghanistan. It is not considered an insult, but rather an honour and a highly respectful act. See Razmjou 2012: 124.

The reference to Cyrus as restorer of peace seems to have been a quite widely used expression, probably because of his reputation or due to the narratives circulating at the time. It appears that the word 'peace' is used more in texts related to Cyrus than in texts related to other Mesopotamian rulers. In one line in the Cyrus Cylinder (24), Cyrus refers to his troops marching peacefully (*šu-ul-ma-niš*) in Babylon. There is also a reference to peace (*šu-lum*) in the Nabonidus Chronicle, while recounting the acts of Cyrus after entering Babylon:

> Nabonidus Chronicle (19): . . . the state of peace was imposed upon the city . . . (Grayson 1975).

The same expression of peace in connection with Cyrus might have even reached the Greek world, in a rare and exceptional case. Thus, a sentence in a play by Aeschylus might have had a link to the narrative which Cyrus was known for:

> Cyrus blessed in good fortune, came to the throne and established peace for all his people. (*The Persians*, 769)

It is not possible to relate the text to any particular Babylonian source but it can only be the result of travelling narratives about Cyrus that might have reached the Greek settlements at the western borders of the empire.

In Isaiah the expression 'bird of prey' is used as a metaphor for Cyrus. Although there is no reference to such a wording in the remaining parts of the Cyrus Cylinder, it is also rare in the Old Testament. From five references in the Old Testament, this one in Isaiah is the only case where the term 'bird of prey' is used in such a context.

> Isaiah (46:11): From the east I summon a bird of prey; from a far-off land, a man to fulfil my purpose . . .

This can be seen more like a metaphor borrowed from neighbouring civilisations rather than a Judean concept. Representations of such a bird can be seen, for example, in Egypt, as the god Horus, and in the Assyrian reliefs from Nimrud a bird of prey (falcon?) accompanies the victorious Ashurnasirpal. The bird of prey is also a Persian term. In Iranian mythology, a 'bird of prey' is a representation of the 'Divine Glory'[9] and also one of the embodiments of Verethragna or Bahram, the

---

9.   Khvarenah/Farr(ah).

deity of war and victory. The description is probably adapted from these virtual or literary traditions to present Cyrus as a victorious king who is selected by god.

It is not easy to track such traditions through the whole of Ancient Near Eastern history, and we cannot do so in the present paper. The major point is how an ancient textual tradition might be adopted by another totally different narrative tradition with a totally different perspective.

Although the dating of sources is important for drawing conclusions, it is not easy to read and interpret the texts, especially if these have been rewritten, updated and edited a number of times by several authors in the course of history. This is evident in the books of the Old Testament, which have been edited and updated by a number of authors. By contrast, the date of the Cyrus Cylinder is fairly clear (Bahrani 2017: 295). The text speaks about finishing some construction projects at Babylon, including the Imgur-Enlil wall, where the cylinder was probably found. Therefore, it might have been written in 538-537 BC, a year after the fall of the city, when some of the projects were finished. The time period of the Old Testament scriptures, on the other hand, shows that the sections relating to Cyrus were written between the Jewish exile in Babylon through the Persian period and into the Hellenistic period.

The Cyrus Cylinder was a sort of declaration to the Babylonian audience. The first nineteen lines were probably composed by Babylonian priests or scribes, then followed by the words of Cyrus with a combination of older Mesopotamian royal texts. Although the text written on a clay cylinder was meant to be a foundation inscription to be buried under the Imgur-Enlil wall, there were also other copies of the text that were kept in the Babylonian archives. The recent find at the British Museum of two fragments containing the same text on a flat tablet confirms the existence of the text in other formats in Babylon, not used as a foundation deposit (Razmjou 2010: 37-38; Finkel 2012: 18-19; Curtis 2013: 45). Such texts were probably read aloud to the people and their content might have been circulated to different audiences in the society. Therefore, the Judean population of Babylon could have been perfectly aware of the contents of the Cylinder, which might have been heard and adapted by the second Isaiah or some other Jewish scribe. Of course, the Judeans did not share the same view as the Babylonians in believing the events recorded to be the divine will of Marduk. Most certainly, they must have seen these as the will of their own god, Yahweh. This seems to have been the case for the Judeans who were still residing in Babylon. However, it is perfectly possible that the Judeans outside Babylon were also aware of the text. As we know, news about important events was transmitted to other parts of the empire. Thus, Darius the Great, in his Bisitun inscription, says that he had ordered different copies and sent those to the people:

> (DB IV: 88-92): By the favour of Ahura Mazda this is the inscription which I made. Besides, it was in Aryan, and on clay tablets and on parchment it was composed . . . And it was inscribed and was read off before me. Afterwards this inscription I sent off everywhere among the provinces. The people unitedly worked upon it (Kent 1953: 132).

Accordingly, parts of the Babylonian version of the Bisitun inscription were found in Babylon, while an Aramaic version was found on papyri fragments from a Jewish military colony in Elephantine, Egypt (Seidl 1976; Schmitt 1990; Bresciani 1998).

The Judean scribes and elite were certainly familiar with Aramaic. The Cyrus decree mentioned in the Book of Ezra is written in both Hebrew and Aramaic versions. The Aramaic version (6:1-5) of the decree has more details than the Hebrew version (1:1-8). The original decree issued by Cyrus was probably written in Babylonian or more probably in Aramaic.

The familiarity of the Jews with Mesopotamian texts is not surprising. Many documents throughout the Neo-Assyrian, Neo-Babylonian and Persian periods were written in Aramaic and the existence of Aramaic archives can be attested. Evidence from the Persepolis Fortification tablets confirms the existence of an Aramaic archive, operating alongside the ordinary Elamite archive at Persepolis.[10]

In addition to the literary similarity of the phrases, the Old Testament and the Cyrus Cylinder present common aspirations. The Old Testament demonstrates the Jewish point of view, in which the fall of Babylon was interpreted as the divine will of Yahweh and as a divine revenge to punish the Babylonians for taking the Jews into captivity and destroying their temple in Jerusalem. In their view, Cyrus was aided directly by Yahweh to capture Babylon, in order to free them and restore their temple, as stressed in Ezra. To the Babylonians, Cyrus was a saviour, who had liberated the city from their infidel king, Nabonidus, who did not believe in Marduk, the patron god of Babylon. In their view, Cyrus had been led to Babylon by the aid of Marduk. This appears to be a common understanding shared both by the people of Babylon and the Jews, but through different gods.

---

10. For example, the reverse of the journal text (PF 1955) features the word '*nsh*', meaning 'copied' (Hallock 1969: 560).

Whereas Isaiah introduces Cyrus as a ruler chosen by Yahweh, the Babylonian texts present Cyrus from a Babylonian point of view and the events occurred at the hands of Marduk. Both sources consider Cyrus as a divinely chosen monarch and liberator. In this respect, they also share the same perspective.

There is a clear attempt by the Babylonian and Jewish traditions to relate Cyrus and his Babylonian victory to themselves by connecting him directly to their own god and their own institutional beliefs. This looks like a competition between the two faiths to claim Cyrus for their own and to demonstrate the divine power of their gods, although in fact Cyrus did not originally belong to either tradition.[11]

Apparently, Old Testament authors were fully aware of the contents of the Cyrus Cylinder. There are three possible explanations for the connections between the Cyrus Cylinder and the Old Testament: first, the presence or employment of Jews in the Babylonian archives, chancelleries and scribal houses; second, the contents might have been read aloud to the public or displayed in a public monumental format, making it accessible for the literate minority to read; and/or third, copies were sent to different regions, in accordance with the Achaemenid tradition of sending royal decrees to the provinces, in which case a copy might have reached those who had returned to their homes.

Conclusion

The Cyrus Cylinder was composed within the Babylonian scribal tradition and was a continuation of Neo-Babylonian and Neo-Assyrian texts. The existence of the same contents in the books of the Old Testament is not surprising: the Jewish people residing in Babylon were in close contact with the same tradition and the texts, either as scribes and elite, or as a public audience. As we know, royal decrees were read aloud to the inhabitants, who also included Jews. Therefore, the contents, with strong Mesopotamian undertones and layers, might have been simply transferred into the Jewish tradition and historical memory.

The Jews shared a feeling with the inhabitants of Babylon. They regretted that their god had been insulted and his temple destroyed, and the Babylonians also felt that their god and his temple, Esagila, had been insulted by Nabonidus with his construction of a counterfeit temple for

---

11. Curtis and Tallis 2005: 59. In Isaiah (45:2-3) there are references to Cyrus, not knowing Yahweh: '. . . I summon you by name and bestowed on you a title of honour, though you do not acknowledge me. . . . I will strengthen you, though you have not acknowledged me . . .'

his god, Sin, in front of Esagila (Cyrus Cylinder, line 5). Both Jews and Babylonians shared the same feeling about their gods and temples being insulted, and were looking for a saviour to change it.

The fall of Babylon was a great turning point in Jewish history and could by no means have been ignored by the literate Jewish elite and scribes. The Babylonian declaration and decrees seem to have been used by the scribes to write their own version of the story. The Jews reproduced Mesopotamian textual traditions by incorporating them into the context of their own religious history.

Bibliography

Arnold, B.T., and P. Michalowski. 2006. 'Achaemenid Period Historical Texts concerning Mesopotamia', in M.W. Chavalas (ed.), *The Ancient Near East*, Oxford: Blackwell Publishing, 426-30

Bahrani, Z. 2017. *Mesopotamia: Ancient Art and Architecture*, London: Thames & Hudson

Black, J., and A. Green. 1999. *Gods, Demons and Symbols of Ancient Mesopotamia*, London: British Museum

Bresciani, A., 1998. 'Elephantine', *Encyclopaedia Iranica* VIII: 360-62

Curtis, J.E. 2013. *The Cyrus Cylinder and Ancient Persia: A New Beginning for the Middle East*, London: British Museum

Curtis, J.E., and N. Tallis. 2005. *Forgotten Empire: The World of Ancient Persia*, London: British Museum

Eilers, W. 1971. 'Der Keilschrifttext des Kyros-Zylinders', in W. Eilers (ed.), *Festgabe Deutscher Iranisten zur 2500 Jahrfeier Irans*, Stuttgart: Hochwacht Druck, 156-66

Finkel, I.L. (ed.). 2012. *The Cyrus Cylinder: The King of Persia's Proclamation from Ancient Babylon*, London: I.B. Tauris

Grayson, A.K. 1975. *Assyrian and Babylonian Chronicles*, Texts from Cuneiform Sources 5, Locust Valley, NY: Augustin

Hallock, R.T. 1969. *Persepolis Fortification Tablets*, Oriental Institute Publications XCII, Chicago: University of Chicago Press

Harmatta, J. 1971. 'The Literary Patterns of the Babylonian Edict of Cyrus', *Acta Antiqua Academiae Scientiarum Hungaricae* 19: 207-31

Kent, R.G. 1953. *Old Persian: Grammar, Texts, Lexicon*, American Oriental Series 33, New Haven, CT: American Oriental Society

Pritchard, J.B. (ed.). 1969. *Ancient Near Eastern Texts*, Princeton, NJ: Princeton University Press

Razmjou, Sh. 2010. *The Cylinder of Cyrus the Great: Historical Background and Complete Translation* (in Persian and English), Tehran: Farzan-e Rouz

Razmjou, Sh. 2012. 'The Cyrus Cylinder: a Persian perspective', in Finkel (ed.) 2012: 104-25

Roaf, M. 2002. *Cultural Atlas of Mesopotamia and the Ancient Near East*, New York: Facts on File

Schaudig, H. 2001. *Die Inschriften Nabonids von Babylon und Kyros' des Großen*, Alter Orient und Altes Testament 256, Münster: Ugarit-Verlag

Schmitt, R. 1990. 'Bisotūn iii. Darius's inscriptions', *Encyclopaedia Iranica* IV: 299-305

Seidl, U. 1976. 'Ein Relief Dareios' I in Babylon', *Archäologische Mitteilungen aus Iran* NF 9: 125-30

Spek, R. J., van der. 2014. 'Cyrus the Great, Exiles and Foreign Gods: A Comparison of Assyrian and Persian Policies on Subject Nations', in M. Kozuh et al. (eds), *Extraction and Control: Studies in Honor of Matthew W. Stolper*, Chicago: University of Chicago Press, 233-64

Strassmaier, J.N. 1889. *Inschriften von Cyrus, König von Babyon (538-529 v. Chr.)*, Leipzig: Pfeiffer

Taylor, J. 2012. 'The Cyrus Cylinder: Discovery', in Finkel (ed.) 2012: 35-68

Weissbach, F.H., 1911. *Die Keilinschriften der Achämeniden*, Vorderasiatische Bibliothek 3,

Leipzig: J.C. Hinrichs

7

Interpreting Sasanian Beards:
Significant Images in an Interconnected World

P.O. Harper

In the art of the pre-Islamic Near East beards are such a constant feature of divinities, kings and heroes that it is easy to assume they are no more than a standard part of an established iconography. Drawing such a conclusion would, however, be a mistake as there is often a message to decypher in the appearance and style of a beard. The comments below on some Sasanian beards are dedicated to my late good friend and colleague, Terence Mitchell, in recognition of his wide range of interests as Keeper of Western Asiatic Antiquities at the British Museum and in appreciation of a long life of scholarship generously shared with others. Biblical studies were one of his chief interests, and it is relevant to note here that beards receive at least some attention in the Old Testament, which draws upon ancient oriental traditions, while in the New Testament, written in a Greek cultural environment, references to beards are no longer in evidence. This disregard for beards and their symbolism is reflected too in early images of Jesus in the third century, at Dura Europos and Palmyra, where the new Messiah is sometimes bearded and often beardless. Only later, in the sixth century, is the presence or absence of a beard on images of Jesus interpreted by some to have symbolic significance as a reflection of the dual nature of Jesus, divine and human (Kraeling 1967: figs 5-6; Weitzmann 1976: 27; Weitzmann [ed.] 1979: 404; Mathews 1993: 98, 123, 177; Ruprechtsberger [ed.] 1993: 153).

To turn to Sasanian beards is to return to the oriental world. Following a long period of Hellenisation in the Near East, the art of the Sasanian era (AD 226-651) illustrates a return to more ancient eastern modes. One phenomenon that serves as an indication of this cultural shift is the iconic appearance of the bearded rulers on Sasanian works, notably coins. Over the centuries stylised Sasanian royal beards are a significant feature which changes only slowly: long and spade-shaped to long and bound and finally to a short, chin-length style. In contrast, the more naturalistic, Hellenised, royal beards of the preceding Arsacid kings illustrate a variety of styles frequently changing on the coinage from reign to reign: long and short, curled and straight. A deviation from these naturalistic types occurs, notably, with the last Arsacid ruler, Artabanus IV (AD 216-24) who is depicted on the coinage and on a sculpture with a unique and, one can only suppose meaningful, stylised, forked beard (Sellwood 1971: 297-99; Ghirshman 1962: 56, fig. 70). While forked beards have a long history in the art of the Ancient Near Eastern and the Graeco-Roman worlds, the adoption by the last Arsacid ruler of this distinctive mode, otherwise unparalleled on Arsacid coins, makes a statement about the royal identity which was not lost on Artabanus' Sasanian successor. On the relief of the first Sasanian king, Ardashir I (AD 224-40) at Naqsh-e Rustam the slain Arsacid king, Artabanus IV, lies under the feet of Ardashir's horse and has a clearly rendered, forked beard (Herrmann 1969: fig. 4, pl. 4). We do not know what particular significance the forked beard had for the last Arsacid ruler but it seems that on the coins this iconographic feature was considered by Artabanus to be as important as the inscription in establishing his identity. On his early coin 'portraits', it is only the forked beard which distinguishes Artabanus IV from his brother Vologases VI (AD 208-28) as they wear identical headdresses (Sellwood 1971: Type 88/17, Type 89/1).

The standardisation of Sasanian royal beards on the coinage and rock reliefs makes variations in the design or mode particularly noticeable when they occur. The three types of beard considered below represent innovations, the first, a long-lasting one and the other two, single unique instances: the early Sasanian, bound beard of the king on the coinage and works of art (Figs 1-3); the unusually rendered portion of the facial hair appearing immediately beneath the lower lip of a Sasanian king on a silver plate in the Hermitage Museum (Fig. 4); the lengthy, pointed beard of the god Ohrmazd as it is depicted on the rock relief of Khusro II (AD 591-626) at Taq-e Bustan (Fig. 6).

The Bound Beard

The early appearance of a bound or gathered beard on the victory relief of Ardashir I at Firuzabad and then, later, on this same king's investiture/ victory relief at Naqsh-e Rustam is unparalleled in Arsacid royal

Fig. 1. (left) Sasanian silver drachm of Shapur I (AD 240-72), BM
1894,0506.1309. © Trustees of the British Museum.

Fig. 2. (right) Sasanian silver drachm of Narseh (AD 293-303), BM
1862,1004.37. © Trustees of the British Museum.

imagery (Herrmann 1977: 88, 90). At Naqsh-e Rustam this treatment
of the royal beard is one of the features that clearly distinguishes the
king from the god who has a lengthy spade-shaped beard. At Salmas, the
two equestrian figures, Ardashir I and his son, the future Shapur I, in a
period of co-regency, have their beards bound (Alram, Gyselen 2003: 31-
33, pl. 45, fig. 6). With the reign of Shapur I (AD 240-72) this beard style
becomes for the first time part of the canonical royal image on coins, and
it remains a constant feature on the coin images through to the reign of
Yazdgird II (AD 438-57), with the exception of Wahram I (AD 273-76)
(Figs 1-2). On some examples only the presence of short ribbons at the
base of the beard testifies to the existence of the mode (Göbl 1971: pl. 10;
Schindel 2004: 368, 378-79).

The replacement of the bound beard with a spade-shaped beard by
Wahram I on his coin images is a change from the mode his father,
Shapur I, had established and appears to be a return to the beard style
of Ardashir I on his coins. The reason for this change is unknown and
it raises questions about the tied beard of Wahram I represented on his
Bishapur investiture relief (V) (Herrmann 1981: 11-20). It is possible
that the unexpected form of the beard of the king on the rock relief is
another modification to that relief made at a later date by Narseh (AD
293-302) when he replaced the name of Wahram with his own in the

Fig. 3. Silver, gilded head of a Sasanian king, fourth century AD.
The Metropolitan Museum of Art, acc. no 65.126, Fletcher Fund.
Photo courtesy of the Metropolitan Museum of Art, New York.

accompanying inscription, added a dead figure beneath the relief and, in
all probability, carved away the points of the crown of Wahram I so that
a plaster replacement showing the crown of Narseh could be depicted.[1]

1.   Herrmann does not mention re-carving in the damaged beard area. For the
     spade-shaped beard on Bishapur VI and P. Calmeyer's suggestion that this may
     be Bahram I, see: Herrmann 1981: 37.

Fig. 4. (left) Sasanian silver, gilded plate from Strelka, Perm region, Russia, sixth century AD. Hermitage Museum, acc. no S520.
Photo courtesy of the Hermitage Museum, St Petersburg.

Fig. 5. (right) Silver, gilded plate from near Cherdyn, Perm region, Russia, late fifth or early sixth century AD. Hermitage Museum, acc. no S216.
Photo courtesy of the Hermitage Museum, St Petersburg.

On Sasanian silver vessels the depiction of a royal beard bound at the base is an inconsistent feature. This is true of vessels executed in the two different styles defined by distinctive depictions of the drapery folds, shown either as paired lines or as a series of closely-spaced parallel lines (Harper and Meyers 1981: 189, Table I, 2; 191, Table II, 2). The occasional absence of the bound beard on some early royal plates where other types are shown was apparently an acceptable variation from the established royal imagery on the coins. A variation of the bound beard appears on a fourth-century, silver, life-size head of a king in the Metropolitan Museum where the beard is shown as meticulously braided (Harper 1966: 131-46; Splendeur des Sassanides 1993: 165, cat. no 23) (Fig. 2). Similarly held together over some length (knotted or braided?) is the beard of Shapur II as depicted on a seal impression in the Ahmad Saeedi collection (Gyselen 2007: 77, Figs Aa, Ab)

It is possible the new and distinctive, forked-beard type adopted by the last Arsacid ruler, Artabanus IV, influenced his Sasanian successors to assume an original mode as well. Two works of art from the latest Parthian and earliest Sasanian period indicate that prototypes for the bound-beard mode may predate its use by Ardashir I and his successors. However, on neither of these examples do the bearded figures wear

Fig. 6. Sculpture of Ohrmazd, iwan of Khusro II at Taq-e Bustan, Iran.
Photo: Fukai and Horiuchi 1972: pl. XIV (full-length figures).

crowns or headdresses although they are clearly elite, prestigious persons.
On a silver bowl in the British Museum (Barnett and Curtis, J.E. 1973:
127, pl. 79) the image is of a figure on a couch similar to many scenes
in Palmyrene art and in the Parthian art of Elymais/Susiana (Mathieson
1992: 62, cat. nos 4, 10, 18, 212). The reclining male on the silver vessel
has a beard which is simply shown as a narrow line beneath the chin.[2]
More clearly rendered, bound beards are depicted on a second work, a
horse-shaped rhyton in the Cleveland Museum of Art which probably
dates to the beginning of the Sasanian period or, conceivably, to the end
of the Parthian period when foil gilding was still the norm. Two male
figures are represented as half-figures within fluted roundels on the front
of the recumbent horse (Shepherd 1966: 289-311, figs 6, 7 and back cover;
Harper 1978: 28-30, cat. no 1). Both males have chin-length wavy hair.
One figure holds out to the other a jewelled ring signifying investiture or

2.   I am grateful to Vesta Curtis for checking the image on this bowl in the British
      Museum for me.

contract, and the scene probably represents an agreement or the passing of some level of high authority to a successor. Because the ring-holding figure rests his hand on his sword and the images appear on a caparisoned horse, a military significance is possible. The beards are simply but clearly bound. Both of these works of art suggest that the bound beard of the first Sasanian rulers may have been a mode which already existed in the late second/early third century before being adopted by Ardashir and becoming under Shapur I an exclusive symbol of Sasanian royal authority.

Non-royal personages and Zoroastrian deities in Sasanian art are always depicted with their often lengthy beards unbound. However, on the northern and eastern borders of the Sasanian kingdom the style of wearing the beard bound was recognised as a meaningful indication of supreme power. The mode was taken over by the Kushano-Sasanian rulers in northern Khorasan and Bactria/Tokharistan (Stavisky 1986: 47-55) and occasionally by their successors in the region in the fourth and fifth centuries, the Kidarites and Alkhon/Hephthalites who countermarked and imitated Sasanian coins on which the bound beard appears (Mitchiner 1978: 201, no 1270; 206-207, nos 1318-26; Alram and Pfisterer 2010: 17, Type 33; Cribb 2010: 143, fig. 42; 146, figs 71, 72, 74; Lerner 2018: 1-19).[3] On a fragmentary, silver roundel in the Hermitage Museum, apparently from a vessel, there is an image of a crowned male bust whose long beard passes through a ring. Identified as a Hephthalite noble by Lukonin, the figure is shown over a plant base as a bust, his head in profile facing to the viewer's right (Trever and Lukonin 1987: 42, fig. 1).[4] He wears a 'crown' composed of a wing and a crescent (and possibly a profile crenelation), which is clearly modelled on Sasanian crowns as they appear on the coinage and in works of art. The shoulder-length, uncurled hair and the straight hairs of the long beard give the image the appearance of a Parthian or East Iranian rather than a Hephthalite personage whose hair is short on coins, seals and silver vessels and who is usually beardless (Mitchiner 1978: 224-37; Lerner and Sims-Williams 2011: 35, fig. 5, 43, 53, fig.11, 107, AB 3.2, 3.3, 113, AB 4.1; Marshak and Krikis 1969: 55-81). The medallion portrait type, the wing and crescent on the crown, the diadem ends framing the bust and the ringed beard point to Sasanian influences but the straight hairstyle and the necklet with a single, large bead reflect Parthian prototypes.[5] Whoever this personage may be, he

---

3. Bactria became known as Tokharistan during the course of the Sasanian period and both terms will be used here for consistency.

4. The roundel was found with much later material dated to the eighth to tenth century in the extreme north of Russia (Bolshezemelskaia Tundra).

5. On Sasanian coins ribbons spreading out on either side of the bust only appear

is unequivocally portrayed as a 'ruler' following Iranian modes which became widespread in Iran and western Central Asia by the mid-first millennium AD. A date no earlier than the fifth century is indicated by the diadem ends framing the bust and by the crown elements.

As with the Arsacid ruler's choice of the forked beard, there is some uncertainty about the significance of the new Sasanian beard mode. Hubertus von Gall observed that the rather summarily bound hair above the head of Ardashir on the Firuzabad relief may have been intended to portray the ruler in an active battle mode (von Gall 1990: 27-28). In the absence of a helmet or headdress, gathering the king's long locks was a practical solution for a warrior pursuing his enemy. Similarly, the long beard of the Sasanian monarch must have needed to be held away from the face in the heat of battle. One solution to this problem is illustrated by a Parthian terracotta head of a warrior found at Old Nisa in Turkmenistan. On that sculpture, which is dated to the second century BC, the earflaps of the helmet, bound under the chin, effectively contain the beard while at the same time securing the helmet in place (Invernizzi 2001: 150, fig. 11). It is possible that in Sasanian art the image of the king having a bound beard, a notable iconographic feature, gained dynastic significance as a potent symbol associated with concepts of battle and ultimate victory.

Facial Hair Immediately Beneath the Lower Lip of the King
as Depicted on the Strelka Silver Plate, Hermitage Museum,
St Petersburg, Russia

On a gilded silver plate in the Hermitage Museum in St Petersburg decorated with the image of an enthroned Sasanian monarch a curious triangular pattern appears just under the monarch's lower lip surrounded by the tight curls of the short beard. The precious vessel was found near the village of Strelka in the Kisherskii region of the Perm Krai to the west of the Ural Mountains, far from any place of probable manufacture (Fig. 4). Technically and stylistically the plate is recognisably late Sasanian, probably a work of the sixth century, although the dress of the king might suggest a slightly earlier date [Harper and Meyers 1981: 67-68, 100-102, 114, 122, 129, 173, pl. 19; Trever and Lukonin 1987: 77-78. 109, 125, cat.

regularly with Peroz' third crown (AD 474/7-484) but are a feature on some Kidarite coin images dated by Mitchiner to around AD 400 (Mitchiner 1978: cat. nos 3621, 3622; Cribb 2010: 91-146). For coins of the Parthian king, Darius (?) c. 70 BC, wearing a necklet with a large, single stone, see: Sellwood 1971: 96, Type 35.

no 9, pls 18,19: Les Perses sassanides 2006: 94, cat. no, 34 (Marshak)].
The crown of the king depicted follows a model seen on the coins of
many late Sasanian kings: Kawad I (AD 488-96, 499-531), Khusro I (AD
531-79), Hormizd IV (AD 579-90), Wahram VI (AD 590/91), Khusro II
(AD 590/1-628) and Kawad II (AD 628). In design and iconography this
vessel is unique among standard Sasanian works of art. A brief summary
of points made previously in more detail follows for those persons
unfamiliar with this late Sasanian vessel.

In the divided composition of the scenes on the plate, the larger, upper
scene includes a frontal image of a Sasanian king seated upright on a
banqueting couch 'throne', an uncommon image in Sasanian art. The
king is framed by two pairs of standing attendants wearing the same
distinctive dress. One figure is bearded and one is beardless in each
pair. Below this scene and separated from it by a horizontal division is
a smaller, secondary scene of a royal hunt in which the hunter wearing
a simple crown with crenellations has a bound beard. This image may,
therefore, be a generalised reference to the long history of the Sasanian
dynasty as the bound beard no longer appeared on Sasanian coins minted
in the period when the vessel was made.

The articulation of the circular field into two unequal parts and the
inclusion in the smaller segment, the exergue, of an associated image
which supplies context for the main scene is a familiar device in the art
of the Graeco-Roman world and is seen as well in the art of Bactria/
Tokharistan (Dalton 1964: pl. 37, no 196, pl. 38, no 208). In that region
Hellenising motifs and designs persisted for centuries following the
conquests of Alexander the Great and the rule of Graeco-Bactrian kings.
Dividing the field of the design into two distinct parts is not a usual
compositional device employed by Sasanian artisans on silver plates as
far as can be determined from the works that survive.

Also owing its popularity to the Graeco-Roman world is the banqueting
couch as the seat of significant personages who recline upon it. This piece
of furniture was widely adopted at an earlier period in the Hellenised art
of Iran, in Parthian Elymais and in the hybrid Graeco-Roman/Iranian/
Semitic art of early first millennium AD Palmyra in Syria. Similarly,
Hellenistic influence dictated the appearance of the banqueting couch as
a throne in the East. In Kushan Bactria, the ruler Huvishka (second half
of the second century AD) appears somewhat awkwardly enthroned, on
some of his copper coins minted at Kapisa, partly reclining with one leg
up on a couch and partly seated with one leg down (Mitchiner 1978: 429-
30, nos 3225-45). [6]

6.   The date of Huvishka follows a dating of Kanishka to c. AD 127.

Sasanian illustrations of a frontal, enthroned king appear on two early Sasanian rock reliefs at Naqsh-e Bahram and Bishapur where the Sasanian monarch is seated upright with both feet on the ground, as on the Strelka plate, but on a simple bench throne (Harper and Meyers 1981: 100-101, figs 25-27). In contrast, the image on a unique gold plate inlaid with coloured stone and glass medallions of late Sasanian date but not certainly of Sasanian manufacture shows the banqueting-couch throne as the seat of a personage who is portrayed as a crowned Sasanian king (Harper and Meyers 1981: 110-111, 113, 115, pl. 33). Typologically closest to this vessel in the Bibliothèque Nationale in Paris is a 'Hunnish' deep bowl which once held similar medallions set in the walls of the vessel (Daim et al. 1996: 161, no 4.303). The gold plate has a Middle Persian inscription indicating that at some point in its history it was in a region where the script was in use but the unusual form and decoration suggest that the place of manufacture lay in a region where artisans followed 'Hunnish' rather than Sasanian forms and designs.

If important features of the scenes on the Strelka plate are derived from Graeco-Roman modes that persisted in the arts east of Iran, other iconographic details point to the nomad peoples who entered the region of Bactria and Gandhara during the early first millennium AD. The four attendants have an unusually styled, short, seemingly uncurled head of hair. As noted above, one figure in each pair has a short beard depicted as a mass of curls and one is beardless. The faces and tall caps contribute to the impression of rather long heads having prominent noses similar in appearance to representations of defeated enemies, perhaps Hephthalites, on stucco panels attributed to the fifth century at Bandian in north-eastern Iran (Rahbar 1998, 238-39, fig. 5; Gignoux 1998: 251-58).

The respectful stance of the figures on the Strelka plate with arms folded across the breast and hands covered has a long history in Parthian and Sasanian art and by the second half of the first millennium AD this posture appears widely in the arts of the Eurasian trade routes and China (Kawami 1987: cat. nos 21, 31, 49; Herrmann 1980: 42-43, fig. 5; Herrmann 1981: fig. 3). More unusual in a Sasanian context are the clothes worn by the four attendants on the Strelka plate. The garments are characterised by the cut and drape of the tunics which curve upward at the front and fall to lower, slightly rounded points at the sides where the skirting can, in one instance, be seen as divided (Vogelsang-Eastwood 2004: 210-15).[7] A prototype for this square-shaped tunic style curving down at the sides exists in the Parthian Near East and is seen on Kushan

---

7.   I thank Betty Hensellek for advice on the garments depicted and for her constructive thoughts and comments.

and Kidarite coins and other artifacts of the third, fourth and fifth centuries where the upward curve of the skirt becomes more exaggerated with the passage of time and the folds at the sides are sharply pointed (Mathieson 1992: 153, fig. 27; 208, fig. 73; 219, fig. 85; Mitchiner 1978: 462, nos 3536, 3540; 467, nos 3570-75; 476, no 3618). East of Iran, this style of tunic persists, as the dress of fifth/sixth century terracotta 'royal figures' excavated at Erkurgan (Uzbekistan) demonstrates (Isamiddinov 1991: 173-76, pls. 71, 72). Slightly later in date is a terracotta ossuary from Yumalakatepa (Uzbekistan) where the side slits of a related form of tunic worn by a priest are also visible (Berdimuradov et al. 2008: fig. 1). The only certain Sasanian depiction of the type of square-skirted tunic which appears on the Strelka plate with divided longer, side folds having rounded hemlines, occurs at the end of the period where it is worn by personages accompanying the Sasanian king and his court on the boar hunt relief in the large iwan at Taq-e Bustan in Iran (Fukai and Horiuchi 1969: pl. 33; Mode 2006: 393-413). The ethnicity of the three personages wearing this form of tunic at the end of the Sasanian period is impossible to know as the heads which might provide some indication are badly damaged. On one head, chin-length, wavy (not curled) hair can be detected beyond the line of the break, not typically a hairstyle of Sasanian Iranians (Fukai and Horiuchi 1969: pl. 39). The tunics of the figures called elephant beaters, servants or nobles in publications are richly decorated and the figures wear belts from which straps are suspended, the number differing according to the placement of the individual on the relief moving from top to bottom (Bálint 1992: 325-27). These features are indications that the persons are of some importance, courtiers perhaps, and they are clearly distinguished by their dress from Iranian figures, similarly mounted on elephants and taking part in the hunt.

Not certainly attributable to a central Sasanian court workshop are two precious vessels on which figures clad in the square-shaped tunic under consideration are depicted. The only variation in the cut of their garments is that the hem ends at the sides in sharply pointed corners as on Kushan and Kidarite coins rather than in the more rounded corners seen on the Strelka plate and the relief at Taq-e Bustan. The first vessel is the gold plate in the Bibliothèque Nationale in Paris which has been mentioned above. The second is a silver plate in the Hermitage Museum (Fig. 5). The vessel was found near the city of Cherdyn in the Cherdynskii region of the Perm Krai to the west of the Ural Mountains and can be distinguished from works of central Sasanian manufacture in the design and details of the scene, in technical aspects and in the composition of the silver (Trever 1937: 6-8, 26-28; Harper and Meyers 1981: 79-81, 111,

113, 130-31, 177, pl. 27; Trever and Lukonin 1987: 73-74, 108-109, 126, pls 16, 17; Splendeur des Sassanides 1993: 206-207, cat. no 61). There is a dotted monogram on the reverse side (Trever and Lukonin 1987: 109).[8] The 'king' has a prominent jaw or, possibly, a short beard now largely worn away and no longer visible in photographs. He wears a crown closely, but not exactly, the same as the third crown of Peroz (AD 474/7-84) as it appears on that king's coinage. The hair is oddly shown as a short bunch behind the ear and gathered as a ball under the forefinger of the bowstring hand. This is a stylisation appearing on late coins of Peroz bearing Hephthalite countermarks and on Hephthalite copies of Peroz' coins (Mitchiner 1978: 227-30, nos 1450-79; Alram and Pfisterer 2010: 27-32). The sword of the king, as Marshak noted, is not a Sasanian type but is comparable to the swords of east Turkestan in the fourth to fifth centuries and to the sword worn by a Hephthalite hunter on a mid-fifth-century Kidarite/Hephthalite bowl in the British Museum (Marschak 1986: 33; Dalton 1964: no 201, pl. 31).

It is beyond the scope of this article to do more than suggest that the vessel from Cherdyn is best understood as a work of the late fifth century or early sixth century, commissioned by a newly-powerful Hephthalite, who ruled over some part of a vast region controlled by Hephthalites, including Sogdiana, as well as lands south of the Hindu Kush and in western Central Asia (de la Vaissière 2003: 119-32). Having overcome the Sasanians in battle in AD 474 and having forced them to pay a massive tribute in silver coins and probably silver plate, the Hephthalite rulers undoubtedly saw themselves as the successors to the Sasanian dynasty. On this plate, made by an artisan familiar with Sasanian works, the ruler chose to depict himself wearing a near replica of the third crown of his defeated enemy, Peroz. As noted above, the Hephthalites used not only countermarked Sasanian coins of Peroz wearing his third crown but also minted local imitations of the coins of that Sasanian king. In this environment, the production in a region under Hephthalite control of a prestigious court silver vessel decorated with the Sasanian theme of the royal hunt would have underscored the Hephthalite claim to be the dominant authority in the region.

To return to the Strelka plate, tall boots into which long leggings are tucked serve as the footwear of the four, distinctively dressed attendant figures. Consistently portrayed over centuries in the art of the Near East and western Central Asia, boots are a persistent feature in the dress of nomadic peoples – whether short and elaborately decorated as on Palmyrene sculptures in the early first millennium AD or tall and more

---

8.   I do not know of an illustration of this detail.

simply defined as on the mid-fifth-century, silver Kidarite/Hephthalite bowl in the British Museum and in a fifth- or sixth-century painting from Dilberjin in Bactria (Dalton 1964: no 201, pls. 29-31; Lerner and Sims-Williams 2011: 39, fig. 6). On Sasanian works of art boots are not part of the court dress although it must be acknowledged that on the latest Sasanian relief at Taq-e Bustan it is difficult to determine whether boots or some form of leg guard are being depicted.

It is probable, that the four distinctively clad figures beside the king on the Strelka plate are intended to represent foreigners, possibly Hephthalites, who are viewed in this instance as supporters and allies of the Sasanian king. Iconographic parallels in the art of the Byzantine West are provided by earlier and contemporary images on silver plates showing enthroned rulers with the support of foreign allies: Theodosius (AD 378-95) flanked on either side by German guards, identifiable by their dress and hairstyle, and David appearing before Saul, flanked by similar guards (Weitzmann [ed.] 1979: 74-76, cat. no 64; 475, 477-79, cat. no 427).

If the design and iconography of the scene on the Strelka plate point to influences from Hellenised cultures which flourished on the northern and eastern borders of Iran, modified in turn by Kushans, Kidarites and Hephthalites who controlled the region in the first millennium AD, another indication of a connection with the region of Bactria is the presence on the reverse of the plate within the foot ring of a Bactrian inscription in cursive Graeco-Bactrian script reading 'Property of Lord Khatul' (Sims-Williams 2009: 192; Sims-Williams 2010: 148, no 518)[9]. While this inscription does not provide information on the precise date or place of manufacture of the vessel or even on the ethnic or regional identity of the original owner, it does indicate that at some point in its history the silver plate was in the region east of Iran where this language and script were in use.

To turn finally to the beard of the king, the unusual stylisation of the facial hair immediately beneath the lower lip of the king on the Strelka plate is a small but surprising deviation from standard Sasanian dynastic imagery. On an early Sasanian plate in the Hermitage Museum found at Malaia Pereshchepina, the almost undetectable, simply hatched, lower-lip hair of the bearded king in the hunting scene is not comparable to the clearly defined patch of facial hair beneath the lower lip on the Strelka plate (Harper and Meyers 1981: 82, pl. 28). Because of the small scale of the image on the Strelka plate it is difficult to know whether the triangular form apparent under the lower lip is intended to define an open or shaved space between two curls as it is rendered on a fine third-

9.   My thanks to Nicholas Sims-Williams for his comments on this inscription.

century head from Palmyra or whether this is a carefully trimmed and shaped patch of hair (Tanabe [ed.] 1986: 486, no 460). In either case, the mode as it appears on the Strelka plate, places the image of the Sasanian monarch outside the Sasanian norm.

In the periods preceding the Sasanian era, the treatment of facial hair beneath the lower lip is realistically defined on a Hellenised Parthian, terracotta head of around the first century BC from Old Nisa in Turkmenistan (Invernizzi 2001: 149-50, figs. 10, 11). Later, on Roman works of art, images of emperors and notables often have realistic tufts of hair beneath the lower lip variously distinguished from the rest of the beard (Inam and Rosenbaum 1966). This western mode is one which spread with other influences from the Hellenistic and Roman worlds to the East. It appears in Palmyra and on works found in Iran, such as the beautiful bronze head from Shami variously dated between the second century BC and the second century AD (Curtis, V.S. 1993: 63-70). Closer in date to the Strelka image are the heads of defeated enemies, thought to be Hephthalites, who are shown on the Sasanian stucco panels excavated at fifth-century Bandian with short lines, representing hair, immediately beneath the lower lip (Rahbar 1998: 238-39, fig. 5). At a later date, in the former Hephthalite lands in Bactria/Tokharistan, the presence of trimmed and styled hair beneath the lower lip remains a feature of images of persons at the highest levels of society. On two silver, gilded plates in the Hermitage Museum, attributed by Boris Marshak to post-Sasanian, eighth-century workshops in Tokharistan, 'royal' figures, shown banqueting and hunting, wear low, generic 'Sasanian', crenellated crowns and have facial hair arranged in two tufts, simplified and stylised variations of one of the Graeco-Roman modes, beneath the lower lip (Marschak 1986: 276-78, 437, fig. 193; Trever and Lukonin, 1987: 79-80, pls 22,23, 32,33; Agostini, Stark 2016: 32-33).

In any discussion of the definition of facial hair beneath the lower lip, it is important to mention, at least briefly, the existence of another long tradition of representing such hair on male visages. In China, a single dart of hair beneath the lower lip appears in the arts by the early third century BC on some of the terracotta warrior figures from the tomb of the Qin Shihuangdi (Ying Zheng 260-210 BC) (Sun 2017: cat. nos 3, 4, 5; Nickel 2013: 413-47).[10] This distinctive mode persists over the centuries in China and is noted here because it became widely known and adopted in parts of western Central Asia by the mid-first millennium AD. Images of non-Han, Central Asians in the arts of China indicate that the Chinese

10. Nickel discusses possible cultural contacts between the Greeks and Chinese in the third century BC but without reference to facial hair modes.

treatment of this detail was known and adopted in the West (Watt 2004: 242-43, cat. no 237; Valenstein 1997-1998: 2, fig. 1; 8, fig. 13). By the end of the first millennium AD the Chinese mode was taken over by Turkic peoples in Central Asia as it appears on local stone monuments and in paintings (Juliano and Lerner 2001: 267, fig. A; Along the Ancient Silk Routes 1982: 169-70, cat. no 108). What, if any, influence the Chinese under-lip hair style may have had on the Hephthalite fashion portrayed on the heads of the defeated warriors at fifth-century Bandian is difficult to assess but the later style of two, crescentic hair tufts, seen on the eighth-century, silver plates from Bactria, described above, is more similar to Graeco-Roman than to any Chinese models.

A date in the second half of the sixth century is both historically and art historically possible for the Strelka plate but it is important to recognise that there are few Sasanian remains of the sixth and seventh centuries comparable to the plate which can suggest a precise dating. Whether the plate was made in a central or provincial Sasanian workshop is also open to question. Arguments in support of the former include important technical details, the method of manufacture, the non-decorative tool marks (line beneath the exterior rim), and the analysis of the silver which places the plate in the category of 'central Sasanian' silver vessels (Harper and Meyers 1981: 173, pl. 19). These factors as well as numerous stylistic features underscore the likelihood that the plate is a central Sasanian work of art.

For whom, then, was this example of Sasanian court silver intended? The scene depicted is unusual and features such as the composition and design as well as the appearance and dress of some of the figures are strange in a Sasanian cultural context. However, the image of a Sasanian monarch, having a distinctive facial hair mode, enthroned on a banqueting couch, and accompanied by notables who, in physical appearance and dress, are not typically Sasanian are all features which would not have been strange north and east of Iran, in a Hellenised and Hephthalite cultural environment. If any uncertainty existed in the mind of the recipient concerning the origin of the unusual vessel, the Sasanian source was underscored by the standardised depiction of the Sasanian royal icon, an equestrian hunting scene, in the exergue.

Images on the plate, including the appearance of the facial hair, speak in an original and deliberate fashion of a Sasanian dynastic authority in which diverse cultural traditions – Iranian, Graeco-Roman, Kushan and Hephthalite – are incorporated and assimilated for the benefit of a wider, presumably Hephthalite, audience. In the sixth century, more than one Sasanian monarch, familiar with the cultures of neighbouring lands, might have sent such an image to a regional ruler on Iran's unstable eastern borders, the destination suggested by the inscription on the reverse of the plate. In the east of Iran in the late fifth and sixth centuries relations with the Hephthalite and later Turk realm in Bactria resulted in a protracted Sasanian royal presence in the region: Kawad I (AD 484; 486-97) who is said to have had a Hephthalite wife, the daughter of the Hephthalite ruler, was left as a hostage by his father, Peroz, and then, at a later date, reputedly fled Iran to seek help from the Hephthalites in regaining his throne (Schindel 2004: 447, 459); Khusro I (AD 531-79), with new Turkic allies, defeated the Hephthalites and, in a treaty in AD 560, assumed for a brief period control of their territories in Khorasan and Bactria; Ohrmazd IV (AD 579-90), the son of Khusro I, had a dual cultural heritage: a Sasanian father and a mother who was a daughter of the Turkic *khaqan*. In contrast, the significant relationship for Khusro II was with the Byzantine West and the Emperor Maurice (AD 582-602) with whose assistance he was able to regain the throne of Iran.

Although it is possible that the king represented on the Strelka plate is Kawad I, the long reign of Khusro I and his considerable achievements make him a likely candidate. Within Iran, the Mazdakite revolution had brought economic, social and political developments and upheavals which led, under Khusro I, to a more independent and centralised monarchy, a new court hierarchy and a standing army under royal control in which foreign elements were present, some at high levels of authority (Harmatta 2002: 153-59). These developments may explain the appearance on this silver plate of a design that is innovative and original in the context of Sasanian royal imagery. The many details noted above favour an interpretation of the vessel as an example of imperial Sasanian propaganda, a statement by the Iranian monarch, once again dominant, to a neighbour in the East whose loyalty to the Sasanian dynasty and support for its ambitious political and territorial designs can never have been certain. It is probable that the image on the plate celebrates the return of Hephthalite lands and peoples to the rule of an all-powerful but inclusive Sasanian authority. If so, it is, in a sense, a Sasanian response to the image on the Cherdyn plate, described above.

The Beard of Ohrmazd in the Iwan of Khusro II
at Taq-e Bustan, Iran

Taq-e Bustan lies near the ancient border with Mesopotamia on routes which led to the western lands of the Sasanian kingdom and, ultimately, to Antioch and Byzantium. The date or dates during which the large iwan achieved its final form are still open to discussion and range, according to most scholars, between the reigns of Khusro II (AD 591-628) and Yazdgird III (AD 632-51) (Mode 2006: 393-414; Compareti 2018: 20-36). In this discussion, the high relief sculptures at the top of the back wall of the iwan are considered to have been executed during the reign of Khusro II.

The three figures on the back wall are the goddess Nahid, the central king, Khusro II, and, on the monarch's left, the great god, Ohrmazd (Fig. 6). All three sculptures are on low bases. Somewhat surprisingly, the king is slightly larger than the deities and is placed on the highest base. The figure of the god, Ohrmazd, turns very slightly toward the central figure of the king. Although the beard of Ohrmazd is the focus of this article, details of the dress of that divinity deserve attention too because they are unusual in the context of Sasanian art and unexpected. Earlier representations of the god on Sasanian rock reliefs datable to the third and fourth centuries are located in southern Iran in Fars and to the north at Taq-e Bustan itself where the god appears in an investiture relief attributed to Ardashir II (AD 379-83) (Fukai and Horiuchi 1972: pls 75-80; Azarnoush 1986: 219-47). On the relief of Ardashir II, both the god and the king are depicted wearing traditional early Sasanian dress. A knee-length, long sleeved, light tunic having a horizontal hemline is tied at the waist by a ribbon belt. Over this tunic a light cape covers only the top of the shoulders and is fastened by a double circle brooch. Beneath these garments are trousers and finally, shoes tied at the ankles.

The clothing of Ohrmazd in the large iwan provides a surprising contrast in style and in appearance to the earlier image. On Khusro's relief the god is clad in a garment quite different in appearance from that of the king. The god's belted, long-sleeved tunic has a slightly downward-curving hemline which is decorated with a double pearl trim. Over this garment is a sleeveless, longer, heavy cloak bordered as well with a double row of pearls and held together at the chest by a double circle brooch. This cloak is worn in a way that covers the upper part of the body extending to the god's elbows. The light fluttering appearance of the drapery in the earlier images on the rock reliefs is not apparent on these garments although folds in the fabric are shown. Beneath the hems of the tunic and cloak a small portion of loose trousers are visible just above low boots, an unusual feature, into which the trousers are tucked (Fukai and Horiuchi 1972: pl. 19).

The closest parallels for the appearance and style of Ohrmazd's clothing in the large iwan at Taq-e Bustan are not found among Sasanian works of art but in representations of ecclesiastical figures over a long time in the late antique West: the High Priest Aaron in a third-century painting in the Synagogue of Dura Europos is clad in almost identical fashion, as is the so-called Zoroastrian *magus* from the Mithraeum at the same site (Kraeling 1956: 126-27, fig. 41; Rostovtzeff 1938: 97, fig. 10). Later in date are the similarly dressed *decanos* Leo in a sixth-century icon now in St Catherine's monastery on Mount Sinai and the figures of the <u>*magi*</u> in an Armenian sixth-century Gospel from Etchmiadzin (Weitzmann 1976: pl. 16; Mathews 1982: 199-216, fig. 3). The cloak of the *decanos* is bordered with pearls while the gems on Aaron's cloak are comparable to the pearls that cover the surface of the cloak of Ohrmazd. In the case of Aaron, Biblical descriptions of his sacred vestments allow us to imagine the effect of the Sasanian relief had it too been painted, as seems likely from slightly later descriptions written in the early tenth century (Abka'i-Khavari 2000: 31, fn. 76).

> These are the vestments they shall make: a breastpiece, an ephod, a mantle, a chequered tunic, a turban and a sash. They shall make vestments for Aaron your brother and his sons to wear when they serve as my priests, using gold, violet, purple and scarlet yarn, and fine linen. (Exodus 28:4-5)

The garments worn by Ohrmazd belong to a long tradition which had developed in the eastern Mediterranean world where similarly cut and styled garments appear on images ranging in date from the second to the seventh century. Originally derived from oriental modes (trousers, tunic and cape), these forms of dress became widespread during the Parthian era (Kawami 1987: 140-45; Curtis, V.S., 1998: 61). By the reign of Khusro II, the garments which had long been represented in a particular form and style in the eastern Mediterranean world were specifically associated with images of priestly and ecclesiastical figures in Jewish and early Christian art. In Sasanian art there are no parallels or prototypes for the heavy, static style and appearance of the garments worn by Ohrmazd in the iwan at Taq-e Bustan and it is probable that a familiarity with ecclesiastical figures in the arts of the eastern Mediterranean world contributed to the late Sasanian image.

In a Sasanian context, the long, pointed beard of Ohrmazd, composed of lengthy, wavy but uncurled hairs, is an even more striking departure from Sasanian norms (Fukai and Horiuchi 1972: pls 14-16; Harper 1999: 317; Harper 2006: 72-73). The beard of Ohrmazd on earlier Sasanian reliefs is a variant of the spade-shaped beards of Assyrian/Achaemenid monuments. This remains true even at the end of the fourth century when the image of Ohrmazd on the relief of Ardashir II at Taq-e Bustan was carved. That beard is still recognisable as a modification of the older type. More naturalistic than earlier depictions, the long wavy lines of the beard in the fourth-century image end in familiar, tight, snail-shaped curls at the sides and on the temples of the god (Fukai and Horiuchi 1972: pls 76, 77).

In the iwan of Khusro II there have been significant changes to the god's beard. These include the fact that the wavy, long hairs of the beard, seemingly without curls, taper to a point and that the beard is much longer than the beard of Ohrmazd on the relief of Ardashir II. In fact, the beard of the god in Khusro's relief at Taq-e Bustan represents a major departure from all other depictions of beards in Sasanian art. A striking contrast is provided by images of late Sasanian royal beards on coins and other works where the beards are short, following the chin line, and are covered with schematic curls. Also different in appearance are pointed beards on some early Sasanian silver bowls and plates where the surface of the beard is variously articulated with short hatched or crescentic lines and, occasionally, with horizontal divisions (Harper and Meyers 1981: pls 3, 6, 23). The immediate source for the unusual beard of Ohrmazd lies, it seems, not in the art of the Sasanian Zoroastrian East but in the Byzantine Christian East where this is the beard of certain saints in early Christian and Byzantine art (Weitzmann [ed.] 1979: 517, fig. 73; 597, fig. 87; cat. nos 454, 474, 478, 494, 554).

Khusro's monument illustrates an awareness and assimilation of the religious imagery appearing in the arts of the other dominant world power, Christian Byzantium, to whom the Persian monarch responsible for the upper sculptures on the back wall in the large iwan owed his throne. Only with the support of the Eastern Roman Emperor, Maurice (AD 582-602), had Khusro II, in AD 591, regained his rightful place as ruler in the Sasanian dynastic line of Iran (Frendo 1969: 78). The extent to which the design of the great iwan at Taq-e Bustan reflects the elite arts and architecture of the Roman and Byzantine worlds has been defined and expanded upon in the studies of Marjorie Mackintosh and later scholars (Mackintosh 1978: 149-77; Canepa 2009: 188-223; Harrison 1989: 77-124). However, architectural forms and decoration are only one level of interaction between Byzantium and the Sasanian state. The new articulation of the great Zoroastrian god's appearance suggests a dialogue at another level. In a well-known letter from Ohrmazd IV (AD 579-90) to prominent *magi*, the Sasanian king states:

> Even as our royal throne cannot stand upon its two front legs
> without the back ones, so also our government cannot stand
> and be secure if we incense the Christians and the adherents
> of other religions, who are not of our faith. Cease, therefore, to
> harass the Christians. . . .(Boyce 1984: 115)

The sculptors at Taq-e Bustan were, apparently, commissioned to place the Zoroastrian god, visually, in a broader, global realm of the sacred. For westerners, elite diplomats and envoys to the Sasanian court, as well as for prominent members of the established Christian hierarchy in Iran who might see the image at Taq-e Bustan, a long-bearded Ohrmazd, wearing a recognisable form of priestly or sacred dress, cannot have seemed an exclusive Zoroastrian icon but rather an inclusive image drawing upon imagery that had developed in the art of the Christian lands west of Iran.

Comparable to the inclusive imagery of Khusro's monument at Taq-e Bustan are slightly later phenomena in the new Muslim world. Scholars have variously interpreted the significance of the presence on the earliest Islamic monuments – the seventh-century Dome of the Rock in Jerusalem and the eighth-century Great Mosque at Damascus – of references to concepts and beliefs of the Christian community (Brisch 1988: 18; Grabar 1996: 65-68; Flood 2012: 246-48; Nees 2015: 104-105). The images at Taq-e Bustan can be seen as forerunners of this intercultural and interreligious dialogue. The Sasanian sculptures speak to members of the Christian communities within and beyond the Sasanian kingdom, as well as to the Zoroastrian faithful. In the years following the reign of Khusro II, the political order in Iran collapsed but the new Arab, Muslim rulers drew upon a rich cultural heritage. That heritage included a long tradition in the Iranian world of cultural and religious dialogue, assimilation and exchange. These phenomena are well-illustrated by the image at Taq-e Bustan of the god, Ohrmazd, in a form of ecclesiastical dress well-known in the eastern Mediterranean world and having, uniquely in the art of Sasanian Iran, a long pointed beard.

Bibliography

Abka'i-Khavari, M., 2000. *Das Bild des Königs in der Sasanidenzeit*, Hildesheim, Zurich, New York: Georg Olms Verlag

Agostini, D. and Stark, S., 2016. 'Zāwulistān, Kāwulistān and the land Posi', *Studia Iranica* 45: 17-38

Along the Ancient Silk Routes: Central Asian Art from the West Berlin State Museums. 1982. New York: Metropolitan Museum of Art

Alram, M., and M. Pfisterer. 2010. 'Alkhan and Hephthalite Coinage', in M. Alram, D.E. Klimburg-Salter, M. Inaba and M. Pfisterer (eds), *Coins, Art and Chronology* II, Vienna: Austrian Academy of Sciences, 13-38

Alram, M., and Gyselen, R., 2012. *Sylloge Nummorum Sasanidarum Paris-Berlin-Wien, Band II, Ohrmazd I - Ohrmazd II*, Wien: Verlag der österreichischen Akademie der Wissenschaften. (please correct in text from 2013 to 2012).

Azarnoush, M. 1986. 'Šapur II, Ardašir II and Šapur III: Another Perspective', *AMI* 19: 219-47

Bálint, Cs. 1992. 'Kontakte zwischen Iran, Byzanz und der Steppe', in F. Daim (ed.), *Awarenforschungen* 1, Vienna: 309-496

Barnett, R.D., and J.E. Curtis. 1973. 'A Review of Acquisitions of Western Asiatic Antiquities (2)', *British Museum Quarterly* 37: 119-37

Boyce, M. (ed. and trans.). 1984. *Textual Sources for the Study of Zoroastrianism*, Manchester: Manchester University Press

Brisch, K. 1988. 'Observations on the Iconography of the Mosaics in the Great Mosque of Damascus', in P.P. Soucek (ed.), *Content and Context of Visual Arts in the Islamic World*, University Park, PA and London: Pennsylvania State University Press

Canepa, M.P. 2009. *The Two Eyes of the Earth: Art and Ritual of Kingship between Rome and Sasanian Iran*, Berkeley, Los Angeles, and London: University of California Press

Compareti, M., 2018. 'The Late Sasanian Figurative Capitals at Taq-e Bustan', in Kadoi, Y. (ed.), *Persian Art: Image-making in Eurasia*, Edinburgh: 20-36

Cribb, J. 2010. 'The Kidarites: the Numismatic Evidence', in Alram, Klimburg-Salter, Inaba and Pfisterer (eds.), 2010: 91-146

Curtis, V.S. 1993. 'A Parthian Statuette from Susa and the Bronze Statue from Shami', *Iran* 31: 63-70

Curtis, V.S. 1998. 'The Parthian Costume and Headdress', in J. Wiesehöfer (ed.), *Das Partherreich und seine Zeugnisse* (Historia Einzelschriften 122), Stuttgart: Franz Steiner Verlag, 61-73

Daim, F., et al. 1996. *Reitervölker aus dem Osten: Hunnen + Awaren*, Eisenstadt: Amt der Burgländischen Landesregierung

Dalton, O. M. 1964. *The Treasure of the Oxus*, 3rd ed., London: British Museum

Flood, F.B., 2012. 'Faith, religion and the material culture of early Islam', in H.C. Evans (ed.), *Byzantium and Islam*, The Metropolitan Museum of art, New York.

Frendo, D. 1969. 'Theophylact Simocatta on the Revolt of Bahram Chobin and the Early Career of Khusrau II', *Bulletin of the Asia Institute* 3: 77-88

Fukai, S., and K. Horiuchi. 1969. *Taq-e Bustan I*, The Institute of Oriental Culture, The University of Tokyo, Tokyo: Yamaka Pub. Co.

Fukai, S., and K. Horiuchi. 1972. *Taq-e Bustan II*, The Institute of Oriental Culture, The University of Tokyo, Tokyo: Yamaka Pub. Co.

Gall, H., von. 1990. *Das Reiterkampfbild in der iranischen und iranisch beeinflussten Kunst parthischer und sasanidischer Zeit*, Teheraner Forschungen VI, Berlin: Mann

Ghirshman, R. 1962. *Persian Art: The Parthian and Sassanian Dynasties, 249 BC-AD 651*, New York: Golden Press

Gignoux, Ph. 1998. 'Les inscriptions en moyen-perse de Bandiān', *Studia Iranica* 27: 251-58

Göbl, R. 1971. *Sasanian Numismatics*, Braunschweig: Klinkhardt und Biermann

Grabar, O. 1996. *The Shape of the Holy*, Princeton, NJ: Princeton University Press

Gyselen, R. 2007. 'Shapur, fils d'Ohrmazd, petit-fils de Narseh', *Res Orientalis* 17: 73-89

Harmatta, J. 2002. 'A Turk Officer of the Sāsānian King Xusro I', *Acta Orientalia Academiae Scientiarum Hungaricae* 55, no 1-3: 153-59

Harper, P.O. 1966. 'Portrait of a King', *Bulletin of The Metropolitan Museum of Art* 25: 137-46

Harper, P.O. 1999. 'Geographical Location and Significant Imagery: Taq-i Bostan', in Alram, Klimburg-Salter, Inaba and Pfisterer (eds) 2010: 315-19

Harper, P.O. 2006. *In Search of a Cultural Identity*, New York: Bibliotheca Persica

Harper, P.O., and P. Meyers. 1981. *Silver Vessels of the Sasanian Period*, Vol. I, New York: Metropolitan Museum of Art

Harrison, M. 1989. *A Temple for Byzantium*, Austin, TX: University of Texas Press

Herrmann, G. 1977. *The Iranian Revival*, Oxford: Elsevier-Phaidon

Herrmann, G. 1980. *The Sasanian Reliefs at Bishapur: Part 1, Bishapur III. Iranische Denkmäler, Lieferung 9, Reihe II: Iranische Felsreliefs E*, Berlin

Herrmann, G. 1981. *The Sasanian Reliefs at Bishapur: Part II, Bishapur IV, V, VI. Iranische Denkmäler, Lieferung 10, Reihe II: Iranische Felsrelief F*, Berlin

Inam, J., and Rosenbaum. 1966. *Roman and Early Byzantine Sculpture in Asia Minor,* London.

Invernizzi, A. 2001. 'Arsacid Dynastic Art', *Parthica* 3: 133-57

Isamiddinov, M.X. 1991. 'Chapelles cultuelles au quartier des céramistes d'Erkurgan', in P. Bernard and F. Grenet (eds), *Histoires et cultes de l'Asie Centrale préislamique*, Paris: Centre National de la Recherche Scientifique, 173-76

Juliano, A. L., and J.A. Lerner, J.A. 2001. *Monks and Merchants: Silk Road Treasures from Northwest China*, The Asia Society, New York: Harry N. Abrams

Kidd, F.J. 2003. 'Costumes of the Samarkand Region of Sogdiana between the 2nd/1st Century BCE and the 4th Century CE', *Bulletin of the Asia Institute* 17: 35-69

Kawami, T. 1987. *Monumental Art of the Parthian Period in Iran. Acta Iranica*, Series 3, XIII, Leiden: Brill

Kraeling, C.H. 1956. *The Excavations at Dura-Europos, Final Report 8, Part 1: The Synagogue* New Haven, CT: Yale University Press; and London: Oxford University Press

Kraeling, C.H. 1967. *The Excavations at Dura-Europos, Final Report 8, Part 2: The Christian Building*, New Haven, CT: Dura-Europos Publications; and Locust Valley, NY: J.J. Augustin

Lerner, J.A., 2018. 'The Visual Culture of Greater Iran: some examples of Kushano-Sasanian Art', in Kadoi, Y., *Persian Art: Image-making in Eurasia*, Edinburgh: 1-19

Lerner, J.A., and N. Sims-Williams. 2011. *Seals Sealings and Tokens from Bactria to Gandhara (4th to 8th century CE)*, Vienna: Austrian Academy of Sciences

Les Perses Sassanides. Fastes d'un empire oublié (224-642) 2016, Paris

Mackintosh, M.C. 1978. 'Taq-e Bustan and Byzantine Art: A Case for Early Byzantine Influence on the Reliefs of Taq-e Bustan', *Iranica Antiqua* 13: 149-77

Marschak, B.I. 1986. *Silberschätze des Orients*, Leipzig: E.A. Seemann

Marshak, B.I., and Y.K. Krikis. 1969. 'Chilekskiye Chashi', *Trudy Gosudarstvennogo Ermitazha* 10 (Kultura i Iskusstvo narodov Vostoka 7), Leningrad: 55-81

Mathews, T.F. 1982. 'The Early Armenian Iconographic Program of the Ējmiacin Gospel', in N.G. Garsoïan, T.F. Mathews and R.W. Thomson (eds.), *East of Byzantium*, Washington, DC: Dumbarton Oaks, Center for Byzantine Studies

Mathieson, H.E. 1992. *Sculpture in the Parthian Empire I, II*, Aarhus: Aarhus University Press

Mitchiner, M. 1978. *Oriental Coins and Their Values: Ancient and Classical World, 600 BC-AD 650*, London: Hawkins Publications

Mode, M. 2006. 'Art and Ideology at Taq-e Bustan: The Armoured Equestrian', in M. Mode and J. Tubach, *Arms and Armours as Indicators of Cultural Transfer*, Wiesbaden: Reichert

Nickel, L. 2013. 'The First Emperor and Sculpture in China', *Bulletin of the School of Oriental and African Studies* 76: 413-47

Rahbar, M. 1998. 'Découverte d'un monument d'époque sassanide à Bandian, Dargaz (Nord Khorassan)', *Studia Iranica* 27: 213-50

Rostovtzeff, M. 1938. *Dura-Europos and its Art*, Oxford: The Clarendon Press

Ruprechtsberger, E.M. (ed.). 1993. *Syrien von den Aposteln zu den Khalifen*, Linz: Philipp von Zabern

Sellwood, D. 1971. *An Introduction to the Coinage of Parthia*, London: Spink & Son Ltd

Shepherd, D.G. 1966. 'Two Silver Rhyta', *Bulletin of the Cleveland Museum of Art*, 53: 289-311

Sims-Williams, N. 2009. 'Some Bactrian Inscriptions on Silver Vessels', *Bulletin of the Asia Institute* 23: 191-98

Sims-Williams, N. 2010. 'Bactrian Personal Names', *Iranisches Personnamenbuch, Vol. II: Mittel-iranische Personennamen*, Fasc.7, Vienna: Austrian Academy of Sciences

Splendeur des Sassanides. 1993. Bruxelles: Musées royaux d'art et d'histoire, Bruxelles.

Stavisky, B.I. 1986. *La Bactriane sous les Kushans*, Paris: Librarie d'Amerique et d'Orient

Sun Z.J. 2017. *Age of Empires: Art of the Qin and Han Dynasties*, New York: Metropolitan Museum of Art

Tanabe, K. (ed.). 1986. *Sculptures of Palmyra I* (Memoirs of the Ancient Orient Museum, Vol. I), Tokyo

Trever, K.V. 1937. *Noviye bliuda ermitazha*, Moscow-Leningrad

Trever, K.V., and V.G. Lukonin. 1987. *Sasanidskoe serebro. Sobraniye Gosudarstvennogo Ermitazha*, Moscow: Iskusstvo

Vaissière, E., de la. 2003. 'Is there a "Nationality" of the Hephtalites?', *Bulletin of the Asia Institute* 17:119-32

Valenstein, S.G. 1997-98. 'Preliminary Findings on a 6th century Earthenware Jar', *Oriental Art* 43: 2-13

Vogelsang-Eastwood, G. 2004. 'Sasanian Riding-Coats: The Iranian Evidence', in C. Fluck and G. Vogelsang-Eastwood (eds), *Riding Costume in Egypt: Origin and Appearance*, Leiden and Boston: Brill

Watt, J.C.Y. 2004. *China: Dawn of a Golden Age 200-750*, New York: Metropolitan Museum of Art

Weitzmann, K. 1976. *The Monastery of Saint Catherine at Mount Sinai: The Icons, Vol. 1: From the Sixth to the Tenth Century*, Princeton, NJ: Princeton University Press

Weitzmann, K. (ed.). 1979. *The Age of Spirituality*, New York: The Metropolitan Museum

Yatsenko, S.A. 2001. 'The Costume of the Yueh-Chihs/Kushans and its Analogies to the East and to the West', *Silk Road Art and Archaeology* 7: 73-120

8

Sasanian-Zoroastrian Intellectual Life in the Fifth and Sixth Centuries AD

Mahnaz Moazami

Late antiquity, that is, the centuries stretching between the third and the seventh century AD, was a time of slow-paced but far-reaching changes and transformations. It was during these centuries that the Babylonian Talmud was compiled, codified and redacted (AD 220-500); the Church of the East (that is, east of the Roman empire) and its doctrines gradually took shape; Manichaeism spread over both the Iranian and Roman empires; and the Zoroastrian religious identity became more clearly defined and articulated.

Textual evidence from the Sasanian period survives in inscriptions and in Manichean texts, the earliest of which date from the third century AD, and in the Zoroastrian scriptures written down in ninth century when, after the Arab-Muslim conquest, Zoroastrian scholars were anxious to preserve as much of Sasanian learning as they could. For the most part, therefore, what they compiled were digests of older texts composed in the Middle Persian/Pahlavi language. These Pahlavi books of the ninth century collectively enhance our knowledge of late Sasanian intellectual life, reflecting its vibrancy and sophistication.

We are also fortunate in possessing two extensive texts in Middle Persian dating from the late Sasanian period that open a window into the Zoroastrian intellectual world of the time. They are the *Pahlavi Vidēvdād* (late fifth century, hereafter PV) and the *Zand ī Fragard ī Jud-Dēw-Dād* (late sixth century, hereafter ZFJ). However, before examining these texts, a word or two is necessary to orient readers not familiar with this literature.

Zoroastrianism was the religion of the Iranians of the Sasanian Empire, although its exact official status remains a matter of debate. Some of the texts date from the second millennium BC onward and were transmitted orally in languages long out of common usage. By late Sasanian times, however, these authoritative texts had been translated into Middle Persian and were the subject of commentaries by late fourth- and fifth-century commentators. We know several of these commentators by name, as they are mentioned in PV and other Middle Persian texts such as the *Hērbedestān* and *Nērangestān* (dealing with the training of priests and liturgical matters, respectively) and others. By the late sixth century, three schools, named after two well-known commentators, and a third, hitherto unknown, seem to have arisen, and their views are presented in ZFJ, along with a later commentator.

The *Pahlavi Vidēvdād* (PV) and the later *Zand ī Fragard ī Jud-dēw-dād* (ZFJ) are of particular importance for understanding the parameters and methods of the Zoroastrian commentators of the time, both in general and in detail. Unlike the *Hērbedestān* and *Nērangestān*, which survive only in fragments, PV and ZFJ appear to be intact: PV gives us a complete text of the *Vidēvdād,* both in Young Avestan and in Middle Persian, along with glosses and comments from both well-known and less-known authorities, and comments from an anonymous redactor or redactors; ZFJ is in many respects a commentary on PV in the form of a *rivayāt*, that is, a collection of *responsa*, since it is made up of about 540 sections, each couched in a question-and-answer format.

Not only are these two texts complete; they are also extensive: PV runs to 55,000 words and ZFJ to 36,000 words. Taken together, they provide us with a secure base from which to assess developments in late Sasanian Zoroastrian thought in the fifth and sixth centuries.

The ancient *Vidēvdād*, part of the Zoroastrian sacred book, is primarily concerned with matters of purity and pollution; it was composed around 1200-900 BC in Young Avestan and transmitted orally for over a thousand years. It provides a mythological/theological view of the world of the Good Spirit's creation, along with practical means of sustaining it by use of various methods of purification, since pollution is one way in which the Evil Spirit attempts to frustrate humanity's role of leading a holy, righteous life and fighting evil. In the course of time – sometime after 250 BC – this work was translated into Middle Persian and furnished with a commentary, which includes comments and disputations from Sasanian authorities of the late fourth and early fifth centuries. Many of these authorities we know by name: Abarg, Sōšāns, Gōgušasp, Kay-ādur-bōzēd, Rōšn, Mēdōmāh, and Wehšābuhr. By the sixth century, three schools had joined together, named after three of these commentators, the third of which is known only from ZFJ, the late-sixth-century text.

These authorities also appear in other Pahlavi books of the late Sasanian period. We have as many as 70 statements for some of them, enabling us to sketch intellectual portraits of their approaches and views on various ritual matters. The version we now have dates from the late fifth century. A century later this was provided with a super-commentary on its specifically legal chapters, the *Zand ī Fragard ī Jud-dēw-dād* (ZFJ).

ZFJ represents a continuation of PV in several respects, but also provides an account of several surprising developments in Sasanian intellectual life in the sixth century, both intellectual and institutional. Among the latter is the development of three schools, either schools of thought and/or actual groups of scholars. Two of them are associated with the names of well-known authorities of the fifth century, Abarg and Mēdōmāh, schools that are mentioned in *Mādayān ī Hazār Dādestān* (hereafter MHD), the Sasanian Law book, dating from the first quarter of the seventh century (Macuch 1993). The third, Pēšagsīr, is named after a scholar not mentioned in the Pahlavi books, although an authority of the same name is mentioned some six times in the MHD (Macuch 1993: chapters 11.10; 26.11; 42.15; 50.17; 52.17; 61.9).

Substantial numbers of positions held by these groups of scholars are recorded in ZFJ – 51 for the Abargites and 48 for the Mēdōmāhites, and 16 for the Pēšagsīrites. As might be expected, due to the telescoping effect of oral transmission over time, the numbers of traditions given in the names of Abarg and Mēdōmāh are much lower in ZFJ than in PV: 11 versus 24, 4 versus 8, respectively; Pēšagsīr is, of course, not mentioned in PV. Still, for some reason these schools are not mentioned in the later Šāyast nē šāyast (Tavadia 1930), 'what is proper and what is not' (hereafter Šnš), a fact that suggests some caution in assessing both the role and existence of these schools.

Is there a political reason for this silence? Did the author of Šāyast nē šāyast ignore them, or did ZFJ invent them? Since they are mentioned in the seventh-century MHD, the possibility that they are an invention of the author(s) of ZFJ seems unlikely. Moreover, there are cases, such as ZFJ 33.25, where the Abargites and Mēdōmāhites disagree over an expansion of an issue that was raised in PV 16.2, illustrating the continuity in legal discussions involving the schools. Perhaps the schools were still functioning in the seventh century, but no longer in the ninth, in the wake of the Arab-Muslim conquest, though that would not in itself explain their absence, since even past disputes are mentioned in Šnš. In either case, however, it is clear that the redactor(s) of ZFJ represent(s) a stream of a somewhat different tradition from that represented in Šnš and the later *rivayāt*s.

Finally, ZFJ provides us with the opinions of a perhaps still later commentator, whose name we do not know, but who prefaces his comments with the phrase *az man*, 'in my opinion', and so, for convenience, I name him Az man. And, of course, the anonymous redactors of ZFJ are not the same as those of PV. For us, the important aspect of ZFJ is that it breaks new ground and the innovations are not of the named authorities or schools, but of the anonymous redactors and the commentator 'Az man'.

The result is a rich and variegated view of a vibrant intellectual culture spanning more than two centuries of the late Sasanian period and, moreover, one which enables us to trace several themes that appeared and developed among the authorities and schools of that time. It also makes it possible to place this regional intellectual life within the broader context of developments in the late antique world, developments that connect Iranian intellectual life both with its ancient heritage and with developments in the Graeco-Roman world.

In particular, a comparison of these late Sasanian compositions with the ancient *Vidēvdād* reveals several underlying trends that Sasanian Zoroastrianism had in common with other religions of the time. Among them was the tendency towards scholasticism, that is, the attempt to rationalise, in the broadest sense, the ritual system that had been transmitted mimetically over the millennia, at least from the early first millennium BC.

Mimetic transmission, by which children are educated into the lifestyle of their society by being socialised into the extended family and clan, is the natural means by which social systems, including religion, are passed on from generation to generation. The attractions of this system of transmission are obvious: religion becomes second nature and thus is not open to challenge. It does not, therefore, require to be supplemented by an educational system as an appendage, with professional teachers to explain and justify the tenets of the religion. However, mimetic transmission lacks flexibility: it does not provide a means of coping with changing conditions or adapting to new knowledge – or new modes of thought.

Thus, Zoroastrian authorities, even in pre-Achaemenid times, had to adapt a religious system developed for a nomadic society beginning to turn to agriculture, and later to that society as it urbanised. Later still, when under challenge by Hellenistic scientific and mathematical advances, the elite authorities of late Sasanian Zoroastrianism adopted and adapted Hellenistic methods of philosophical analysis to the ritual system that they had inherited and for whose continuation they were responsible.

An analysis of the methods and objectives of the redactors of PV and ZFJ reveals features that connect these redactors with the late antique intellectual currents. These had begun centuries before, but some of the aspects which I will point to can be detected in both works. They are as follows: quantification of ritually meaningful substances, chiefly 'dead matter' (nasā, hixr), accompanied by a more precise definition of the differences between them, a process which may require abstraction and/or a systematic approach to Zoroastrian norms so as to derive the principles governing those definitions.

Along with this cognitive revolution came an institutional one: the increased intellectual role of scholars and scholiasts as authoritative interpreters of the religion. The dialectic nature of Hellenistic thought fostered the development of differing views, the recording or memorising of these differing views and their evaluation and analysis, a process that led to second-order analysis and statutory construction, though only the beginning of a dialogic literary structure (e.g. ZFJ 37.16). This was all eventually embodied in the establishment of three schools of scholars, two named after authorities of the early fifth century, Abarg and Mēdōmāh, the third after Pēšagsīr.

As noted, these texts provide us with the makings of a detailed picture of the progressive scholasticism of Sasanian Zoroastrianism during a two centuries of late Sasanian times, at least in regard to issues of pollution and purification. Aside from being a central issue in Zoroastrian ritual law and theology, the unfolding of the development of views on issues pertinent to pollution serves as a medium through which to understand developments in Zoroastrian modes of analysis through those centuries.

One consequence of the Sasanian government's realisation that mathematics could also serve as a tool for governing was to spark a revision of the Sasanian taxation system similar to that introduced by the Ptolemies in Egypt during the third century BC, which was noted for its comprehensiveness and exactness (Satlow 2014: 105; Thompson 2008: 27-38). This census was instituted by Kawad I, during his second term of kingship (AD 499-531), and concluded under Khusro I (AD 531-79) (Wiesehöfer 2001: 190-91; Altheim 1957: 88-95; Christensen 1944: 122-26), during whose reign, or shortly thereafter, ZFJ was probably composed.

It may be that this conceptual leap was aided by the influence of the move by the Athens academy to Iran in AD 529, when Justinian and his philosophers were welcomed in the Persian court.

In his open-mindedness with regard to religious and metaphysical questions, Khusro I, who, according to Agathias, was a great admirer of the works of Plato and Aristotle (Frendo [trans.] 1975: II: 30-31; Christensen 1944: 428-29), invited to the Sasanian court a number of Western philosophers after the closure of their school. This appetite for Greek science was in great part indebted to Khosrow's own partiality for foreign culture and thought. Priscian of Lydia was one of the Athenian philosophers who in AD 531 took refuge with Khosrow. Priscian fully recorded in Greek the answers provided by the Athenian philosophers to the king's questions on philosophy and science (Huby et al. 2016).

With this move came a large increase in the coinage of Greek-influenced loan-translations and the like. According to Mansur Shaki, 'The Greek knowledge of Sasanian scholars has been abundantly reflected in the extant Middle Persian books, especially in the encyclopedic *Dēnkard*, as seen in some of its fundamental concepts', and he lists over a dozen such coinages and additional evidence of Greek philosophical concepts and statements that appear in Middle Persian literature (2003: 321-26). The redactor of ZFJ was not so palpably philosophical; his interests were focused solely on systematic legal analysis without the theological framework of the PV, or its forays into Avestan exegesis.

Moreover, this development coheres with the 'telescopic' phenomenon I pointed to above. The decrease in statements of named authorities and the emergence of the schools and the fact that ZFJ often takes PV as its starting point confirm the relative dating of the two works to the late fifth and late sixth centuries, respectively, and allows us to trace the trajectory of Zoroastrian intellectual history in terms of an increasing interest in quantification.

In Zoroastrian religion the roots of the trend towards scholasticism go back a long way and involve the attempt to determine the exact contours of the divine will as far as possible, including minute, even mundane details of ritual.

It may seem strange to apply a term usually associated with the medieval 'schoolmen' to late antiquity, especially when it is often associated not only with a particular form of intellectual analysis, but with a social and religious movement. However, the roots of scholasticism may be found in the ancient *Avesta* itself. One of the hallmarks of the Avestan *Vidēvdād*'s method is *Listenwissenschaft*, that is, the ordering of the world by making lists of similar objects. The *Vidēvdād* opens in chapter

1 with a list of 'the best of places and settlements' that the Good Spirit created – in order: first was 'Ērān-wēz of the Weh Dāitī (River)', then, second, 'Gawa, inhabited by Sogdians' and so on. This drive for precise definition, aided by advances in Hellenistic mathematics and astronomy, also fuelled Christian and Manichaean concerns on the theological plane; the struggles over definitions of faith and theology in Christianity, and Mani's elaboration of his doctrines, are readily apparent, and both must be seen against this Graeco-Roman intellectual background.

Another aspect of this development was the development of a pluralistic mentality, where disputes were permitted, validated and entered the religious tradition. PV has dozens of disputes among *dastwar*s, ZFJ adds disputes among two, or sometimes, three schools.

The intra-religious dispute was an indispensable part of the decision-making process of the Sasanian Church. The process is well described in *Nāmagīhā ī Manuščihr* (the Epistles of Manuchihr), written in about 881, though the date only appears at the end of the third letter. The subject is a matter of ritual purification. In his letters Manuchihr tells us (Dhabhar [ed.] 1912: 2.1.8: 56) that, when there were differences of opinion regarding practices and interpretations of the tradition (*dēn*), the *magi* assembled at the court in Pārs, where a large number of priests could meet. After discussing and reaching a decision, then they would put their seals on the agreed-upon versions and then the highest authority would enact a law (*dād*) and send an order (*framān*) to the community. A similar procedure must have been used in the Sasanian period. The council organised by Khusro I to impose a single canonical interpretation of Avestan texts in the early sixth century must be seen in this context.

The Final Redactors

It is important to note that the final redactors of the Pahlavi texts remain anonymous, expect for *Mādayān ī Hazār Dādestān,* which was compiled by Farroxmard ī Wahrāmān. From the indications of the scholars mentioned in PV and ZFJ it becomes clear that the redactor(s) of the former can be dated to the late fifth century and the latter to the middle or late sixth. It has also to be mentioned that in the Pahlavi texts, the first person is scarcely used. Only the expression 'it is not clear to me' is common. For example, PV 5.7 (I), where the inspection of a channel is ordered to see whether there is a dead body or not, to the redactor it is not clear, in the event that the inspector finds a dead body in the water, whether he is thus impure and therefore guilty of death, or not. Thus he says: it is not clear to me (Moazami 2014: 128-29).

In the comments, only very rarely does the final redactor participate in the exchange of opinions between the various commentators, although this may sometimes happen. Thus, in a comment to PV 8.22 (G₁), the writer exposes the opinion of many commentators about the days when the *frawahr*s, the guardian angels of the dead, return to the material world. Regarding the number of days of Frawardīgān, it gives different views of several anonymous commentators, but the writer signals that, in his opinion, the guardian angels were there for ten days of Frawardīgān and supports his view with an unknown Avestan passage (Moazami 2014: 236-37).

In ZFJ, as stated before, we find the expression *az man*, 'in my opinion', that often rounds off the collection of differing opinions (there are 24 examples) which does not indicate a final opinion of the redactor, but a later interpolation. This seems to be a feature of ZFJ, which is later than the rest and includes almost all points of views. However, the final redactors are not just unbiased collectors of oral tradition. Their choices and their selections of opinions listed reflect their ideological position.

In the Middle Persian texts there is also a clear distribution of grammatical tenses. For the presentation of divergent anonymous views, the expression usually employed is: *ast kē* ēdon *gōwēd*, 'there is one (authority) that says so' (or other very similar formulations), with the verb in the present tense. To introduce opinions of named commentators, they use similar expressions but always in past tense, for example, *Sōšāns guft*, 'Sōšāns said'. It seems that in PV the redactor distinguishes two markedly differentiated time phases: the old sages mentioned by their proper names belonging to the past and the anonymous commentators who are contemporaries of the final redactor.

In general, the Sasanian exegetical tradition was not entirely uniform nor did the religious authorities interpret it in the same way throughout the centuries. These differences caused disagreements among contemporaneous authorities, as well as in different generations, as evident in the extant literature.

The statement at the beginning of the Šāyest *nē* šāyest (chapter 1.3) provides information on the major doctrinal dependence of old sages:

> In the law of the teachers of old, there were some that disagreed. For Gōgušasp followed the teaching of Ādur-ohrmazd, Sōšans that of Ādur-farrbay-narsē, Mēdōmāh that of Gōgušasp, Abarg that of Sōšans. But all the teachers of old adhered to these four teachings, some more leniently (*susttar*), others more stringently (*saxttar*). (Tavadia 1930: 28)

With this text we can reconstruct two schools of commentators, each of which is identified by the name of the master followed by those of his disciples:

1. Adur-ohrmazd-Gōgušasp-Mēdōmāh;
2. Ādur-farrbay-narsē-Sōšāns-Abarg.

The Šāyest nē šāyest does not mention the school of Pēšagsīr, another doctrinal school, which is very important in ZFJ, presumably because it had not yet acquired the importance that it attained later. However, his doctrine is already mentioned in the introduction to the first chapter of the Hērbadestān. Here we are informed that the first part of this work was composed under the doctrine of Pešagsīr (Kotwal and Kreyenbroek [eds and trans.]1992: I: 26-27).

As stated before, Pēšagsīr appears also in MHD and plays an absolutely dominant role in ZFJ. He is mentioned more often than Abarg, and Sōšāns and his followers are mentioned alongside those of Abarg and Mēdōmāh. The doctrine of Pešagsīr is in line with the doctrine of Abarg.

Often positions of Pēšagsīr and Abarg coincide and are opposed to those of Mēdōmāh. For example, in one passage, the redactor of ZFJ asks whether the egg of an eagle that has eaten from a dead body is pure or impure until the birth of the chick. According to the doctrine and followers of Pēšagsīr and Abarg, the egg is impure but, for the followers of Mēdōmāh who are always more flexible, the egg is pure (ZFJ 525; 24.4).

The Scriptural Movement

Interwoven within this intellectual context of scholasticism is another trend, referred to by Guy G. Stroumsa as 'the scriptural movement', whereby Christianity, Manichaeism and eventually Zoroastrianism turned to their respective scriptures for guidance. The idea of religions of the Book, as we know, was launched in 1873 by Max Müller in his *Introduction to the Science of Religion* (Müller 1873: 102). Müller was enlarging and modernising the Qor'anic concept of *ahl al-kitāb*, 'people of the book', an expression, which usually refers to both the Jews and Christians (Stroumsa 2009: 34-35; 2008: 61-77):

A Jewish parallel to this concept of *umm al-kitāb* is found in a midrash that says God created the world by contemplating the book of the Torah (Genesis Rabba 1.1). In mediaeval and

modern Christian thinking, too, 'the great book of nature' is
conceived as a divine revelation in parallel to Scripture. . . .
That the fundamental religious importance of the idea of
the Book does not appear only with Islam but is present long
before can be best expressed by some capital passages of
the prologue to the Chapters, or *Kephalaia*, a fundamental
theological text from early Manichaeism that survived in
Coptic translation (Stroumsa 2009: 36-37): '[The messenger
of] light, the resplendent illuminator, [Zoroaster, came as a]
Persian to King Hystaspes. . . . [He elected] disciples righteous
and truthful . . . [and he preached] his hope in Persia. [But
nor did he,] Zoroaster, write a book. On the other hand, his
[disciples coming] after him, remembered and wrote [books]
that they read today . . .' (Tardieu 1998: 71; Stroumsa 2009: 37)

Mani pressed this point home as an advantage of his religion over the
others. In his 'ten points letter', he enumerates ten forms of superiority of
Manichaeism; the second goes as follows:

(The second): My church surpasses in the wisdom and . . .
which I have unveiled for you in it. This (immeasurable)
wisdom I have written in the holy books, in the great *Gospel*
and the other writings; so that it will not be changed after me.
Also, the way that I have written it in the books: (This) also
is how I have commanded it to be depicted. Indeed, all the
(apostles), my brethren who came prior to me: (They did not
write) their wisdom in books the way that I, I have written
it. (Nor) did they depict their wisdom in the Picture-(Book)
the way (that I, I have) depicted it. My church surpasses (in
this other matter also), for its primacy to the first churches."
(Gardner and Lieu [eds] 2004: 266)

This argument is preserved in a Middle Persian fragment as well, with
a significant difference:

This religion which was chosen by me is in ten things above
and better than the other religions of the ancients. . . .
   Secondly: The older religions (remained in order) as long
as there were holy leaders in it; but when the leaders had been
led upwards, then their religions became confused and they
became slack in commandments and pious works, and by

> greed and fire (of lust) and desire were deceived. However, my religion will remain firm through the living (. . . tea)chers, the bishops, the elect and the hearers; and of wisdom and works will stay on until the end. (*Ibid.*: 109)

In response to this challenge, the Zoroastrian authorities initiated the writing of the *Avesta*, a task which was apparently completed by the middle of the sixth century (Bailey 1971). Indeed, as Albert de Jong observed:

> in the sixth century, two important developments changed Zoroastrianism drastically. The first was the destruction of the Mazdakite movement . . . which led to a tightening grip of the priesthood on the instruction of the laity. The second, and possibly an even more momentous development, was the writing down of the *Avesta* (with its *Zand,* commentary), which led to a scriptural movement among the Zoroastrians. (De Jong 2009: 27-41)

That event is evident in both PV and in ZFJ, so we tend to date the writing down of the *Avesta before* the composition of those Pahlavi books, though it is not impossible that it is the orally-transmitted text that is being cited. In any case, PV refers to the *Avesta* by name some 35 times and ZFJ does so 54 times, but in both texts there are also other references, for instance, in PV Avestan verses are quoted almost always incompletely; presumably the reader was assumed to be familiar with the whole texts. More importantly, PV's glossators and commentators (more than those of ZFJ) are intensely interested in Avestan exegesis.

Omnisignificant Approach

The new attention to scripture, along with the scholastic concern with precision, led in turn to what has been called by James Kugel (1981: 103-104) an 'omnisignificant' approach to scriptural exegesis, one of the great theological principles shared by Jewish and Zoroastrian religions. Some thirty years ago, James Kugel noted a fundamental principle of the rabbinic approach to scripture, which he named 'omnisignificance', that is, the idea that scripture, and, in particular, the Pentateuch, was formulated in an exceedingly exact manner and for very specific purposes, so that there was not an excess verse, phrase or even letter that did not hold, at least theoretically, either moral, theological or legalistic lessons for the attentive exegete. In a series of studies beginning in 1993, Yaakov Elman applied this insight and traced the history of the use of omnisignificant biblical interpretation in rabbinic thought throughout the centuries. Ten years later, he pointed out that the same approach to the Avesta could be discerned in Zoroastrian texts (Elman 2006: 153-69).

The redactors of PV dealt with a text that was prone to describing matters of interest in triads. An example is PV 6.5 (Moazami 2014: 164-65). The section outlines the proper procedure regarding agricultural work on a field in which a human or a dog has died and resulting in agricultural work being forbidden for a season (PV 6.1-2, the *Avesta*) or a year (PV 6.1-2). The question arises as to which and how many such labours are prohibited and with what penalty. The ancient Avestan text specifies 200 lashes as the penalty, which corresponds to two *tanāpuhls* (or sins), each of which presumably refers to two prohibited agricultural labours and not more.

Following this opinion literally, digging and tilling the ground incur one *tanāpuhl*, while letting water run over it incurs another, but the anonymous *dastwar* concludes that a farmer never incurs more than two *tanāpuhls* for these three agricultural labours. Again, reading the *Avesta* (or rather, the *Zand*) literally, it specifies two hundred lashes for three agricultural labours, this would seem to place a *limit* on the sins that could be transgressed. Any additional agricultural labours would not incur additional sins. The redactor(s) do(es) not address the question of how to consider any additional labours that may have been done, but we may presume that the additional labours incur something less than a *tanāpuhl* each.

This then is the view of PV's redactor(s), but ZFJ's redactor(s) report(s) yet another opinion, that of the priests. They, perhaps to increase their yield of fines, assess one *tanāpuhl* for each labour, presumably even beyond the three; this is the most stringent view of all. The redactor(s) record(s) yet a third and a fourth possibility. The third possibility is that of Az Man, which may or may not be later than the fourth, anonymous possibility of ZFJ 11.5, as I shall discuss below.

> [ZFJ 11.4] (A) (As to) working with oxen (= to till), sowing seeds, letting water run over (the earth) (=irrigating), are they separate (works) or a single one?
>
> The priests have said (these are) separate (works).
>
> (B) And in my opinion [that is, Az Man], however, when someone who works with oxen, sows seeds, lets water run over (the earth) or weeds or performs any (other) work on it, there is a *tanāpuhl* (sin).

> [ZFJ 11.5] If someone moistens (the earth) in a different time, works with oxen in a different time, sows seeds in a different time, how is it?
>
> For him there are three *tanāpuhl* (sins).

The question of whether Az Man's opinion (11.4B) is earlier or later than the anonymous opinion of 11.5 depends on how we date Az Man. It may be that the next opinion, that of 11.5, which is anonymous and therefore likely to be a redaction (?).

We need not assume that there was only one redactor or set of redactors. Indeed, the order of opinions as given in ZFJ may be chronological, since they seem arranged in logical order: first, the *dastwar*s suggest that each labour incurs a sin; Az Man then rejects this view and includes all labours into one count; and, finally a second set of redactors introduces the factor of time.

However, there is still another possibility, one that brings the Middle Persian books a step closer to the rhetorical cultures of late antiquity. It may be that the anonymous opinions of ZFJ 11.4A and 11.5 are to be attributed to the same redactor(s), and that we have here the beginnings of a more extended dialogue than is usual for the Pahlavi books. The fact that the last opinion, that of 11.5, is the most complex, including as it does the factor of time, might indicate that the redactor(s) favoured it and therefore placed it last.

The *dastwar*s consider each individual labour as incurring a *tanāpuhl* (sin); Az Man goes to the opposite extreme, with all labours subsumed under one sin, and 11.5 brings time into the equation. Needless to say, this possibility requires a good deal more investigation and for now we will assume that Az Man is a later commentator than the redactors, simply because he did not remain completely anonymous.

At any rate, this latter anonymous view links the sin to the time period in which the labour is done; each labour incurs one *tanāpuhl* (sin), and, if the labour continued into the next division of time (*gāh*), further sins would accrue – with the condition that each time the farmer chose to pursue a different labour during each division of time.

However, interpolated between the third and fourth opinions is that of a later commentator, that is, Az Man. My suggestion that Az Man is later than the redactors of ZFJ is based on the fact that he identifies himself rather than remaining anonymous. In any case, taken as it stands, Az Man's opinion, that all agricultural labours incur but one *tanāpuhl*, is the most lenient and also somewhat conceptual, since it includes every labour under the general concept of 'labour'. It is interesting to note that PV's lenient opinion is not mentioned in ZFJ at all.

To conclude, to the rich panoply of Hellenistically-inspired scholastic endeavour in substance, method and school, we may now add the Abargites, the Mēdōmāhites and the Pēšagsīrites of late Sasanian times – and the related problem of coming to terms with deciding the law in matters under dispute, a phenomenon that is clear from work that I have done on PV and ZFJ.

PV and ZFJ redactors were part of the intellectual world of late antiquity, and thus share a number of characteristics which joined them to that world that shed light on features of other works. Scholars of late antiquity need to integrate the cultural and intellectual history of the Sasanian empire into their works in order to develop a more interdisciplinary vision of late antiquity and to look across the traditional disciplinary division between Mediterranean and Near Eastern history. Modern interpretations of the philosophers' journey to the court of Khusro I reveal how often this disciplinary division has obscured the richness of intellectual life at the late Sasanian court, as well as the intensity of its contacts with Greek and other intellectuals (Walker 2002: 45-69).

Bibliography

Altheim, F. 1957. *Utopie und Wirtschaft: Eine geschichtlicher Betrachtung*, Frankfurt am Main: W. Klostermann

Bailey, H.W. 1943, repr. 1971. *Zoroastrian Problems in the Ninth-Century Books*, Oxford: The Clarendon Press

Christensen, A. 1944, repr. 1971. *L'Iran sous les Sassanides*, Copenhagen: Ejner Munksgaard

Dhabhar, B.N. 1912. *Nâmakîhâ-î Mânûshchîhar: The Epistles of Mânûshchîhar*, Bombay

Elman, Y. 2006. 'Scripture Versus Contemporary Needs: A Sasanian/Zoroastrian Example', *Cardozo Law Review* 28/1: 153-69

Elman, Y., and M. Moazami. 2014. 'Zand ī Fragard ī Jud-Dēw-Dād', *Encyclopædia Iranica*, online edition

Frendo, J.D. (trans.). 1975. Agathias: *The Histories*, Berlin and New York: Gruyters

Gardner, I. (ed.). 1995. *The Kephalaia of the Teacher: The Edited Coptic Manichaean Texts in Translation with Commentary*, Leiden: Brill

Gardner, I., and S.N.C. Lieu (eds). 2004. *Manichaean Texts from the Roman Empire*, Cambridge: Cambridge University Press

Huby, P., S. Ebbesen, D. Langslow, D. Russell, C. Steel and M. Wilson (trans.) 2016. *Priscian: Answers to King Khosroes of Persian*, London: Bloomsbury

Jong, A., de. 2009. 'The Culture of Writing and the Use of the *Avesta* in Sasanian Iran', in É. Pirart and X. Tremblay (ed.), *Zarathushtra entre l'Inde et l'Iran*, Wiesbaden: Reichert, 27-41

Kugel, J. 1981. *The Idea of Biblical Poetry: Parallelism and Its History*, New Haven, CT: Yale University Press

Kotwal, F.M., and Ph.G. Kreyenbroek (eds and trans.). 1992-2009. *The Hērbedestān and Nērangestān* (with contributions by J. Russell) 4 vols, Paris: Association pour l'avancement des études iraniennes

Macuch, M. 1993. *Rechtskasuistik und Gerichtspraxis zu Beginn des siebenten Jahrhunderts in Iran: Die Rechtssammlung des Farrohmard i Wahrāmān*, Wiesbaden: Harrassowitz Verlag

Madan, D.M. 1911. *The Complete Text of the Pahlavi Dinkard (Dēnkard)*, Bombay: Fort Printing Press

Moazami, M. 2014. *Wrestling with the Demons of the Pahlavi Widēwdād*, Leiden and Boston: Brill

Moazami, M. *Zand ī Fragard ī Jud-Dēw-Dād*, MS TD2 (in preparation for publication)

Satlow, M.L. 2008. *How the Bible Became Holy*, New Haven, CT: Yale University Press

Shaki, M. 2003. 'Greece iv. Greek Influence on Persian Thought', in *Encyclopaedia Iranica* Vol. XI: 321-26

Stroumsa, G. 2009. *The End of Sacrifice: Religious Transformations in Late Antiquity*, Chicago: University of Chicago Press

Stroumsa, G. 2008. 'The Scriptural Movement of Late Antiquity and Christian Monasticism', *Journal of Early Christian Studies* 16/1: 61-77

Tardieu, M. 1998. 'Le Prologue des "Kephalaia" de Berlin', in J.-D. Dubois and B. Roussel (eds), *Entrer en matière: les prologues*, Paris: Cerf, 65-77

Tavadia, J.C. 1930. Šāyast *nē* šāyast*: A Pahlavi Text on Religious Customs*, Hamburg: Friederichsen, de Gruyter & Co.

Thompson, D.J. 2008. 'Economic Reforms in the Mid-Reign of Ptolemy Philadelphus', in P. McKechnie and P. Guillaume (eds), *Ptolemy II Philadelphus and His World*, Leiden: Brill, 27-38

Walker, J.T. 2002. 'The Limits of Late Antiquity: Philosophy between Rome and Iran', *The Ancient World* 33: 45-69

Wiesehöfer, J. 2001. *Ancient Persia from 550 BC to 650 AD*, trans. Azizeh Azodi, London: I.B. Tauris

Index of selected place-names and personal names